# THE ROMAN WEST COUNTRY

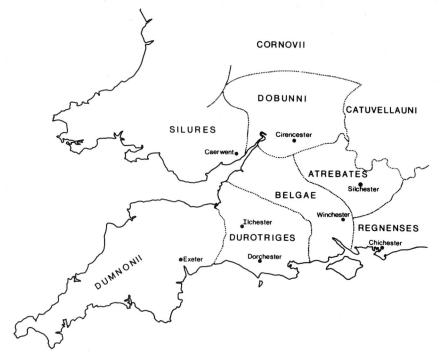

The Roman West Country

# THE
# ROMAN WEST
# COUNTRY

## CLASSICAL CULTURE AND
## CELTIC SOCIETY

EDITED BY
KEITH BRANIGAN AND P. J. FOWLER

**DAVID & CHARLES**
NEWTON ABBOT    LONDON
NORTH POMFRET (VT)    VANCOUVER

TO
AILEEN FOX

ISBN   0 7153 7003 0
Library of Congress Catalog Card Number 75–31328

Set in 11 on 13pt Times New Roman
by Trade Linotype Ltd Birmingham
and printed in Great Britain
by Redwood Burn Limited
Trowbridge and Esher
for David & Charles (Publishers) Limited
Brunel House   Newton Abbot   Devon

Published in the United States of America
by David & Charles Inc
North Pomfret   Vermont 05053   USA

Published in Canada
by Douglas David & Charles Limited
1875 Welch Street   North Vancouver   BC

# CONTENTS

# Contents

# LIST OF ILLUSTRATIONS

## PLATES

## FIGURES

# CONTRIBUTORS

K. Branigan, BA, PhD, FSA
Lecturer in Archaeology, Department of Classics, University of Bristol

H. D. H. Elkington, MA
Housemaster, Wellington School, Somerset

P. J. Fowler, MA, FSA
Reader in Archaeology, Department of Extra-Mural Studies, University of Bristol

H. Hurst, BA
Formerly Director of Excavations, Gloucester City Museum

P. Isaac, MA
Research Student, Department of Classics, University of Bristol

R. H. Leech, BA
Research Student, Department of Classics, University of Bristol

A. D. McWhirr, BSc, MA, FSA
Director of Excavations, Cirencester Excavation Committee

W. H. Manning, PhD, FSA
Senior Lecturer in Archaeology, Department of Archaeology, University College, Cardiff

A. C. Thomas, MA, FSA, Hon MRIA
Professor of Cornish Studies and Director of the Institute of Cornish Studies, University of Exeter and Cornwall County Council

M. Todd, BA, FSA
Senior Lecturer in Archaeology, Department of Classical and Archaeological Studies, University of Nottingham

B. H. Warmington, MA
Reader in Ancient History, Department of Classics, University of Bristol

# NOTES FOR READERS

*References*
References throughout follow the Harvard system, except in the four Appendices where for convenience and economy an abbreviated form of reference has been adopted.

References to classical sources give the author or title of the work, and the number of the book or chapter, and refer to particular lines where necessary.

*Abbreviations*
Abbreviations used are those advocated by the Council for British Archaeology, with the following additions:

| | |
|---|---|
| *CIL* | *Corpus Inscriptiones Latinarum* |
| OS | Ordnance Survey |
| RCHM | Royal Commission on Historical Monuments (England) |
| *RIB* | *Roman Inscriptions in Britain*, R. Collingwood and R. P. Wright (OUP, 1963) |
| *VCH* | *Victoria County History* |

*County Boundaries*
Revised county boundaries were adopted after this book went to press and references to county locations throughout the book are therefore made on the basis of the county boundaries as they were before 1 April 1974.

# PREFACE

The scale of archaeological excavation in Britain has increased greatly during the last decade and now there is some danger that the new, and often fundamental, evidence which is being continuously recovered will simply pile up like a dump of unused coal outside a power station. Only if the evidence is periodically reviewed and related to earlier work will it generate fresh insights into the past and, we can but hope, through them a fuller understanding of our history. This is certainly true of the West Country in the period of the Roman occupation. In recent years there has been so much excavation and other research in this field that a review of south-western Britain and its inhabitants, primarily through their archaeology, seemed desirable, even though (perhaps because?) most of the new primary evidence has not yet been fully published. A linking theme for such a review, implicit if not always explicit, was the interaction of Celt and Roman, of barbarian and bureaucrat, of Atlantic and Mediterranean cultural traditions, during some four centuries of the imperial connection. Was the West Country 'Romanised' and what, if any, was the nature of that 'Romanisation'? A full answer lies many years ahead, but at least the contributions here to what may eventually be at least a fuller answer have been able to draw on fresh evidence.

We gave our contributors no constricting definition of 'the West Country' and consequently the topographical focus changes slightly from chapter to chapter. The book is centred on the historic counties of Devon, Dorset, Gloucestershire, Somerset and Wiltshire, but we happily include relevant material from Cornwall, Hampshire, Herefordshire and south Wales. In terms of the Roman administrative system in Britain, we are therefore dealing with parts of the territories of the Belgae, the Dobunni, the Dumnonii, and the Durotriges and, to a lesser extent, of the Atrebates and Silures too.

Our contributors and their topics were chosen to provide a wide and up-to-date coverage of the Roman West Country – its archaeology and history, its settlements and its society – though we could not achieve comprehensiveness. Religion and roads, for example, are only touched on.. All the contributors have recently been and indeed still are active in fieldwork, excavation and/or other research in the region, so much so that, although the essays presented here are based on papers first read at a conference at Bristol in February 1973, the authors subsequently revised and rewrote them in the winter of 1973–4, incorporating results of excavations during the rest of 1973.

Nevertheless, recognising that no archaeological discussion can remain up to date for long, we have attempted to give some element of permanent value to the book by including appendices to four of the chapters, in which are provided bibliographical references to the main sources of evidence for coin hoards, villas, larger rural settlements and lead pigs from the Mendip mines. We hope, too, that the book may provide a useful starting-point for further advances in our understanding of the Roman West Country during the next decade. Increase in knowledge can indeed be the only compensation for what will be destroyed in the field between 1975 and 1985.

K.B.
P.J.F.

# 1

# THE CONQUEST OF
# THE WEST COUNTRY

The classical accounts of the conquest of the West Country are
tantalisingly few and present a confusing and incomplete picture. Any
account must therefore rely largely on the evidence of archaeology,
although by its very nature this cannot produce the exact chronological
account of the contemporary historian. Before discussing the conquest
itself it is necessary to consider briefly the situation in the years preceding
the Roman invasion. For the present purpose we need concern ourselves
only with the political situation, or as much of it as can be deciphered
from the existing evidence. One thing is clear: the Roman system of
*civitates*, or cantons, cannot be projected straight back into the Iron
Age. In most cases they perpetuate tribal names, but they do not
necessarily reflect their original geographical limits (Radford *1955*; Rivet
*1966* 133). Fortunately some indication of these (fig 1) and of the state
of flux which marked the end of the Iron Age in lowland Britain can
be gained from the Celtic coin distributions so brilliantly studied by
Allen (*1944, 1958, 1961, 1967*).

For a century before the Roman invasion the political scene had
been dominated by the Catuvellauni, who by direct conquest and no
doubt by more diplomatic means had absorbed large parts of southern
England. Among the tribes to suffer in this way were the Atrebates,
originally ruled by Commius. Centred on Hampshire, their territory
had extended into the western parts of Sussex and a large part of
Berkshire and north-eastern Wiltshire. The northern half of this area
had been lost to the Catuvellauni by *c* AD 25, but the southern half
continued to be ruled by descendants of Commius until the eve of the
Roman conquest when Verica, the last of them, fled to seek refuge in
Rome, appearing in the opening of Dio's account of the conquest as
the Bericus who persuaded Claudius to launch the invasion (Dio
60.19,1). Although there is no certain evidence, it is usually assumed
that his departure was the result of the final attack on his kingdom by
the Catuvellauni. Adjoining the Atrebates on the south-west were the

Fig 1   Tribal territories in the West Country

Durotriges, covering Dorset and the southern parts of Wiltshire and
Somerset, with the Dobunni to the north of them occupying Gloucestershire, Worcestershire, much of Somerset and the western edges of
Oxfordshire and Wiltshire. The archaeological evidence shows that
throughout the first century AD the Dobunni were subject to considerable
Catuvellaunian influence (Hawkes *1961*), while the coins indicate that
shortly before the Roman conquest the tribe had split into two halves
under separate rulers (Allen *1944* 36, map VII; *1967* maps 4 and 5; *1961*
89). On the south-east the lands of the Dobunni probably marched with
those of the Atrebates, as did those of the Durotriges further south,
but in the central area between these three tribes around Salisbury Plain
was a region apparently independent of them all – or at least largely
independent of their coinages (Allen *1944* 36, map VII; *1967* maps 4
and 5). If this was a separate tribe we do not know its name, unless it
was the Belgae after whom the much larger Roman *civitas* was named.
The last tribes which need concern us here lie still further to the west,
so far beyond the pale of civilisation that they minted no coins of their
own; the Dumnonii of Devon and Cornwall, and the Silures of south-east
Wales.

16

One of these tribes makes a surprisingly early appearance in the history of the conquest, for immediately after the first defeat and flight of the Catuvellaunian kings Caratacus and Togodumnus, Dio tells us that a part of the *Bodunni* capitulated to Aulus Plautius (Dio 60.20,2). It is now generally accepted that the Bodunni are not an otherwise unknown Kentish tribe but a simple scribal error for Dobunni (Hawkes *1961* 60; Frere *1967* 69).

## VESPASIAN'S CAMPAIGNS

The major part of Dio's narrative ends with the fall of Camulodunum, and for the actual conquest of the west we must turn to the familiar passage in Suetonius' life of the emperor Vespasian:

> In the reign of Claudius he was sent in command of a legion to Germany . . . ; from there he was transferred to Britain, where he fought thirty battles with the enemy. He reduced to subjection two powerful nations, more than twenty towns, and the island of Vectis, near Britain, partly under the leadership of Aulus Plautius, the consular governor, and partly under that of Claudius himself. For this he received the triumphal regalia (Suetonius *Vespasian* 4.1).

We know from other sources that the legion in question was the II Augusta (Tacitus *Histories* 3.44,1) and there is no reason to challenge the accepted view that the scene of these victories was south-western England, but the period involved has been the subject of some controversy. It has been argued that they must have been completed within the conquest year as Vespasian will have returned to Rome in AD 44 to receive his triumphal insignia at Claudius' triumph (Dudley and Webster *1965* 90), an assumption which imposes a very tight time scale for actions of the magnitude recorded by Suetonius. In a recent paper, however, Eichholz (*1972*) has shown that there was no necessity for Vespasian to go to Rome in person; indeed that it is most unlikely that he would do so at such a time. More probably we should allow him several seasons for his conquests, perhaps completing them as late as AD 47 when Plautius returned to Rome.

Unfortunately our present knowledge is not sufficient for any meaningful attempt to restore the details of these campaigns. With the exceptions of the famous war cemetery at Maiden Castle (Wheeler *1943* 118) and the evidence for the artillery bombardment at Hod Hill (Richmond *1968* 32), few of the archaeological remains need date from the actual conquest phase. No doubt forts were rapidly constructed, but the majority must have come after the open military opposition had been defeated. To have left small garrisons here, there and everywhere while still advancing would have dangerously reduced the strength of the field army while major battles were still likely. The client kingdom of the Atrebates, or Regnenses as the southern section was to be called (Jackson *1970* 78), must have been established soon after the conquest, and such a secure base will not have been ignored, as the evidence for a fort at Chichester and a port at Fishbourne shows. But Chichester cannot have been the base for campaigns in the northern part of the area. Here Silchester, soon to become the key junction in the road system to the west, would form a more suitable centre (fig 2). Part of the Dobunni had already surrendered, and if the northern Atrebates also came to terms, which in view of their original hostility to the Catuvellauni is probable, then a barrier of allied tribes will have been created, cutting off the Durotriges and Dumnonii from any possible allies.

Initially the Roman army probably followed the existing trackways, which will have led to the enemy *oppida*, but once the area had been sub-

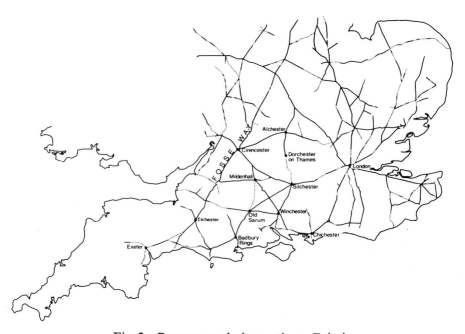

Fig 2   Roman roads in southern Britain

jugated a new road system would be surveyed and built. It has often been remarked that three major Roman roads run from London in the directions taken by these first armies (Haverfield and MacDonald *1924* 106; Frere *1967* 70; Ogilvie and Richmond *1967* 51), and there is no reason to doubt that these roads and their main branches reflect, if not the actual process of conquest, at least the consolidation which followed. If this is true, the road running from London to the west may provide some indication of the area conquered by Vespasian (fig 2). As far as we know it runs more or less directly to Silchester where it throws out four branches. Of these two, that to the north to Dorchester-on-Thames, and that to the south-west to Old Sarum, are somewhat later, but the other two are primary and lead to Winchester and Cirencester. More roads spring from Winchester and from the secondary centres at Badbury Rings, Old Sarum and Mildenhall, while across the western edge of the system runs the Fosse Way marking, as Webster (*1960*) has so convincingly demonstrated, the limit of the province at the time of Aulus Plautius' departure in AD 47. The alignment of some of these roads suggests that the Fosse Way predates them, but this is only to be expected; a system as extensive as this is not the result of a season's work. If we are correct in identifying this part of the road system with Vespasian's command, it suggests that the break between the area occupied by Legion II and that of Legion XIV came somewhere to the north of Cirencester where the roads begin to lead back through Alcester to the Watling Street.

## THE GARRISON FORTS

By AD 47 the west of England was largely conquered and garrisoned, but it is at this point that the inadequacies of our present knowledge become particularly clear, for we can name less than half a dozen forts of this period in the area with absolute certainty. To these can be added rather more sites where the discovery of military equipment or where the topography and the presence of Claudian pottery strongly suggest the existence of a fort. Other sites have been proposed on general grounds at various times but still await supporting evidence. In the area to the north of Old Sarum bounded by the Silchester–Winchester road on the east and the Fosse Way on the west there is at the moment a total lack of proven Roman forts (fig 3). Some military occupation at Silchester is almost certain, for relatively large amounts of equipment are known, although it is not all early (Boon *1969* 44, fig 5). Calleva was a major Belgic *oppidum* and the way in which the road system focuses on it

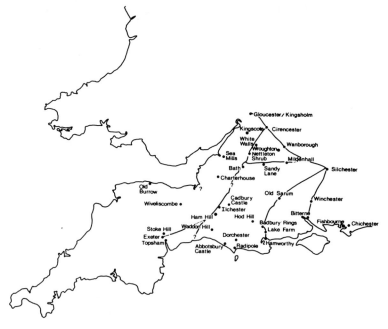

Fig 3   Early military sites and roads in the West Country

shows its strategic importance at the opening of the Roman period. It is unlikely, although not impossible, that a fort lies undiscovered under the city itself, but less is known of the area outside the walls. In a recent paper Boon (*1969* 39) has argued that as soon as the area was occupied by the Roman army the old kingdom of the Atrebates was reconstituted for Cogidubnus and that he at once made Calleva his northern capital, fortifying it with the defence known as the Inner Earthwork. In itself this does not exclude a Roman garrison, for one certainly existed at Chichester which is assumed to be Cogidubnus' southern capital (Wilson *1970* 302; *1971* 284; *1972* 350). Boon also shows that the roads from London and Cirencester were in existence when the new defences were built, but suggests that the road to Winchester was slightly later because it is aligned on the southern entrance of the later defence system (the Outer Earthwork) rather than on the south gate of the Inner Earthwork (Boon *1969* 39 fig 1). The problem is complicated, however, by the fact that immediately west of the entrance through the Outer Earthwork the defences incorporate an earlier dyke (Rampier's Copse), the original length of which has not been tested by excavation, while further south the road skirts another linear dyke which must predate the Roman defences (Boon *1969* 23, fig 1). Both these features were in existence when the road was constructed and could in themselves be sufficient to cause the change of angle in the road as it approached the town. If such was the case, this road would also be primary. The roads to Old Sarum and to Dorchester override the Inner Earthwork and must, therefore, be secondary to the original system.

On the roads to the west, forts are generally accepted at Mildenhall (Dudley and Webster *1965* 126; Annable *1966* 9) and Wanborough (Dudley and Webster *1965* 126), pottery of Claudian date being known from both sites. Their precise locations have yet to be discovered. Between Mildenhall and Bath lies Sandy Lane where another fort has been suggested, but in the absence of supporting evidence its existence is dubious (Dudley and Webster *1965* 126).

West of Winchester the situation is only a little clearer. A fort may exist at Winchester itself, although no sign of it has been found in the recent excavations. The existence of civil defences before the end of the first century and the town's position on the road system, however, indicate its importance in the pre-Flavian period. To the east, Down has shown that Chichester had a long military occupation with several phases of timber buildings (Wilson *1970* 302; *1971* 284; *1972* 350). No doubt the military store buildings found at Fishbourne on Chichester Harbour represent a port for this fort (Cunliffe *1971* 38), but the relationship of these military works to Cogidubnus' presumed capital presents certain problems. Further west a fort should exist at or near Old Sarum, and early pottery is known from Stratford-sub-Castle in the Avon valley below Old Sarum itself (information from Mrs V. Swann).

Other forts must lie between there and the Fosse Way but no trace of them has yet been found. From Old Sarum the road to the south-west runs to a junction near Badbury Rings where a famous series of air-photographs show it crossing the road from Poole Harbour to Bath (Collingwood and Richmond *1969* pl 1b). This relationship need not mean any great difference in date, but it does confirm the importance of the early base at Hamworthy. The discovery of Claudian coins and pottery outside Badbury Rings itself suggests a fort here (information from Mrs V. Swann), but the existence of the important military site at Lake Farm, Wimborne, a few miles to the south-east, may indicate that it had but a short life. The fort at Lake Farm is clearly of great interest, but the excavations under Field and Webster have not yet reached a conclusive stage. At least two forts appear to exist, the later with a sub-

Plate 1   Air-photograph of Hod Hill, Dorset, showing the neat defences of the Roman fort in the north-west corner of the pre-Roman hillfort

stantial rampart and triple ditch system, together dating from the mid-forties until the sixties of the first century (information from Dr Webster). The potter's kiln discovered nearby at Corfe Mullen must have been associated with this fort (Calkin *1935*).

Some eleven miles to the north-west lies the best known of all Claudian forts – Hod Hill (pl 1). Richmond's excavations (*1968*) have given us the only complete ground plan that we have for any fort of this period. The occupation began *c* AD 43–4 and, after a number of the internal buildings had been burnt down, ended before the close of Claudius' reign (AD 54). The familiar air-photographs often give the impression that the Roman fort is small, but this is because it lies within such a large Iron Age fort. Its actual area is ten acres, although of this less than seven acres were suitable for buildings. Perhaps the most interesting detail to emerge from the excavations was that it had housed a mixed garrison formed of a legionary cohort of six under-strength centuries (*c* 352 instead of 480 men), and half a *quingenary ala* of auxiliary cavalry (*c* 250–300 men), each with its own commander. Richmond felt that such an arrangement was largely the result of its dating from the early years of the conquest before the troop dispositions were finalised, but recent work at other pre-Flavian sites suggests that this may have been a common arrangement at that time. Certainly it was not limited to the conquest years, for a similar situation existed at Newstead in the Antonine period and probably in the late Flavian period too (Richmond *1950* 11, 21). The advantage of such a combination was that it provided a miniature field army which could be used for patrol, raiding, foraging or small-scale actions. The disadvantages largely derived from mixing units of different grades: at Newstead it was thought advisable to separate the two by a wall and, probably, to duplicate the social facilities of the bath house (Richmond *1950* 22). It may have been under such circumstances that the men of Legion XIV acquired their hostility to the Batavian auxiliaries (Tacitus *Hist* 2.66). Hod Hill and Nanstallon in Cornwall are the only forts of this period where the size of the garrison can be calculated, and it is important to realise that if Vespasian's command accounted for rather more than a quarter of the total army in Britain, say 12,000 men, then twenty forts such as Hod Hill would have absorbed it entirely!

Further west stood the fort at Waddon Hill, near Beaminster, excavated by Webster. For the details of this work we must await his final report, but apparently it too had a mixed garrison of legionaries and auxiliary cavalry, although as quarrying had destroyed a large part of the site the details can never be as clear as at Hod Hill. It continued in use until after AD 60 (information from Dr Webster). Between Waddon Hill and Hod Hill lay the Roman town of Dorchester, set almost at the foot of Maiden Castle which, like Hod Hill, was stormed by the Roman army. Dorchester is an obvious place for a fort and it has been suggested as a possible site for the original base of Legion II (Frere *1967* 74). Support for the existence of a fort is provided by its position in the early road system and by the discovery of military equipment, but recent extensive excavations have failed to find any trace of such a fort, and although one could still exist in the unexcavated areas of the town a large base probably could not (information from Professor Cunliffe).

Associated with these southern forts there appears to have been a series of ports or supply bases. Two are known with certainty, Fishbourne (Cunliffe *1971*) and Hamworthy on Poole Harbour (Dudley and Webster *1965* 104; Webster *1960* 57), from which a road runs to the Lake Farm fort and ultimately to Bath. Others probably existed at Bitterne on Southampton Water, where a large group of pre-Flavian pottery was found (Waterman *1952*) and whence lead pigs from the Mendips were exported to Gaul (Frere *1967* 284) and, if the spur road from Dorchester is significant, at Radipole on Weymouth Bay. Either Bitterne or Fishbourne must have been the base from which the attack on the Isle of Wight was launched and through which communications with the mainland were maintained. Of the two, Bitterne would seem the more logical both from its position and from its relationship to the road system, but it must be admitted that the evidence for the base at this date is less satisfactory than at Fishbourne. In most cases these ports must date from the time of consolidation after the conquest. The problems of liaising with a fleet during the actual conquest would probably have been too great for its regular use; nor was the Roman army accustomed to working with a naval force in this way. But once the conquest was completed the advantages of seaborne supplies would be obvious, the more so as all material or men brought from the Continent would have to be embarked to cross the Channel no matter where they landed. Associated with the forts may have been a system of observation posts and signal stations. One of these has been recognised in the corner of the Iron Age hillfort at Abbotsbury Castle overlooking the English Channel in west Dorset (RCHM *1952* 10); another has been excavated a few miles to the north at Blackdown, near Winterbourne Steepleton (Fowler *1971* 20). Other probable signal stations are currently being investigated by Putnam.

## THE FRONTIER FORTS

Beyond these forts lay the frontier zone itself, centred on the Fosse Way. Although here at its western end it was separated from the most obvious enemy, the Silures of south Wales, by the Bristol Channel, the defence system was presumably continued to its end, originally perhaps at Axmouth where the road reaches the sea, but soon extended to Exeter. Only the ends of the system, the forts at Exeter and Cirencester, are known with certainty in the south-west. On the assumption of a regular series of forts, an assumption which is not necessarily correct, other forts have been suggested at Ilchester, where the recent excavations have failed to produce supporting evidence although the remains of a bank below the Civil War defences could be connected with a fort (Fowler *1970* 46; *1971* 27), at Bath, where the Fosse Way crosses the Avon, and at White Walls, Easton Grey, between Bath and Cirencester, although here again there is little firm evidence. The fact that the excavations in Bath have produced no evidence of a fort does not disprove one, for the area around the thermal spring is an inherently unlikely site, and some early material is known from the area to the north of the springs (Cunliffe *1969* 1). Several of the tombstones from the city are of first-century date, but as a spa – even a military one – Bath is too atypical for much emphasis to be placed on this. Of all the tombstones, the memorial to Lucius Vitellius Tancinus (*RIB* 159), a trooper in the *ala Vettonum*, dated by Birley (*1952* 10) to the closing years of Claudius or at latest the reign of Nero, is the most likely to represent a garrison. The absence of the title Victrix, probably granted after AD 61, from the two Legion XX tombstones (*RIB* 158, 160) means nothing as its other title, Valeria, certainly used before 61, is also omitted. If the system of forts was more or less regular, another should exist between Bath and Ilchester, possibly at the point where the road from Old Sarum to Charterhouse crosses the Fosse Way, while a final one may have stood near the mouth of the Axe on the south coast.

Such a system on its own would be too perfect, and other forts reflecting local problems and other phases of the conquest must still wait to be found. A number were suggested by the O'Neils (*1952*), mainly on or near the Fosse Way, but such subsequent work as there has been has not supported their suggestions. Many small rectangular enclosures are known in the area, but without excavation a medieval date is at least as likely as a Roman one; and even if they are Roman, they need not be military. Other fort sites have been suggested at Camerton (Wedlake *1958* 45; Dudley and Webster *1965* 109, fn 37), and White Walls (Dudley and Webster *1965* 126; Hoare *1821* 101), both on the Fosse Way, but in neither case is the evidence at present sufficient for their acceptance. The discovery of Claudian material and a baldrick loop at Kingscote south of Stroud suggests the possibility of a military site there (Eagles and Swann *1973* 61), and another has been claimed at Nettleton Shrub on the Fosse Way north of Bath (Fowler *1969* 22; *1970* 49). The military equipment from Ham Hill, just to the east of the Fosse Way, has led to its being widely accepted as a fort site (Webster *1960* 54), but no details are known and the same hillfort has produced an Iron Age hoard (Manning *1972* 230), suggesting that the Roman material may have been a votive offering comparable with the Seven Sisters hoard from south Wales (Grimes *1951* 223, fig 40). Of the possible military occupation of another hillfort in Somerset, South Cadbury Castle, more will be said below.

The Fosse Way system cannot have consisted solely of forts along the road itself, and in any event it seems improbable that the relatively narrow strip of land between the road and the sea would have been left unoccupied. As Frere has pointed out (*1967* 75), the regular spacing both from the Fosse Way and from each other of the early sites at Broxtowe, Mancetter, Alcester, Gloucester and Sea Mills is suggestive of a planned screen of forts which would be completed in the south-west if another had existed on the river Parrett near Bridgwater. The fort at Charterhouse (Wilson *1971* 277, fig 12, and information from Professor Barri Jones and P. J. Fowler) does not readily fit this pattern, but lead was being produced there by AD 49 (Elkington *infra*), and that Legion II had a hand in the work is shown by a pig bearing their stamp and the name of the emperor Nero from the harbour at St-Valery-sur-Somme (Gowland *1901* 379). The Roman government, however, continued to keep close control over the production of lead well into the second century (Frere *1967* 286), and the fort need not necessarily date from the first years of the conquest. Air-photography and fieldwork by Fowler suggest that it has two phases with a change of axis in the second phase. Other rectangular earthworks in the area are likely to be medieval.

A fact which recent work throughout Britain has revealed is the extreme flexibility of the pre-Flavian troop dispositions. Once a suitable spot for a fort had been found it was utilised for as long as the necessity remained. But, as the military situation throughout the province constantly changed, the movement of units and combinations of units will have been frequent, and these changes are often reflected in the archaeological remains. Forts were modified, rebuilt to a different size, or moved to a new site only a short distance from the old, with the result that the picture is often confused even after intensive excavations. A similar situation existed in Germany in the first century with almost identical results (Wells *1972*). Multiple sites are already known at Exeter, Cirencester, Gloucester and Usk, and future work will undoubtedly make the position more rather than less complicated.

One final question concerning Vespasian's share in this work is outstanding: which were the two tribes that Suetonius says he conquered (*Vesp* 4.1)? Commentators are now universally agreed that the Durotriges were one of them (Richmond *1955* 23; Dudley and Webster *1965* 92; Frere *1967* 74), but there are a number of contenders for the second. The Dumnonii are perhaps the least likely. Even if the army had reached as far as Exeter by AD 47, probably the latest date at which Vespasian can be assumed to have been in Britain, the greater part of their territory would still lie outside the province. It could be that half of the Dobunni which did not surrender to Plautius; it could be the group occupying the Salisbury Plain area who were later incorporated in the *civitas* of the Belgae; or it could even be the northern Atrebates who had been under Catuvellaunian control before the conquest; but on the present evidence any suggestion is little more than a guess.

## THE GOVERNORSHIP OF SCAPULA

It is often suggested that the original Roman intention was merely to occupy the lowlands of England and that the Fosse Way marks the frontier of this intended province (Frere *1967* 76; Webster *1960* 49; *1970* 179). The conquests which actually followed are then seen not as the result of Roman ambition but as the inevitable consequence of the unremitting hostility of the tribes beyond the frontier, especially the Silures and Ordovices, and of the failure of the client kingdom system. Certainly the Fosse Way with its forts suggests a frontier system, but the evidence for its being intended as permanent is not conclusive. At that stage in the conquest, with the three armies strung across the country, some form of lateral communication would have been a necessity, and its possibilities as part of a temporary frontier system would be obvious. Behind such a frontier, cutting across conquered and allied territory alike regardless of existing boundaries, the newly won lands could be garrisoned and Romanised without straining the available manpower. But once these had been digested, distant as that day might be, further advances may always have been intended. It is unlikely that the Roman intelligence system was so defective that the government was under the illusion that the Welsh tribes would be pacific, but it may have underrated their ability to make real trouble, the more so if they were separated from the Roman forces by a chain of buffer states including the northern Dobunni and perhaps the Cornovii (Frere *1967* 76). The probability of such a system is confirmed by the reason given by Tacitus for the advance under Ostorius Scapula, namely that the enemy had attacked the territory of a tribe allied to Rome (*Annals* 12.31), a situation in which the Romans had little alternative but to assist their ally. It is, however, noticeable that Scapula was not content with a punitive expedition of the type so often launched in support of Cartimandua in Brigantia, but began a major attack on Wales after occupying the territory between the Severn and the Trent. Such action suggests that plans already existed, and that the pause on the Fosse Way, if it actually occurred, was no more than temporary.

Various writers have assumed the attack mentioned by Tacitus to refer to a move by the Silures against the Dobunni (Collingwood and Myres *1937* 91; Hawkes *1961* 66), but Scapula's subsequent actions suggest that the trouble was further north. He took three measures (*Annals* 12.31,32): he disarmed the tribes in his rear; he occupied the area between the rivers Trent and Severn; and he struck against the Deceangli of Flintshire, almost reaching the Irish Sea during this campaign. These last two steps must indicate that the initial trouble was in Wales and probably in north Wales. Tacitus makes it clear, however, that even if the Silures were not the prime movers they were soon involved, and the remainder of Scapula's campaigns were directed against them and the Ordovices. Even after the defeat of Caratacus, who had been commanding the Welsh tribes, the Silures continued the war until after Scapula's death in AD 52, and it was left to his successor Didius Gallus to contain them. In Tacitus' generalised and confusing account of these events are certain facts of considerable importance to the present discussion: (i) the frontier is moved forward into the territory of the Silures (*Annals* 12.38); (ii) a legion (no doubt **XX** Valeria) previously based at Colchester is brought forward against the Silures in AD 49

Fig 4   Possible military dispositions in the south-west, *c* AD 52

(*Annals* 12.32); (iii) a series of forts was built in Siluria (*Annals* 12.38); (iv) the legions were not always used as single units but often in large detachments – in one case we hear of an incident involving more than one cohort during which a camp prefect and eight centurions were killed (*Annals* 12.38) – some of which had auxiliary support; (v) Tacitus' narrative appears to indicate that more than one legion was involved (*Annals* 12.39); and (vi) Didius Gallus built some forts in outlying areas (*Agricola* 14.2).

It is clear that by AD 52 the effective frontier of the province had moved forward an unknown distance into Wales but the archaeological evidence for this is still very slight. Only a handful of sites can be dated to the pre-Flavian period, let alone to the reign of Claudius (fig 4). In south Wales, the forts at Llandovery, Clyro, Clifford near Clyro, Abergavenny, Coed-y-Caerau and Usk are claimed as pre-Flavian. Of these Llandovery (Nash-Williams *1969* 95) and Clyro, which has two phases (Nash-Williams *1969* 77), are dated to this period on a few sherds of pottery which defy a closer dating. Coed-y-Caerau is unexcavated but is assumed to be pre-Flavian because its proximity to Caerleon renders it irrelevant to the Flavian system of forts. It seems unnecessarily large (2.5 acres) to have been merely an observation post for the fortress (Nash-Williams *1969* 81). The large fort at Clifford, Hereford, only some two miles from Clyro, is probably not contemporary with Clyro, and is so poorly sited that it is most unlikely to be later in date (St Joseph *1973* 238). Considerable quantities of pottery are known from Abergavenny (Probert *1969* and recent excavations by P. Ashmore) but this suggests a somewhat later date, although still within the pre-Flavian period, while at Usk, the pre-Flavian fortress dates from the mid rather than the early fifties. Further north, at Wroxeter, the fortress believed to lie under the Roman city is generally thought to be rather later in date, although the auxiliary fort lying outside the town may be Scapulan (information from Dr Webster). In view of this one wonders how far Scapula's fort-building parties had advanced at the time of his death. In describing the battle in which the camp prefect and eight centurions died, Tacitus makes it clear that they were saved from annihilation by the Silures only by the arrival of support from neighbouring forts (*Annals* 12.38), a fact which suggests that they were still close to the old frontier. Thus it seems possible that Scapula's work of consolidation, in contrast per-haps to his campaigns, was more limited than has at times been suggested.

## THE WORK OF DIDIUS GALLUS

Tacitus presents Scapula's successor, Didius Gallus, in a rather unfavourable light: 'burdened with years and covered with honours, he was content to act through his officers and to hold back the enemy' (*Annals* 12.40). From the *Agricola* we learn that he 'kept a firm hold on what his predecessors had won, and even pushed some forts into outlying districts, so that he could say that he had extended his sphere of duty' (*Agricola* 14). Such phrases must mean that he was consolidating the conquests of Scapula, work which Scapula's death had prevented him from doing. Among these forts may well have been Wroxeter, Usk and quite probably Clyro or Clifford, between them covering the valleys of the Usk, Wye and Severn. The speed with which his successor Quintus Veranius was able to take the field on his arrival in AD 57 confirms that the necessary preparations for a further advance had been completed by Gallus (*Annals* 14.29).

This great move forward must have had a considerable effect on the troop dispositions in the west of England. It was at about this time that Hod Hill was closed (Richmond *1968* 119). Although the fire which destroyed some of the internal buildings may have hastened the process, it is unlikely to have been the sole cause. The replacement of the first fort at Cirencester may also date from this period, although there is as yet no certain proof (Wacher *1965* 99). It is now certain, however, that the legionary fortress at Gloucester, for so long held to have been founded in AD 49 to receive Legion XX, in reality dates from at least fifteen years later as Neronian coins from primary positions show (Hurst *1972* 50). Tacitus makes clear that the legion was brought against the Silures, and it is difficult to reconcile this with a base at Gloucester some twenty miles from the river Wye, the generally accepted frontier of Siluria (Nash-Williams *1969* 3). On the other hand, the vital crossing of the river Severn at Gloucester, the main route into south Wales, would not have been left unguarded: the fort at Kingsholm, on the outskirts of Gloucester itself, may be a Scapulan foundation if it had not already come into existence as part of the forward defences of the Fosse Way scheme. Whether it was ever intended to be a legionary fortress is more doubtful.

To the west of the Severn no sites as early as Scapula can be identified with certainty. The size of Clyro (twenty acres) and Clifford show them to be major bases, but although Clifford is probably earlier than

Plate 2 The *caldarium* and *tepidarium* of the legionary (?) baths excavated at Exeter in 1972 in the cathedral close by the site of the demolished St Mary Major church (2m pole)

Clyro, Clyro itself is ill-dated. The fortress at Usk, which covers *c* 48 acres, cannot have been founded much before AD 55. Weston-under-Penyard has produced Claudian coin copies and is a likely site for a fort, but the evidence for more precise dating is lacking (Webster *1960* 66).

The situation in the south-west of England is hardly clearer. As noted above (p 23), no major base is likely at Dorchester, but Exeter and possibly Cirencester are more probable sites.

No surviving account mentions the conquest of the Dumnonii. Indeed

31

until quite recently it was held that the Roman conquest had largely passed them by, a suggestion which Lady Fox's work has effectively ended. Four forts are now known: Wiveliscombe, six miles west of Taunton, which has been trenched by Webster (*1959a* 81), unfortunately without producing any dating evidence; Exeter, where more than one fort appears to have existed (Fox *1968* 4; Collis *1972* 7; information from M. Griffiths); North Tawton, as yet unexcavated; and Nanstallon, excavated by Fox and Ravenhill (*1972*). To these must be added a probable port at Topsham on the Exe below Exeter (Dudley and Webster *1965* 104; Webster *1960* 56), and several fortlets and signal stations, namely Stoke Hill (Exeter), Broadbury, near Halwill in west Devon, and Old Burrow and Martinhoe on the north Devon coast (Fox *1959*; Fox and Ravenhill *1972* 89; *1966*).

The excavation in 1964–5 which finally discovered the long-suspected fort at Exeter failed to produce the evidence for a closer date than 'certainly pre-Flavian and probably Claudian' (Fox *1968* 13). On

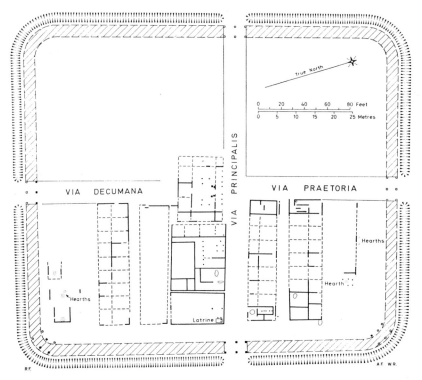

Fig 5   The fort at Nanstallon

historical grounds one would expect a fort to be built there as soon as the Fosse Way reached the site, and even if this was not in AD 47 it cannot have been long after. The more recent excavations of Collis and Griffiths have revealed early military remains under the city, including barracks, a granary, or granaries, a fabrica and a massive bath house (pl 2), all indicating a site of considerable importance and permanence whose garrison must have contained legionaries. The exact date within the pre-Flavian period for the establishment of the fortress is, however, not yet certain. A fort at Exeter may in any case merely mark the end of the Fosse Way system and need not necessarily presuppose the permanent occupation of the western half of Dumnonia.

Here the evidence from Nanstallon is of particular importance. Nanstallon is a small fort of 2.2 acres with a single bank and ditch. Somewhat over half of it was excavated, sufficient to allow a restoration of the complete plan if the two halves are assumed to be mirror images (fig 5). The principia, the commander's house and four barracks were found, probably leaving no more than four more barracks undug. The garrison appears to have been a *cohors quingenaria equitata*, around 380 infantry and 120 cavalry, although a mixture of legionaries and cavalry as at Hod Hill cannot be excluded (Fox and Ravenhill *1972* 84). The site produced an interesting group of coins: two republican denarii, a denarius each of Augustus and Tiberius, three bronze issues of Nero AD 64–6, a denarius of Otho and three (possibly four) bronze coins of Vespasian (Fox and Ravenhill *1972* 88). As the excavators say, the absence of coins of Claudius must put the foundation of the fort into the reign of Nero, AD 54–68, but, as is well known, no bronze coins were issued during the first ten years of Nero's reign with the result that copies of the existing Claudian bronzes appear to have been the normal small change in Britain. Such copies are completely absent from Nanstallon and if we assume, as we must, that the bronze coins reflect a random loss, the series suggests that Nanstallon was founded late in the reign of Nero, certainly after AD 64, a date with which the samian ware from the site would agree (Fox and Ravenhill *1972* 100).

The fortlets at Martinhoe and Old Burrow must imply a stronger Roman presence in the area than their size suggests. Old Burrow was a Claudian foundation which appears to have had a relatively short life, not surprisingly in view of its bleak and exposed situation. Martinhoe may logically be regarded as its successor; although there may have been a gap between the occupation of the two, Martinhoe was apparently not built before AD 55 or perhaps even a few years later. Unlike Old Burrow, it contained timber barracks for some 65–80 men (Fox and Ravenhill *1966* 22). The excavators suggest that the function of these fortlets was to watch, probably in collaboration with a Roman fleet, for Silurian raids across the Bristol Channel, but they may also have been intended to observe the movements of refugees fleeing from the Roman campaigns in Wales.

We have few details of the military situation in the west under the governors who succeeded Gallus. Quintus Veranius, who survived only one year in Britain (57–8), campaigned against the Silures (*Annals* 14.29; *Agricola* 14). Within two years his successor, Suetonius Paulinus, was able to launch a major attack on Anglesey, a fact which strongly suggests that in the intervening years he had reduced the Silures to a state in which they presented no immediate danger. This work was brought to an end by the Boudiccan revolt during which part of Legion XX is found in Paulinus' army (*Annals* 14.34), suggesting that it had been involved in the Anglesey campaign and reminding us that the whole of a legion need not be kept in one area when campaigns were in progress elsewhere. It was at this time that a part of Legion II failed to obey the governor's summons to join his army after the revolt had begun, presumably because the camp prefect in charge felt it too dangerous to move (*Annals* 14.37). The detachment was probably in the south-west, though it could conceivably have been in south Wales, and so the threat is not likely to have come from Boudicca's own army but from local disaffection.

Paulinus was in turn succeeded by Petronius Turpilianus who continued until AD 63 when Trebellius Maximus became governor. During his term of office, which appears to have been free from military actions, Legion XIV was removed from the province. Turpilianus remained until AD 69 when he was forced to flee from Britain after a quarrel with his legionary commanders during the Civil War. His successor, Vettius Bolanus, had a much depleted army, for 8,000 legionaries, about half the total, had been removed by Vitellius, and although Legion XIV returned in AD 69 for a year it was hostile to Vitellius and can hardly have improved a difficult situation. It was not until Petillius Cerialis arrived in AD 71 with a new legion (Adiutrix II) that major campaigning could begin again, and then it was against the Brigantes. The final conquest of the Silures was reserved for Julius Frontinus, governor from AD 74 to AD 78, and with his work the conquest of the west was finally completed (*Agricola* 17).

34

## THE FINAL PHASE

One of the results of the survival of an historical account is a tendency to try to fit all the archaeological material into it, no matter how terse and generalised that account may be. Occasionally, however, archaeology provides material which cannot be neatly dovetailed into the Tacitean framework. One such anomaly was the discovery that the fortress at Gloucester, which had been firmly dated to AD 49 many years before it had been found, must date from after AD 64; while another is that an even larger fortress existed on the other side of the Bristol Channel at Usk. Further south the excavations at South Cadbury Castle have produced more complications, while in Cornwall the late date for Nanstallon suggests considerable military activity in a period which has been traditionally regarded as absolutely peaceful.

This is perhaps the point at which to summarise the archaeological evidence for this final phase, limited though it is. The fort at Nanstallon was probably founded after AD 64 and continued into the reign of Vespasian (Fox and Ravenhill *1972* 88). The fortlet at Martinhoe was apparently built in the reign of Nero, possibly after AD 64, and continued in use until the Flavian period (Fox and Ravenhill *1966* 26). The situation at Exeter is complex, but Griffiths suggests that the sequence began in the Claudian period with the establishment of an auxiliary fort on a site to the south of the later city. This was then superseded by a fortress containing legionaries who remained until the opening of the Silurian campaign when they were replaced by an auxiliary unit. The fort at Waddon Hill was also built under Claudius and continued until *c* 60 or a little later (information from Dr Webster). At Cirencester there is evidence for three possible forts, or only two if the ditches found in the Watermoor Hospital Gardens and the Sands are, as Wacher has suggested, part of the same fort. The relationship between them is still somewhat obscure but, if there are three, the sequence would appear to be: (i) the Watermoor Hospital fort occupied until *c* 49 and forming part of the Fosse Way scheme (Wacher *1965* 99); (ii) the fort under the basilica occupied until *c* 60–5 with its abandonment dated by a great mass of pottery from the ditch (Wacher *1962* 3); (iii) the Sands Watermoor fort built *c* 60+ and abandoned by the last quarter of the first century (Brown and McWhirr *1967* 192; *1969* 222). Tombstones indicate at least two cavalry regiments in garrison during this period (*RIB* 108, 109).

At Gloucester the Kingsholm fort was replaced by a fortress of 43.25 acres after AD 64 (Hurst *1972* 29, 50). This is distinctly small for a full

Plate 3 A large granary at Usk, represented by a regular pattern of slots and holes for horizontal and vertical timbers. Recent excavation has shown it to belong to a major military base of the late sixties AD (2m poles)

legionary fortress, which is usually around 50 or more acres, and compares rather with Lincoln (41.5 acres); it may indicate that the legion was divided and brigaded with auxiliaries, only a part being at Gloucester. The fortress may have continued in existence until the reign of Nerva, but whether it was fully garrisoned as late as this is another matter, and the probability is strongly against it. At Usk a full fortress was built apparently early in the reign of Nero (pl 3), which continued until it was replaced by a smaller fort in the Flavian period. The fort at Clyro may also have been occupied in this period and, if the early bank at Llandovery is accepted as evidence of a pre-Flavian fort (Nash-Williams *1969* 96), it too would fit best in this context of the campaigns of the late rather than the early fifties.

With the exception of Gloucester, these sites end in the seventies, a date which would agree with the necessity for moving troops to garrison the north of England and Wales. Even at Gloucester it seems unlikely that the fortress had more than a caretaker garrison after the mid-seventies when all the legions have known bases elsewhere. But it is the dates at which the majority of these forts were built which presents a problem for they must indicate major troop movements in the mid to late sixties. Whether the fort at Nanstallon represents the occupation of Cornwall for the first time or merely the shuffling around of the available troops cannot be decided without more evidence, but until it can be disproved the former appears likely. The relatively late occupation at Waddon Hill serves as a corrective to any theory based on the early abandonment of Hod Hill. Clearly the Durotriges were not regarded as thoroughly pacified until well into the reign of Nero. The work at Gloucester and Usk must mark something more. Clearly the fortresses at Gloucester and Usk must have held legionary garrisons, perhaps with auxiliaries as well, but the redating of Gloucester must make it doubtful if Legion XX was the original garrison. The situation is complicated by the removal of Legion XIV from Wroxeter in AD 66, for this will have left the northern marches unprotected, and it is possible that Legion XX was moved there and Legion II regrouped at Gloucester (Frere *1967* 93). The tombstone of a soldier of Legion XX from Gloucester (*RIB* 122) came from between the city itself and Kingsholm and was found with the better-known memorial of Rufus Sita (*RIB* 121), a Thracian cavalryman. Both facts suggest that the Gloucester tombstone is as likely to represent the Kingsholm garrison as that of Gloucester itself. At Usk the discovery of a small medallion bearing a charging boar motif (pl 4) suggests that Legion XX had a hand in building the fortress there, although whether it formed the garrison is another matter.

The evidence from the fort sites in the south-west is fairly straightforward and indicates that the area was held in some strength until the Flavian period when it was thought practical in most cases to remove the garrisons. But the excavations at South Cadbury Castle, although they do not contradict this picture, add a complication. As at a number of other Iron Age hillforts, the excavators found clear evidence of a massacre in the last phase of the Iron Age occupation, in this case with the bodies left to decay unburied in the south-west gateway. The dating evidence for this massacre consists mainly of the brooches found with the bodies. Although the subject of some controversy, they are now generally agreed to indicate a date after *c* AD 44 when the area first came under Roman domination (Alcock *1972* 160). A date well within the Roman period for this assault is confirmed by the incorporation of more

37

Plate 4   A bronze medallion with a boar, the insignia of Legion XX,
excavated from the Roman military site at Usk

brooches and samian ware in the final refurbishing of the defences which
preceded the destruction of the hillfort (Alcock *1972* 169).

An indication that the Roman army found it expedient to occupy the
fort at least for a short time is seen in the discovery of the base of a field-
oven with fragments of military equipment and samian ware around it
(Alcock *1972* 172). Unfortunately this samian ware is undecorated and
cannot be dated with great precision. Originally it was held to indicate
a date after AD 70, but the excavator now considers a date some ten
years earlier to be more probable on historical grounds. What is certain
is that it is not Claudian and must reflect military activity at South
Cadbury Castle some years after the sacking of Maiden Castle and Hod
Hill. In summary, the evidence from South Cadbury, as at present interpreted, suggests that the Iron Age occupation continued unchecked and
largely uninfluenced by the Romans until well into the reign of Nero
when, after an ineffectual strengthening of the defences, the fort was
attacked by Roman troops who then occupied the site themselves for a
short time.

The main objection to this reconstruction is that the massacre and the Roman occupation around the field-oven are not linked beyond question. On the other hand, the evidence for a long period of native occupation, after the Roman conquest, of a hillfort within sight of the Fosse Way appears incontrovertible and in itself requires explanation. When the date for the destruction of the hillfort appeared to be after AD 70 the interpretation of this evidence presented very great problems, but now that a date of *c* AD 60 is acceptable an obvious explanation is available in the Boudiccan revolt. In terms of Iron Age political geography, Cadbury lies near the northern edge of the Durotriges as defined by their coinage, but a few Dobunnic coins are known from the area, including one from Cadbury itself (Alcock *1972* 12, fig 1). It is by no means impossible that at the time of the Roman invasion it was actually part of the southern Dobunni, or that the Durotriges were already divided into two groups as they certainly were in the Roman period when they had capitals at Dorchester and Ilchester (Stevens *1952* 188). In either case, the tribe in whose area South Cadbury lay may have made terms with the Romans and become a client kingdom, able to maintain its old ways into the Neronian period. That there was active hostility to Rome in some part of the south-west during the Boudiccan war is shown by the refusal of Poenius Postumus, camp prefect of Legion II, to obey the governor's orders and join him (*Annals* 14.37). Only an obvious and immediate danger to his troops once they left the security of their forts could lead to such a decision, and, as such a threat in the south-west could hardly come from Boudicca's army, the revolt must have had repercussions in that area. This is not surprising. If we are correct in assuming that Cadbury lay within a client kingdom, the provocation which caused the Boudiccan rising would at the least produce the sympathy of self-interest, while her initial successes might suggest that a total Roman defeat, a disaster of truly Varan proportions (p 47), was likely and would be greatly increased if Legion II, like Legion IX, could be stopped from joining the main army. Under such circumstances, supporting the revolt might seem both politic and patriotic, but once Paulinus was victorious a day of reckoning was inevitable, when the 'tribes that wavered or were hostile were ravaged with fire and sword' (*Annals* 14.38).

It is unlikely that any theory based on our present manifestly inadequate knowledge will stand for long, and what follows is merely an attempt to produce a reasonable explanation of the position as it appears today.

The initial phase of the conquest lasted from AD 43 or 44 until 47, by when it was possible to draw a temporary frontier along the Fosse Way. A number of the tribes in the west were probably admitted as client kingdoms, although this did not prevent the Fosse Way with its chain of forts from crossing their territories. The main garrison in this area was provided by Legion II and its auxiliaries. The second phase, in the ten years after AD 47, was marked by a move forward into south Wales, largely in response to the continued aggression of the Welsh tribes, during which Legion XX was brought up and probably formed the core of the army in the new territory. The process of fort-building which followed lasted well into the mid-fifties, and the legions were almost certainly divided between a number of major bases including Exeter and at least one other, at present unknown, further north or east. The size and date of the fortress at Usk must give it the chief claim to be the base of Legion XX, but there may have been detachments at Clyro, and perhaps Kingsholm as well. North Devon must have been occupied at this time if not in phase I, and Old Burrow was built to watch the Bristol Channel, possibly to warn of Silurian landings but perhaps also to observe any attempt by Caratacus and his supporters to cross to Dumnonia. Whether west Devon and Cornwall were occupied at the same time is an open question, but the existing evidence suggests that they were not.

Additional campaigns of unknown extent took place in south Wales in the late fifties, perhaps reaching as far as Llandovery. The situation was sufficiently uncertain in the south-west during the Boudiccan revolt for part of Legion II to refuse to leave its base, and the destruction of South Cadbury Castle may be a result of this rising. The military arrangements in the west then remained static while the pacification and Romanisation of eastern England continued, but by AD 66 the situation was regarded as sufficiently stable for the removal of Legion XIV, stationed at Wroxeter, and no doubt its auxiliaries from Britain. If north Wales was not to be left without a legionary garrison either Legion II or Legion XX must have been moved to Wroxeter, and all the evidence suggests that it was Legion XX. In the absence of literary evidence the exact date of the building of the fortress at Gloucester must remain uncertain, but there would seem to be two likely possibilities. It could have been constructed between *c* 64 and 66 when the south-west of England was judged sufficiently pacified for Legion II to be moved, perhaps as part of the preparations for a renewal of the Welsh campaigns. Gloucester would be well placed for this, for it could serve as a command centre for the south-west, while providing support for the army in south Wales. Alternatively, it may have been the result of the decision to remove Legion XX from Usk, which will have left south Wales unprotected. Although it would seem that the obvious move was to regroup Legion II in the vacated fortress, Usk lies on the western side of the Forest of Dean and is ill-placed for controlling south-west England where a large though divided garrison was still maintained. Under these circumstances Gloucester would again be an obvious site for a new fortress, although the old one at Usk must have retained a caretaker or much reduced garrison for the archaeological evidence makes it clear that it was not abandoned. In any event either Usk or Gloucester will have been almost empty in the last years of Nero's reign, and will have formed a suitable base for the dissident Legion XIV when it was returned to Britain during the Civil War. Of the two Usk may have been thought a better choice, for its supply route crossed the river Severn at Gloucester effectively putting it at least partially under the control of the legion in garrison there.

Not until 74, after the conclusion of the Civil War and the conquest of Brigantia, were the Welsh campaigns resumed, but by 78 the conquest was complete.

# 2

# NERO, BOUDICCA
# AND THE FRONTIER IN THE WEST

According to Suetonius (*Nero* 18), Nero 'was never moved by any desire or expectation of enlarging the empire, and even thought of withdrawing the army from Britain, only desisting from shame at appearing to disparage his father's glory. He merely provincialized the kingdom of Pontus on the abdication of Polemo, and the Alps on the death of Cottius'. Tacitus, who is complete for Nero's reign to AD 66, does not mention the project and such is his authority that his silence on such a point might seem to give substance to the view that the statement is a typical piece of Suetonian rumour-mongering. Some, for example Syme (*1958* 490) and Townend (*1959* 292), have gone further and suggested that it is a veiled criticism of Hadrian's policy of withdrawal from Trajan's conquests in the east by associating a policy of withdrawal with Nero – by definition the worst of emperors. On the other hand, most specialists on Roman Britain have accepted it. Richmond, for example (*1946* 61), associated the proposal with the revolt of Boudicca, and Frere (*1967* 85) regarded this as the most likely date; but the only detailed arguments about possible dates have been put forward by Stevens (*1951* 4) and E. R. Birley (*1961* 1), the former suggesting a period between AD 54 and 58, with the notion decisively rejected by Nero on reading the will of Veranius, the latter a shorter period ending in AD 57 when Nero appointed Veranius with instructions to pursue a forward policy in Britain. The purpose of this chapter is to suggest that the arguments for the traditional date, Boudicca's rebellion, are far more powerful than those for the other dates. The relevance of the Roman position in the south-west to the discussion will appear in due course.

It must be admitted at the outset that we cannot prove that Suetonius' statement is true, but that goes for a great deal of material in the *Lives* which is generally accepted. Townend's arguments referring the statement to Hadrian's policy are ingenious, but his view that Suetonius does not elsewhere suggest so strongly that the expansion of the empire was an obligation on emperors gives entirely the wrong picture. In his highly laudatory biography of Augustus, Suetonius actually praises the non-expansive policy (as he considered it) of that emperor in terms very similar to those he uses of Nero: 'he waged war on no people without just cause or unless forced to do so, and was far from any desire to enlarge the empire or increase his military reputation regardless of the means' (*Augustus* 21). In fact this has been said by one scholar (Brunt *1967* 69) to be an anachronistic attribution to Augustus of the non-expansive policy of Hadrian – in which case of course he is praising, not criticising, the policy by associating it with the first and greatest of emperors! This shows that there are serious problems of method involved in identifying such oblique references to current events in Roman historians' accounts of the past. The same criticism of method has been made against Syme who, in his Tacitus, saw oblique criticism of Hadrian at many points in the *Annals* and precisely in the Neronian books (see Sherwin White *1959* 140–6). In fact, in all the lives except those of 68–9, Suetonius lists the campaigns undertaken by the emperors in person or, more usually, through *legati,* together with acquisitions of territory (*Augustus* 20, 21, *Tiberius* 37, *Gaius* 43, *Claudius* 17, *Vespasian* 8, *Domitian* 6). Except in the case of Augustus, who of course did enlarge the empire considerably, as Suetonius says, acquisitions of territory were mostly the reduction of client states to provincial status, precisely as in the Nero reference. *Nero* 18 and 19 in which his two projected tours in the east are mentioned, with his planned campaign to the Caspian Gates, are strictly in line with similar summaries in the other lives, and are included by Suetonius under the heading of actions of Nero which were either blameless or even worthy of considerable praise. Finally, although Suetonius unquestionably mixed fact with gossip in an irresponsible way, it seems clear that it all comes from the copious store of Julio-Claudian and Flavian historiography, and it has never to my knowledge been demonstrated that he went in for the plain invention of alleged historical detail. I conclude therefore that the statement is derived from a Flavian source on Nero, in all probability one of the three named and used by Tacitus – Pliny the Elder, Cluvius Rufus and Fabius Rusticus (Warmington *1969* 1–8).

## THE GOVERNORSHIP OF VERANIUS

Stevens's choice of date was based on the view that when Nero read the will of Q. Veranius, in which the governor said that he could have conquered the whole province for Nero if he had had two years longer to live (*Annals* 14. 29), he gave up the idea of abandoning Britain and appointed Suetonius Paulinus, as an expert in mountain warfare, to press on into the island. Meanwhile Seneca, who had not appreciated the finality of Nero's decision to retain Britain, called in his loans to the Britons, thus adding to the grievances which led to the rebellion of Boudicca. The prime objection to this hypothesis from the historical point of view is the position of Seneca. Leaving aside the disputed question as to whether Seneca really did lend and recall all that money, the idea that Nero was taking decisions of such magnitude at the date suggested without the knowledge or advice of Seneca, Burrus and others, cannot be sustained. Our sources are, it is true, not clear as to the precise mode by which Seneca and Burrus exercised their influence – nor could they be, in view of the fact that it was exercised in the emperor's privy council, not in open senate – but that the two senior and respected figures exercised a dominant influence over Nero's governmental actions till AD 62 is their consistent view (Warmington *1969* 27ff).

Birley, without dealing with the point about Seneca, suggested that Nero's change of mind came before, not after, the appointment of Veranius, who was the man chosen to lead a new advance in Britain. It is an eloquent testimony to the acuteness of this scholar that he was able to demonstrate the importance of Veranius' rapid career as a possible indicator of a new policy before the publication of the important sepulchral inscription of Veranius which showed that he had had a five-year term as governor of Lycia and Pamphilia, precisely with operations against mountain tribes and strongholds – an eminently suitable preparation for advance in Wales. It is not surprising that this solution was favoured by, among others, Webster (*1970* 192) and Jarrett (*1964* 33).

There are, however, some serious objections to be made, the most obvious being why Nero and his advisers should think of abandoning Britain at this date. There appear to be two suggestions, one economic, the other military. Birley suggested that the early hopes of great mineral wealth had been disappointed, and it had not yet been possible to reduce the garrison of the province appreciably. Webster (*1970* 191–2) concentrated on the difficulties of the Romans on the western frontier and regarded the situation in the last years of Claudius as serious. On the first point I know of no evidence at all to suggest that the Romans were seriously disappointed at what they had won at this date, and indeed the report on Nanstallon (Fox and Ravenhill *1972* 91) shows the army, in Nero's reign, still prospecting and working metal. Furthermore, just as economic benefit was never the chief ground for the acquisition of territory (Ogilvie and Richmond *1967* 50, 183), though it was of course hoped it would accrue, so a profit and loss account of the worth of a province seems to have been primarily a second-century attitude, as I will mention later, and never, in any case, led to abandonment of a province.

As for the military difficulties, Webster, in his latest treatment of events in Britain (*1970* 191f), in my view quite correctly painted a far less gloomy picture than that given in his earlier *Revolt of Boudicca*, though still regarding it as perhaps serious enough under Didius Gallus for Burrus and Seneca to advise Nero to consider withdrawal and for Seneca to call in his loans. Yet, as he points out, it is clear that Didius solved the problem of the Silures, probably in the early part of his governorship, since they are not mentioned as attacking or raiding Roman territory again. It should be observed, too, that Tacitus, who alone gives an account of the guerrilla warfare conducted by the Silures, himself says (*Annals* 12. 40) that the reports of Roman reverses prior to the arrival of Didius were exaggerated both by the Silures and by the general himself 'to increase his fame if he won and improve his excuse if resistance continued unbroken'. Archaeologically the only certain traces of this period in south Wales appear to be the important sites at Usk and Clyro, no doubt part of a series to control the Silures (*supra* p 29). There may also have been advances in south-west Britain in Devon and Cornwall, probably without much difficulty, even though Nanstallon appears to belong in the later Neronian period (*supra* p 33). In the north, Roman intervention was required to maintain Cartimandua, but Tacitus does not suggest that the task was difficult, merely complaining that Didius left the task to a subordinate, surely an unjustified sneer at a normal piece of delegation in a simple situation. As for Veranius, the most that we know for certain is what Tacitus says (*Annals* 14. 29), that he conducted some minor operations against the Silures, though it is no doubt legitimate to conclude that he completed the intimidation of the tribe, and thus of most of south Wales, begun by Didius.

It may also be argued that too much can be made of the supposed military expertise of the generals as an indicator of changes in policy and that there is little to choose between the three governors of the years AD 52–62. Tacitus' sly suggestion that Didius Gallus was an elderly has-been is difficult to sustain (Jarrett *1964* 32; Frere *1967* 83f). He had been *legatus* of the difficult province of Moesia *c* 46, with responsibilities as far away as the Crimea, and had held other unknown governorships. The interval of sixteen years between his consulship and his governorship of Britain is almost exactly the same as in the case of Suetonius Paulinus. The latter is conventionally regarded as an expert in mountain warfare on the strength of campaigns in Mauretania no less than seventeen years earlier. If this is true, it ought to make us think hard about the whole concept of military experience when applied to Roman generals. Veranius must have been younger (eight years since his consulship), but his five-year tenure of Lycia and Pamphilia with a campaign in mountainous territory is only superficially impressive. It is true that Lycia had just been provincialised after internal quarrels and added to Pamphilia, provincialised long before, but it is not clear that there were disturbances except in the mountains between the new province and the province of Cilicia, where the tribes were admittedly turbulent at all periods. But the fact that his sepulchral inscription can mention as an achievement the storming of a single native fort leads one to think that his campaign was as inflated as his will was boastful. (On Veranius, see Gordon *1955* 939ff; on the chronology of the three governors and references to sources, A. R. Birley *1967* 65–6.) The rapidity of his career as demonstrated by E. R. Birley *(1953)* can be explained in terms of patronage in a typically Roman manner – the son of a former companion of Germanicus was likely to do well under Germanicus' son and brother. Finally, though one must agree with Birley that the governors of imperial provinces received detailed instructions before taking up their posts, it must be a matter of debate *how* detailed they were, since we have no examples. I see nothing in Tacitus' narrative or in the archaeological record to prevent one from thinking that governors of Britain could have been free to make advances in Wales at any time if such advances would improve the security of the rest of the province, and that there was no dramatic change with Veranius or Suetonius Paulinus. There would seem to be little difference in principle between the suppression of the Silures, the most active opponent in the field, and the attack on Anglesey, the refuge for dissidents from the province.

## THE BOUDICCAN REVOLT

We may turn now to the years 60–1, when the military and economic situation of the province was truly serious. We should look at the development of the rebellion, beginning in the early summer of AD 60, as it would have appeared, after several weeks' delay, to Nero and his council. The first report would have come from the procurator, Catus Decianus, who fled to Gaul after the destruction of the *colonia* Camulodunum and the defeat of Legion IX with the loss of part of its infantry. If only to excuse his own flight and his failure to save the colony in the absence of Suetonius, he would certainly have painted the situation in the blackest colours, emphasising that the general was campaigning well over 200 miles away from the rebel area. This news would soon have been followed by the report that Suetonius had got through rebel territory as far as London with his cavalry, but had found the position so serious that he had had to give up the town, his main supply base, and much of the most prosperous part of the province, together with the *municipium* Verulamium, and retreat into the interior of the island *away* from the area closest to Gaul, through which lay his most obvious route for escape or for receiving reinforcements. Legion IX was licking its wounds in its fortress at Langthorpe and it was perhaps known that Legion II in the west had failed, for whatever reason, to join the governor. Thus four legions, dispersed in at least three widely separated bases, were cut off in the island by successful rebels. This surely was a situation in which the island could be regarded as actually or potentially lost, and it has not to my knowledge been sufficiently observed that all our sources for the event apply this term to the situation. In the *Agricola* (16) Tacitus summarises: if Paulinus had not brought rapid assistance on hearing of the rebellion, Britain would have been lost. According to Dio, also summarising before his main account of the events, 'a terrible disaster occurred in Britain. Two cities were sacked, 80,000 of the Romans and their allies perished, and the island fell into the hands of the enemy'. Finally, according to Suetonius (*Nero* 40), Nero comforted himself in the final crisis of his reign with the thought that 'having lost and recovered both Britain and Armenia, he had already suffered the misfortunes which fate had in store for him'. Elsewhere (*Nero* 39) Suetonius speaks of 'a disaster in Britain in which two important towns were destroyed with great loss of Roman citizens and allies'. This is generally and rightly held to come from the same source as Dio, and thus the whole notion of the loss, actual or potential, of Britain will come from one of the accounts of Nero's reign published soon after his death.

Looked at in this light, the idea of trying to get the army out before another loss on the scale of the *clades Variana* in Germany over fifty years before was attractive. An evacuation could be mounted, I suggest, through south-west Britain alone, since the whole east coast was controlled, or easily threatened, by the rebels. The kingdom of Cogidubnus was still loyal, but was extremely isolated, even if the Durotriges had not actually joined the rebels. Much depended on the location of Legion

47

II at this date, when its *praefectus castrorum* Poenius Postumus disobeyed his orders to join Suetonius. Gloucester appears to have been generally favoured, but the legionary fortress lying under the later *colonia* dates to AD 64 or later (*supra* p 35), while an earlier fortress at near-by Kingsholm is presumed, but not yet proved, to have existed. In any case, if it did exist, it need not at this time have been the base of Legion II. Webster, it may be noted, gives no view at all in his latest study of its location in AD 60/61. Frere on the other hand (*1967* 74–5, 90) argues strongly for Exeter (*supra* p 35), or for two separate fortresses at Exeter and Dorchester. If this location is correct, an evacuation through this part of Britain was feasible. We can never know why the unfortunate Postumus disobeyed – whether the Durotriges and other tribes were in revolt (*supra* p 39), whether he lacked Suetonius' ruthlessness in abandoning the pro-Roman civilian population, or even whether he had an eye on a possible escape if Suetonius suffered a disaster. After all, since he committed suicide on Suetonius' victory, it looks as though his behaviour was such that no extenuating circumstances could be offered. Such a situation, I suggest, would be one likely to provoke a hasty, panic-stricken reaction from the young Nero, the most unmilitary emperor of the first century, and one who never showed interest in, or concern for, the army or even visited an army unit. The stories of his alternating moods of panic and euphoria on hearing of the revolt of Vindex in AD 68 no doubt lost nothing in the telling (Warmington *1969* 162), but his demoralisation then seems to have been real enough. In AD 61 he was talked out of his notion, as he was out of other politically dubious projects like the abolition of all indirect taxes throughout the empire. The man who did this, we may suppose, was Burrus, who is praised by Tacitus for his military efficiency (*Annals* 13. 2), though we are ignorant of what this consisted in detail. Apart from general considerations about the bad effect on opinion of a precipitate withdrawal *(infra)*, Burrus must have urged at least waiting for the result of a major engagement, in which the Romans had never had any difficulty in Britain since the invasion, knowing that with the time factor involved in communications a result might have been reached before any orders could reach Suetonius. Perhaps it was also known that the rebels had not attacked or taken any forts (*Annals* 14. 33), a fact which could indicate that they were less dangerous than they might seem to the militarily inexperienced Nero on hearing of the widespread destruction of unfortified places.

A date immediately following the rebellion is likewise a possibility if it is considered that long-term economic and manpower factors were discussed, and not merely a hasty idea of Nero's. The economic devastation caused by the rebellion, with the destruction of Camulodunum, Verulamium and Londinium, was added to both by the widespread repression of its aftermath by Suetonius, and by continued resistance. It is generally assumed that when the new procurator Classicianus complained to Nero that the war would not end till Suetonius was superseded as governor, he was thinking about the massive drop in revenues which must have occurred and which he wanted to restore to their old level. As is well known, an imperial freedman Polyclitus was sent to investigate the situation in Britain. Tacitus claims to know (how?) of Nero's hope that Polyclitus would reconcile governor and procurator and also induce the rebels to make peace. But he says nothing further about this; he concludes merely that Polyclitus toned everything down in his report – no doubt a typically bureaucratic exercise saying that things were not as bad as had been painted (*Annals* 14. 39).

It is certainly true that from the point of view of the overall defence of the empire a good case could be made for withdrawal from Britain. We tend to concentrate on the events in Britain to the neglect of the far more important situation which had developed in the east, and to which Tacitus gives several times the amount of space he devotes to Britain. For eleven years the Roman and Parthian empires confronted each other, while the Roman forces in the east had been increased from four to seven legions with the transfer of legions from Moesia and Pannonia. The position on the Danube was stretched, and the troops used in Britain, it might be argued, could be far more use to the empire as a whole on other frontiers. Indeed it was precisely from Britain *c* 66 that Nero withdrew Legion XIV for his planned expedition to the Caspian Gates. Frere (*1967* 85) suggested the Armenian situation as a possible reason for an appraisal of Britain early in Nero's reign, but it did not become serious till after AD 60 (Warmington *1969* 91ff). However, the general argument is valid for the whole Roman period; Britain was strategically unnecessary to the Roman empire and thus a permanent drain on military manpower. The fact that it was never given up till the last necessity of Rome does not prove that the Romans were stupid but simply that great imperial powers, especially those with a sense of destiny as the Romans undoubtedly had, simply do not judge by such apparently rational standards.

This applies also to any notion that Britain might have been given up in AD 57, 58 or 61 for economic reasons. We know now that the great imperialist adventurers of the late republic like Pompey and Caesar, and likewise the more cautious strategist Augustus, were keenly interested for their different reasons in the money which could be extracted from the provincials, yet the number of cases in which an economic motive for annexation can even plausibly be argued as the main one are negligible. Strabo, it is true, gives an economic motive for Rome's failure to annex Britain after Caesar's expeditions, namely that the revenue would not pay for even the one legion which conquest would require (4. 200), but this is secondary to the statement that the island was effectively dominated already through client chiefs. But in any case the passage should surely be recognised as the basis of the official explanation given by Augustus for his failure to undertake an invasion frequently demanded by public opinion in Rome. The master propagandist manages to suggest no less than three excuses – the island is already dominated by Rome; it is no threat since only one legion would be sufficient to annex it; but it is so poor that even this would not pay. Much later, Appian under Antoninus Pius writes of Britain (*Proem.* 5 and 7): 'the Romans possess the better half of it having no need of the rest; indeed the part they possess is no profit to them . . . Emperors on the whole have refused to extend the empire to poverty stricken and profitless tribes of barbarians . . . on some of their subjects they spend more than they receive, thinking it dishonourable to give them up even though they are expensive'.

The fact is that the prestige of Rome and the emperor were of far more concern than economics once a province had been acquired. The loss of a province in circumstances akin to what happened in Britain, only worse, was for Florus in the mid-second century a blot on the reputation of Augustus: 'If only he had not thought so much of conquering Germany; its loss was more disgraceful than its conquest was glorious' (2.30). He also judged, with reference to Roman expansion before Augustus, that the subjection (though not formal annexation) of Armenia and Britain was honourable and glorious, and, even if they served no practical purpose, constituted solid titles to imperial greatness (1.47). The notion of honour and possible disgrace at territorial loss brings us back to the reason given by Suetonius for Nero's abandonment of his idea – shame at appearing to disparage his father's glory. At first sight this concern for Claudius' reputation might seem to restrict the project to the first few months of Nero's reign when Claudius was given divine honours and a temple to Divus Claudius was begun in Rome, but to be unsuitable later when Nero and his advisers sought popularity by ridiculing Claudius and some of the unpopular features of his reign. Yet Nero's connection with Claudius was still important to Nero, dynastically, at least up to AD 62 (Warmington *1969* 50), and his conquest of Britain had been an important event. Strategically and economically dubious though the advantages might be, there is no evidence that anyone seriously criticised this first major departure from Augustus' final advice on the optimum size of the empire. On the contrary, an immense amount of publicity had surrounded the conquest. There was Claudius' triumph, the massive arch set up at Rome, important series of coins celebrating the event, and the naming of his son Britannicus. Claudius had sought, perhaps not without success, by his prestigious British victory to overcome the handicaps of his obscure and unmilitary background on the fringe of the imperial family, and the fortuitous, not to say humiliating way in which he had become emperor. The young Nero had not the slightest interest in the army and the military affairs of the empire, and it could be argued that he was incapable of feeling shame at anything; but he could presumably appreciate the argument that a withdrawal from Britain would appear to an important section of opinion to be a rejection of an important achievement of Claudius and that this would reflect on Nero's own standing.

# 3

# COIN HOARDS AND HISTORY IN THE WEST

The evidence of coin hoards can be made to appear convincing in terms
of crises – social, economic and political – but in matters such as these
it can oversimplify and even mislead. For the historian the evidential
value of coin hoards lies in the study of the chronological and geographical contexts of discovery. Accordingly I will begin by establishing a
framework in terms of time and space. The period covered in this chapter extends from the pre-Roman Iron Age to the last phase of the Roman
occupation of Britain and its immediate aftermath. The area here considered embraces the modern counties of Cornwall, Devon, Somerset,
Dorset, Wiltshire, Gloucestershire, parts of Hampshire and Herefordshire
and, on historical and geographical grounds, the southern counties of
Wales. Thus the territories of the Atrebates, Belgae, Dobunni, Dumnonii,
Durotriges, Demetae and Silures will all be involved.

## THE CHRONOLOGICAL PATTERN OF HOARDING

Pre-Claudian commercial transactions are indicated by two Somerset
hoards composed solely of republican denarii. These echo the larger
total of such hoards in the south-east of Britain, with its closer continental contacts. Then comes the conquest itself. Monmouth has a hoard
of aurei of Claudius I as a regional counterpart to the Bredgar, Kent,
hoard of aurei from Julius Caesar to Claudius, both marking the new
presence in native affairs. Perhaps the most notable of the small number of south-western hoards closing in issues of Claudius I is that from
Nunney (Som). This hoard, however, is indicative of a rather later
period when republican and early imperial denarii and bronze issues
of the early emperors could circulate freely enough to enter hoards with
British gold and silver coins. The bronze coins, at least, are likely to
have come, ultimately, from military pay.

The rest of the first century seems to have produced few hoards. The
most remarkable feature of them is the continued hoarding of mixed
groups of British and Roman coins, as on the Hampshire sites at Bitterne

and Timsbury. In the latter years of the first century Roman currency may have been in short supply in the south-west. Taken with the nationally reflected habit of hoarding British with Roman coins, this suggests that the scarcity of hoards may indicate a scarcity of Roman coins among the native population.

While the province as a whole underwent consolidation in stone and saw increased security in the early second century, the south-west appears to have progressed at only a modest economic pace. What little there seems to have been in terms of surplus wealth appears to concentrate in the towns. Bath, for example, has yielded a hoard of about a hundred denarii, closing in those of Trajan. In south Wales, by contrast, the hoards occur on military sites, with Hadrianic hoards at Caerleon and Y Gaer. Nowhere except in a reputedly primitive area of Hampshire does the rural native population seem to have money to hoard. The 'Southants' hoard continues the practice of hoarding British and Roman coins together, one of the latest hoards to do so, having Hadrianic coins as its latest Roman issues. To make generalisations on the basis of a small sample is dangerous, but military and urban sites seem better sources of hoards than rural settlements in the early second century, a reflection as much of continuing small-scale farming as of urban development.

Hampshire continues to provoke interest during the second century with two hoards that terminate in issues of Marcus Aurelius. In general, however, hoards of Trajanic, Hadrianic and early Antonine denarii are rare in the south-west. The most likely reason is that in this area the period was one without serious political disorders in which economic life may well have achieved moderate levels of prosperity.

The late Antonine period provides the first real peak in south-western hoards. Rather than occurring on military or urban sites, most of these hoards belong to areas somewhat too remote to relate to prudent town-dwellers hoarding in the local countryside. These hoards form part of a national pattern of late Antonine hoards, the reason for which is not obvious. Warfare in the north is archaeologically and epigraphically attested but its effect on the morale of the native population of the south-west is likely to have been small.

More to the point is the fact that hoards of 100 and 200 denarii were now being amassed and buried. Of the four well-recorded examples one is from a military site, Caerleon, and one from the mines at Lydney; together they attest the volume of silver circulating in the south-west. Two notable bronze hoards from the region also close in coins of

Marcus Aurelius. It has been suggested that a shortage of bronze coins may have been felt in the mid second century (Sutherland *1937* 30). Hoarding was a usual reaction to such a shortage and could explain a Hampshire hoard of bronzes from Nero to Marcus Aurelius at Bitterne and a gallon of bronze coins closing with Marcus Aurelius at Barton on the Isle of Wight.

It is not surprising that very few hoards of the Severan period have been recorded in the south-west. A considerable number of hoards of this period occur in northern Britain, as might be expected in view of the Severan military campaigns there. Meanwhile the south-west entered into what has been called a period of relative peace and poverty (Laing *1969* 227). This period, the first half of the third century, is one where the onus has to be on negative evidence. The few known hoards are, however, expressive of current economic conditions. Until the time of Severus Alexander hoards are generally of silver; thereafter the debasement of the antoninianus is encouragement to hoard, instead, large brasses. Of these the south-west has a notable example in the Ham Hill (Som) hoard of 2,000 sestertii, ending in issues of AD 267.

The currency manipulations by which the mid-third-century emperors and usurpers completed the debasement of the coinage left many in Britain prey to well-founded fears about the value of their money. Inflation and uncertainty have very often been given as the reasons for so many hoards of this period being buried and never recovered. In the south-west the majority of those where a terminus is recorded belong to the period of the Tetrici or to the circulation-period of their coinage.

These hoards are the first clear reflection of a mass reaction. The traditional theory of general alarm, marked by hoarding, is difficult to replace but may at least be modified. If the currency was so badly debased, why not circulate it rather than trust to better times later? All who were able would surely put their wealth into the form of goods and property, leaving only the less fortunate to hoard base coins and false hopes. If this is so, we may consider the possibility that the undoubted misery and ruin affected only the non-land-owning labouring classes in agriculture and industry. At the end of an economic chain, paid in poor coin for goods and services, largely able to circulate money only among themselves, many might choose to hoard in hope of coming improvements.

Despite the apparently nationwide dislike of Aurelian's reformed coins, they appear with some regularity in south-western hoards, even 167). Small hoards of bronze coins, often in remote rural areas, contrast a third of the British hoards closing with coins of Aurelian were buried north of the Midlands. With this figure in mind, the south-west's total may be considered quite significant. It might be that this region was able to recover economically during the steadying period of Aurelian's brief reign and to move towards a moderate prosperity. An alternative view would reflect on the possibly violent end of Gallic authority in Britain and the destruction of anti-Aurelian factions. Most remarkable of all were two Somerset hoards closing in Aurelian's coins, both possibly of over 10,000 bronzes. Whether military chests, tax collections, mercantile revenues or none of these, they are certainly a high-spot in a period more noted for economic and political distress.

Once the rash of inflation-reaction hoards had passed there is hardly any hoarding in the south-west until the period of the British empire. Perhaps little is seen of official coinage too, since barbarous radiate production and circulation are widespread until the time of Probus or Carinus. Sites such as Whitchurch (Som) and Coygan Camp (Carmarthen) gave suitably remote locations for the production of radiate copies (Boon and Rahtz *1966* 13–51; Boon *1967* 110–26).

Carausius is generally considered to have been more powerful in the south of Britain than in the north, the south-west being particularly associated with the abrupt collapse of his island empire. In a circular way, support for this theory is drawn from the large number of coin hoards of this period found in the south-west. Be that as it may, normal commerce had to function and, Carausian coins being both available and, for a while, superior to central government issues, they were doubtless widely used. Pirates and the central government's attempts to reconquer Britain provide the usual reasons for hoarding at this time, but some hoards may be thought too far inland to reflect fears of sea-raiders. Meanwhile Carausius was defeating all efforts to crush his rebel regime. It is possible that despite the external dangers and uncertainties, a measure of stability was achieved in the south which either allowed some to hoard up savings or encouraged the concealment of surplus wealth for fear of enforced contributions to the national defence budget or the exchequer in general.

When Allectus fell before Rome's troops, many contemporary hoards seem to have been buried. It appears likely that such hoards were concealed in fear of looting by troops of either army rather than in face of threatened arrest as rebels and traitors. This would account for the great number of hoards rather more satisfactorily than a theory involving rich political fugitives since, in terms of numbers, the latter group seem strangely large. The concentration in the south-west of Britain may be an indication of native fears when the reconquest began. The Roman force landed in the Southampton area and the hoard of Allectan coins found at Bitterne near-by may be only the most obvious example of a panic reaction in which many, implicated or not, buried their wealth.

The period of the Tetrarchy overlaps that of the British empire, and as a result hoards closing in coins of these years have been recorded variously as of Carausian, Allectan and Tetrarchic date. In many cases no indication of the exact closing date is recorded, and many Tetrarchic hoards are left as belonging to the British empire period but are equally likely to be later. In the south-west, hoards with terminals in Diocletian, in Maximian and more vaguely in the Tetrarchy mostly have in common their considerable size. A hoard from a villa at Rockbourne (Hants) contained 7,717 coins, and a contemporary hoard in the villa's out-buildings contained some 4,020 coins. The larger hoard was of silver and bronze, the other solely of bronze coins. A villa at Lillyhorn, near Bisley (Glos), produced a hoard of 1,223 bronzes closing with the Tetrarchs, and the Somerset sites of Tickenham and Clapton-in-Gordano yielded bronze coin hoards of the same period as Lillyhorn. Further contemporary examples are known from Wiltshire and Cornwall.

Diocletian's currency reforms and his efforts to control prices were alike granted only limited success. Making due allowance for the allocation of some of the 'Tetrarchic' hoards to the period of the British empire, as is true of the two Rockbourne hoards, there is still a significantly high level of hoarding in the earliest years of the fourth century. While this is true throughout Romanised Britain, the south-western hoards are more often found on civilian sites, whereas military sites account for many of the hoards in other regions. It is now that hoards become more frequent in villas perhaps, as was suggested for Rockbourne, in antici-pation of raids (Morley-Hewitt *1971* 24), or perhaps in order to conserve domestic finances for daily running costs. The current inflation would be enough to encourage hoarding by anyone who could manage it.

In the lengthy period of rule by the Constantinian dynasty it is possible to establish that the majority of the coin hoards belong to the reign of Constantine I. Having thus limited the period to AD 307–37 it is rarely possible to be more precise. Two isolated, closely datable examples are from near Aston Blank (Glos) of about AD 307–18, and from Okehampton (Devon) of about AD 320–30. Apart from these, some twenty hoards are labelled with Constantine I terminals but yield no further details of their date of deposition.

That all these hoards are composed solely of bronzes is to be expected and is recorded. In this period, AD 307–37, when many of the hoards contain hundreds or even thousands of coins, it is noteworthy that hoards of ten to seventy coins also occur. For the poor as well as for the rich, or perhaps for the individual as much as for commercial organisations, the army and the government, it was a period when much currency was in circulation and opportunities existed to hoard it against worse times or future needs. If this is a criterion of prosperity, then the south-west, in common with much of Roman Britain, seems to have enjoyed a measure of it under Constantine I.

After the first Constantine's death a confusing mass of hoards labelled 'House of Constantine' has to be assessed. These divide into portions of the period from 337 to 361. Within this group the more closely datable hoards form a series in which about ten close in coins of Constantine II, about half a dozen terminate with Constans, and ten close with issues of Constantius II. The steady hoarding of bronze continued, but now as a result more of the already worsening economic situation than of any anticipation of such developments. *Fel Temp Reparatio* copies began to circulate and entered hoards with the official coins. The eagerness of the copyists to produce coinage indicates among other things that the south-west functioned as a money-using economy.

For a few people silver was becoming more common again by AD 360. The later years of the Constantinian dynasty saw a hoard of silver of the greatest rarity in that it closed in coins of Julian II and was indeed largely formed of these relatively rare issues. Found at Willersley (Glos) buried in a cemetery – though apparently not a funerary deposit – this hoard is among very few of this period yet found in Britain. That the south-west should have a silver hoard when nationally the contemporary silver currency was rare points forward to the end of the Roman administration when this region saw the deposition of numerous silver hoards.

The transition to the dynasty of Valentinian was marked by an increase in the gold and silver coinage circulating in Britain. This is reflected in the hoard from East Harptree (Som) containing some 1,500 silver coins, buried in about AD 375. As yet this is exceptional; most hoards are still of bronze, as at Shapwick (Som) where a hoard of 1,121 bronze coins was found. More typical of Valentinian dynasty hoards in the south-west was a small hoard of some forty bronzes at Constantine (Cornwall). A similar find at Wookey Hole (Som) suggests that some turned to cave life, perhaps during seasonal herding and hunting (*infra* p 167). Small hoards of bronze coins, often in remote rural areas, contrast with the as yet small number of large silver hoards and suggest that all who could hoarded what they might, in many cases only bronze. From the towns, villas and military sites comes little evidence of hoarding, while the rural areas contribute a sizeable quota of small hoards. The indications are of a situation in which the agrarian sector continued to function at a modest level, life in the towns and their attendant villas began to decline, and there was little military activity, beyond garrison duties. In fact, the hoards suggest that this was a period of decline in Roman influence in the south-west.

The decline became more abrupt in the Theodosian period. Incursions of raiders may have been a factor, but more important were the troop withdrawals which reduced markets for agricultural and other products and services. The poor economic position may help to explain the very small number of hoards of Theodosius I's reign. The site at Shapwick (Som) produced a bronze hoard, and a silver hoard of this reign and a similar hoard of bronzes were found at Gloucester. All three finds contained over 100 coins, the Shapwick bronze hoard over 1,000. With silver and bronze generally circulating, the opportunity to hoard would seem available to many. That more did not may indicate a minimal fear of raids, economic upheaval or any other alarm. As yet the majority apparently felt safe, complacent or possibly too poor to hoard surplus currency.

The circumstances of the Romano-British population in the early fifth century may be reflected by the numerous contemporary coin hoards. From the Scillies to Somerset many owners of silver currency hoarded it now. That they did so will not be unconnected with the loss of the military market and the end of the Roman administration. Devoid of these assets, many traders would have to find new markets or go out of business. It is not unlikely that such men would hoard capital while attempting commercial reorganisation.

There were also those who hoarded their wealth in bronze coinage. The statistics of hoards whose metal is recorded show that approximately equal numbers of early fifth-century silver hoards and bronze hoards occur in the south-west. Where figures are recorded, most of these hoards comprise over 100 coins, and in the case of the bronzes some contain over 1,000. The distribution of these late bronze hoards shows that most types of site have produced examples, including towns, villas and hill-forts, the latter perhaps now sheltering subsistence farmers, rebellious peasants or other groups of economic or political refugees or dissidents. It is against this background that we might see a minor south-western revival in the late fourth century. The temple complex at Lydney (Glos) and the Jordan Hill and Maiden Castle temples in Dorset all rose, flourished and declined between AD 350 and AD 450. From Maiden Castle came a small hoard of gold solidi of Arcadius and Honorius, and a hoard of bronzes closing in early fifth-century issues was found at Jordan Hill. Even at this late point in time, it seems that the temples continued to attract wealth.

## SOUTH-EAST AND SOUTH-WEST

An examination of the coin hoards of south-east England demonstrates the relative frequency of hoards at key periods in the history of the south-west. Hoards of the pre-Claudian period occur in small numbers in the south-east but outnumber contemporary south-western hoards. With some of the Belgic tribes of the south-east already developing trade relations with the Continent, this is not surprising. Conversely the south-east has less hoards combining British with Roman coins and the practice seems to end much earlier there than in the south-west. This presumably indicates the greater speed with which large amounts of Roman currency entered general circulation in the more commercial and urbanised south-east. This difference in the levels of social and economic sophistication is a marked feature of Roman Britain. Far more concerned with agriculture than with commerce and largely avoided by major overland trade routes, the south-west demonstrates rural development at a patient domestic pace in contrast to the brisk growth of the towns in the south-east.

The peak observed in hoard frequency under Marcus Aurelius in the south-west is part of a national pattern in which the south-east is strongly represented, as befits an area at once prosperous and perhaps unsure of the future. It is at such peak periods that site comparisons are valuable. While the south-western examples occur mostly on native settlement sites, the south-east has several urban examples including two from London.

In some later periods the south-west outdoes the south-east and the rest of Roman Britain in terms of coin-hoard totals. The hoards recorded as closing in Carausius and Allectus concentrate strongly in the south-west. It is noticeable that few hoards of this period come from towns and villas; native settlements and military sites give much larger totals. Constantius Chlorus had to reorganise the national defences, and it may be that hoard evidence showing greater levels of hoarding in the countryside than in towns indicates that much commercial rebuilding was also needed.

The south-west stands high above the rest of Britain in its total of late silver hoards. This demonstrates a degree of prosperity in the region at a time when the country as a whole was reputedly in dire political and economic trouble. Trade would still be possible and necessary, so silver still circulated. Some reorganisation might be undertaken, and at the same time travel on business might become increasingly unsafe. For both reasons the hoarding of silver coinage might become standard mercantile practice.

If this was so, why did the south-west share the fate of the rest of the province after the Roman withdrawal and enter an economic decline? It is a question of how much effect the Roman withdrawal would have had in the south-west. The towns and their mercantile communities amounted to only a minority group in the south-west's total population. The villas were a part of the town-oriented economy (Rivet *1969* 214ff) and the standard of living attained in them depended on the maintenance of good communications. This suggests that for the villas, the end of their occupation was not necessarily attendant on the removal of Roman authority. Where the occupation of villas extends beyond the period of the Roman withdrawal, it would suggest either an absence of danger or an adequate defence against it, and also an ability to maintain economic stability and self-sufficiency. One group of villas that survived unscathed the 'barbarian conspiracy' of AD 367 (*infra* p 139) was situated in the Cotswolds, but though surviving military danger, their success or failure in responding to the changing economic situation is less clear. Few fifth-century hoards have been recorded in villas and it has been questioned whether any authentic fifth-century hoards have ever been found in them (Rivet *1969* 234). It was a period when self-sufficiency or ruin were the alternatives. By AD 400 the rural communities could do without coinage when barter was adequate. Once the towns had begun to decay and the villas had perhaps ceased to be sound economic units only the native subsistence farmers could hope to continue as before with some success.

## THE DISTRIBUTION PATTERN OF THE HOARDS

A study of the various types of site on which coin hoards have been found in the south-west indicates some general factors in the history of the region. The first is that the great majority of these hoards come from civilian sites, and this raises the question of why the military sites of the south-west have provided relatively few hoards. This may be answered by recognising the cumulative effect of the comparatively sparse military occupation of the region after the early years of conquest, and the political and economic stability which the region subsequently achieved.

A further examination of civilian hoards shows that they occur on many types of site. A small proportion come from towns in the south-west, notably from Cirencester and Gloucester, some are directly associated with industry (mainly mining), some are from hillforts, and others are from villas. But by far the largest proportion of the hoards from civilian sites are either associated with known native settlements or with locations devoid of any so far recorded remains of the Roman period. Many of the hoards in this last category have been found in relatively remote areas.

From this pattern of evidence the following broad conclusions may be tentatively drawn. The small number of hoards from south-western military sites seems to reflect the low level of military activity in the south-west at most periods. Life in the towns seems to have attracted only a minority of the native population in the Roman period. While some concealed their wealth in towns, the majority of the Romano-British hoarders committed their wealth to rural concealment. In the countryside, the villas echoed the small total of urban hoards. If we assume that all hoards buried in the countryside have no connection with soldiers, townsfolk or villa-dwellers, then of course we allow a dangerous generalisation. There are no adequate grounds for excluding these groups. However, many of these hoards surely will have belonged to the non-villa-occupying majority of the rural population. Subdividing this total of rural hoards, we can separate out hoards found in native settlements of the Roman period in which the coins correspond with independent evidence of the sites' occupation, those found in hillforts, others discovered beside Roman roads or native tracks, examples from ports, and those from known or suspected sites of rural habitation or activity.

Perhaps the most intriguing of these groups are those found in the hillforts and in the mines. Of the former, those that have been recorded in sufficient detail belong largely to the mid third century, to the period of the Gallic empire and of that period's coinage-circulation. Whether the hillforts in question were occupied when these hoards were buried there is not always clear. There may be no good reason, however, to exclude this possibility; a third-century hillfort occupation may in fact be archaeologically acceptable, at least on a limited scale.

61

The hoards associated with mines in south-west Britain are concentrated in three areas – the Forest of Dean, the Mendips and western Cornwall. The Mendip silver mines are well known as sources of the metal and as a focus for hoards of late Romano-British wealth in the form of siliquae. From the Forest of Dean mines has come an earlier silver hoard, of denarii from Antony and Nero to those of Commodus. Like those buried in the reign of Aurelius, this hoard may reflect a scarcity of silver coinage and the usual reaction to this situation. That bronze hoards of the period from the reign of Gallienus to that of Allectus are found in the Dean mining area is probably less significant, as such hoards appear wherever money circulated in those uncertain years. It is in Cornwall that the application of coin-hoard evidence to mining areas is of the greatest value. Here the hoards give an accurate history of at least some phases of the area's Romano-British history. After some success early in the first century AD the Cornish tin industry declined and was abandoned by AD 100. It was not revived until after AD 250, but once this had happened a pattern of hoards appeared which indicates the prosecution, and perhaps the prosperity, of the revived industry. One such hoard was even found in a tin jug, at Carhayes, buried like some of the others near a creek and indicating the use of water transport in carrying the tin to its wider markets. These Cornish hoards demonstrate both the changing fortunes of the tin industry, with their largest concentration in the period AD 250–340, and, by their geographical distribution around harbours on the west coast, the method and routes of transportation.

4

# GLOUCESTER (GLEVUM):
# A COLONIA IN THE WEST COUNTRY

*Coloniae* (colonies) were an old-established institution by the time they appeared in Britain, and their history and development as an institution can be traced from an abundance of inscriptions and other literary evidence as well as from archaeology. With such a background, the British examples are a good index to urbanisation in the province: we can, for example, put questions about the adaptation of the *colonia* to a British

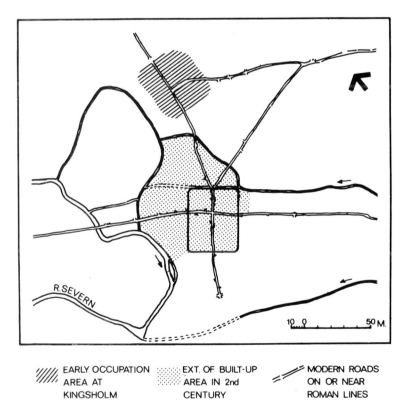

EARLY OCCUPATION
AREA AT
KINGSHOLM     EXT. OF BUILT-UP
AREA IN 2nd
CENTURY     MODERN ROADS
ON OR NEAR
ROMAN LINES

Fig 6   The topography of Roman Gloucester

63

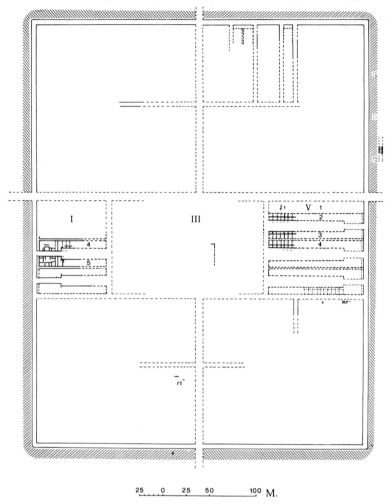

Fig 7   The legionary fortress at Gloucester

context which could not be formulated in the case, say, of the *civitas* capitals. Many of these questions were raised and discussed, and the then state of knowledge summarised, by Richmond *(1946).* The aim of this chapter is to reconsider Gloucester in the light of present information.

The *colonia* at Gloucester occupies a hillock beside the river Severn where it divides into two channels (fig 6). Until the Industrial Revolution this was the lowest bridgeable point on the river, controlling the main route from England into south Wales. The site of Gloucester was therefore bound to be strategically and commercially important from the moment when the first permanent bridge was constructed. The evidence at present suggests that the earliest Roman occupation may have been at Kingsholm, about half a mile to the north of the present river crossing (Green *1942* 40ff). Green's conclusions about the plan of the fortress and its attribution to Legion II are now unacceptable, as is his suggestion that there was no military occupation on the *colonia* site. The presence of an early military site at Kingsholm has, however, been confirmed by the writer's discovery of timber buildings and associated military finds in 1972. Occupation on the site of the *colonia* seems to begin not earlier than the late Neronian period (Hurst *1972* 39, 50, 53). There is now clear evidence for a legionary fortress with its defences established on all four sides and several internal buildings have been excavated (fig 7). The date of the latest coins found in occupation contexts within these is AD 77/8, but their demolition may have been a decade or more later (*infra* p 66). Evidence is also accumulating for an extensive *vicus* outside the fortress.

Plate 5   Between the baulks of an archaeological excavation at Gloucester lie the stone foundations of colonial buildings and, top left, the wall trenches of an earlier wooden barrack block (2m pole)

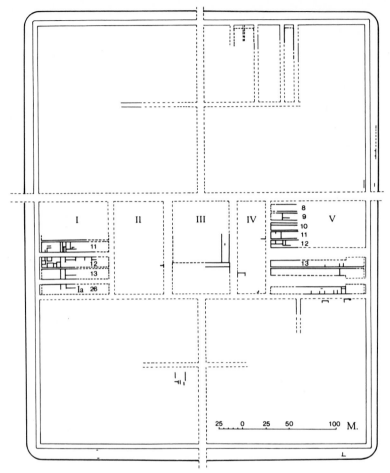

Fig 8   The *colonia* at Gloucester in the late first century

Three widely scattered sites outside the northern defences have produced early Flavian buildings (Hurst *1972* 64–5). Green drew attention to the early pottery from the dockside area west of the fortress (*1942* 48) and part of a probable early timber building was recorded in Quay Street in 1960.

## THE FOUNDATION OF THE COLONIA

Within the defences, the demolition of the timber and clay fortress buildings (Period 1) seems to have been followed immediately by a general rebuilding (Period 2). The Period 2 floors usually rest directly on the Period 1 clay and plaster destruction layer and, at 10 Eastgate Street (Insula V) and 13–17 Berkeley Street (Insula I), the outline plan of the Period 2 buildings almost exactly follows that of Period 1 (fig 8, pl 5). The same metalled roads divide pairs of building blocks except in one case in Insula V where a Period 1 road is overlain by a Period 2 building (Hurst *1972* 38ff). In construction the Period 2 buildings are a mixture of masonry and timber-framed walls, masonry always being used for main walls and minor internal partitions usually being based on timber ground sills. The internal layout of the buildings has been recovered in most detail at 13–17 Berkeley Street (Insula I). Both here and at 10 Eastgate Street coins of AD 87 were found in contexts where they antedated a Period 2 building (Hurst *1972* 40, 50). Finds from occupation contexts suggest that the buildings were still in use in the early second century, and a coin of AD 111 is probably from such a context at Berkeley Street.

Plate 6   A tombstone in Rome, adduced as evidence that the *colonia* at *Glevum* was founded during the reign of Nerva

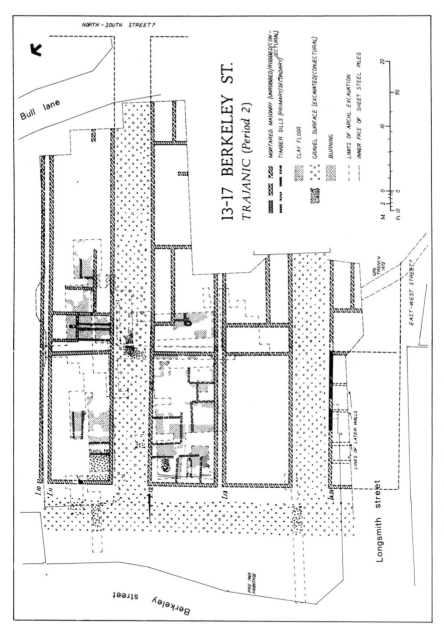

Fig 9　Details of Trajanic buildings at Gloucester (Berkeley Street)

## Gloucester (Glevum): A Colonia in the West Country

Evidence for Gloucester's foundation as *Colonia Ner (via/viana) Glev (ensis/ensium)* is derived from two tombstones: one, in Bath, of a decurion COLONIAE GLEV. (*RIB* 161), the other in Rome of a *frumentarius* of the VIth legion, which mentions NER ... GLEV for the man's birthplace (*CIL* vi, 3346: pl 6). Mommsen suggested that NER was used instead of the Roman voting tribe as an epithet for Glevum, as is often the case with cities with imperial titles, and that this probably meant that Gloucester was a Nervan foundation. With Period 2 dated archaeologically to AD 87 or later and occupation continuing into the second century, there seems to be a good case for identifying it with an AD 96–8 *colonia* foundation. However, there are difficulties: while Nerva's name may have been in the official title of Gloucester, it does not necessarily follow that the *colonia* was founded in his reign. Forni cites a series of examples such as Drobeta in Dacia, with the title Claudia, but in territory conquered under Trajan, and Hadrianopolis, founded by Hadrian, with the title Ulpia. The *colonia* could therefore have been founded after AD 96–8. From the point of view of military history, however, an earlier foundation date would be preferable since Gloucester seems to be somewhat redundant as a legionary fortress from the time when Caerleon was founded and wholly so by the time of the military redispositions after the conquest of Wales and the north in the late eighties.

With these difficulties in mind it is worth looking at the archaeological evidence in more detail. The extensive evidence for Period 1 (O'Neil *1962, 1965*; Hurst *1972*) now leaves little doubt that the site was occupied by a legionary fortress, whether or not its small area (just over forty-three acres) means that it never housed a full legion. There has so far been no indication that its buildings underwent a different use in a later phase. The Period 2 layout differs in detail from Period 1 in spite of its outline similarity. At both 13–17 Berkeley Street (Insula I) and 10 Eastgate Street (Insula V), in areas corresponding to former *contubernia*, there are variations in the internal plan of building blocks and differences from Period 1. Particularly at Berkeley Street there is the suggestion of building plots of a certain size, which may not always have been completely covered by the structures built on them (fig 9). There are also variations in structural details which are perhaps best explained as being due to individual choice or varying functions: the stone sills in Building I,11, for example, as opposed to the more common timber, and the substantial mortar floor in Building I,13 which was the only one of its kind at this period. Civilian use of the buildings is suggested by the domestic

69

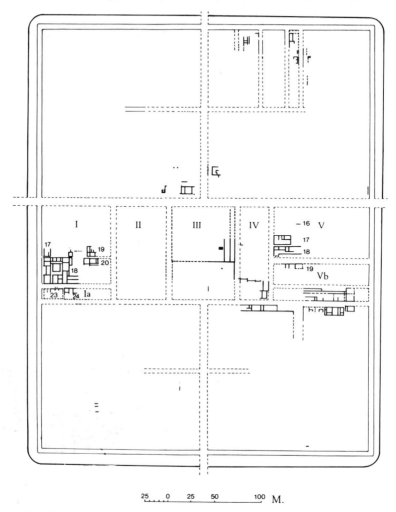

25    0   25   50      100  M.

Fig 10   The *colonia* at Gloucester in the mid second century

ovens in I,11 and I,12, the ironsmithing hearth (?) in I,12 and a steel-yard deposited at this period on the site of I,11. No serious difficulty arises from the fact that, in the two excavated cases, Period 1 centurions' quarters are overlain by buildings of similar internal plan. Since the centurion's house as a type is clearly based on a civilian model, it is perfectly acceptable in a civilian context. A further explanation of it appearing in Gloucester at this period might lie in the social structure of the initial *colonia* (*infra* p 72).

70

Allowing for the variations of detail in Period 2, this and Period 1 are the only occasions when there is a uniform general occupation sequence in different areas. At 13–17 Berkeley Street, directly after Period 2 the sites of some buildings appeared to be open ground, indicated by a deposit of disturbed clayey loam. Above this on the former site of Building I,12 a small building, I,14, was constructed some time after AD 111, perhaps about 120. A pottery kiln to the east of this seems to have been in production at about the same date. The whole area was fairly soon after, perhaps *c* AD 130–40, covered by a large stone court-yard house, I,18 (fig 10: Hurst *1972* 40ff). To the south of this area, occupation in Building Ia,26 seems to continue uninterruptedly from Period 2 until the construction of the fully stone Building Ia,23 at perhaps *c* AD 130. Building I,14 contained a tiled hearth with an *RPG* tile *in situ*. Accepting that the letters stand for *Res Publica Glevensis*, this is evidence that Gloucester was a chartered city by the date of deposition (*c* 120?) and so would suggest an early second-century date at the latest for the *colonia* foundation. The initial phase of the *colonia* would surely be before Building I,14 was constructed, since it does not appear to be associated with any general change on the site. The obvious context is therefore Period 2. This makes a more convincing reason for accepting the Rome tombstone at its face value.

We know little about the early *colonia* defences because their potential line has everywhere been obliterated by the later city wall. But in the excavation at 41–51 Eastgate Street there was an indication of some sort of revetment retaining the front of the legionary rampart – perhaps a narrow stone wall (Hurst *1972* 32). An inscription found in contractors' operations on this site may be a direct record of military building activity in a *colonia* context (pl 7). This was a centurial building stone and, though strictly unstratified, appeared to have been dug out of the ground from the same spot as the stone pillar base (or capital) and respond. At the New Market Hall and 22 Southgate Street sites, terracotta antefixes with military parallels were found in contexts which suggest that they may have adorned colonial buildings.

The military character of the *colonia* is apt, in view both of evidence from elsewhere in Britain of the army's part in urbanisation and what we know generally of military colonies. Gloucester matches up to Tacitus' requirement of Camulodunum, to be a *subsidium adversus rebellis* (*Annals* 12.32), or might, like Lugdunum, be described as *coloniam Romanam et partem exercitus* (*Histories* 1.65). Moreover, its social order may have been no less military than the construction of

71

Plate 7   Part of a military building stone, probably from a colonial building, found in King's Walk, Gloucester. It bears the legend CO(H——) I(——)

its buildings. Jones has drawn attention to the passage in Tacitus (*Annals* 14.27), where, in contrast to the Neronian foundation at Puteoli, the old style of *colonia* is described: 'Whole legions were settled with their tribunes and centurions and soldiers of all ranks in order to ensure the harmonious and agreeable conduct of public affairs.' Jones (*1973*) points out that this seems to be the meaning of some inscriptional evidence in southern Etruria, for example in the case of Caius Musanus, a veteran colonist of Lucus Feroniae. He was *primus pilus* (twice), military tribune, *praefectus stratopedarci* then *duovir quinquennalis*, the implication being that he owed his civilian position to his rank at the time of discharge from service. The general Period 2 layout in Gloucester, and particularly the apparent use of centurions' quarters as accommodation units, makes it tempting to see this occurring there also in the original *colonia*.

The best example of a *colonia* whose size and original population are known is Aosta. There the site of about 100 acres was planned for 3,000 veterans of the Pretorian Guard (Haverfield *1906a* 89–90). At Timgad Haverfield suggested that the 70ft* square insulae were divided into between one and four accommodation units. He estimated from the total of insulae occupied by private buildings that the original draft of veterans was not more than 400 (*ibid* 110). The walled area there was just under twenty-nine acres. At Augst a similar attempt has been made to break up an excavated insula into its original colonial plots, producing units 80ft × 30ft (Laur-Belart *1966* 128, fig 92). The evidence of the Berkeley Street site at Gloucester allows some dubious speculation of this sort. There was some suggestion of a barrack-sized building block (*c* 250ft × 36ft) being divided into four, giving three units *c* 56ft × 36ft and the fourth (centurion's quarters) *c* 70ft × 36ft (fig 9). As five such building blocks and the adjacent streets occupy an acre, this gives a suggested twenty units to the acre. Allowing for public buildings, the average density per acre would work out at about seventeen, with a total of *c* 720–750 units throughout the forty-three-acre defended area. Comparable densities per acre would be thirty at Aosta and about fifteen on the Timgad calculation. For obvious reasons the Gloucester figures are not to be taken too seriously, but the calculation is worth doing merely to stress that further excavation of the *colonia* should eventually allow an accurate estimate to be made.

In fact an original veteran settlement of 720–50 seems reasonable. With an average of about five per household, this would mean a *colonia* population of 3–4,000. This would not, however, be the total population of Gloucester at the time. It is now quite clear that occupation continued on the site of the earlier *vicus* and by the mid second century there appears to have been a densely built-up area outside the defences two or more times the size of the area within. Structures found within this area include a possible Roman quay (Fullbrook-Leggatt *1968* 56), a monumental building partly excavated at 63–71 Northgate Street (Hurst *1972* 63–4), a colonnaded range, probably of shops, at 96 Northgate Street (Rhodes, *forthcoming*) and several buildings with mosaics (Fullbrook-Leggatt *1968* 57–9). The area is thus not to be dismissed as one of suburban sprawl or scattered extra-mural occupation. Without greater knowledge of the character and history of the occupation in this area we are still very far from an understanding of Roman Gloucester as a whole. A particularly crucial point will be how extensive occupation

*Roman feet, here and throughout this chapter.

here had become during the life of the fortress, for it may be that the military *vicus* had made Gloucester a considerable urban centre before the first colonist settled there. The little evidence we have at present, both negative from within the defended area and positive from without, suggests that the latter was always the scene of most of the city's commercial activity, as it must have been originally in the fortress period. The colonists' initial role may therefore have been a largely passive one, of providing a continued market and institutional respectability for an otherwise unstable trading community. The two elements making up the city's population would presumably correspond to the distinction often made between *coloni* and *incolae* or that implied by the title of a second-century census official at Camulodunum, the *censitor civium Romanorum* (*CIL* XIV, 3955), which suggests that there were also *peregrini* in the urban population subject to a different form of taxation.

Evidence for the institutional civic life of the colony is recorded in a series of tiles stamped *R(es) P(ublica) G(levensis)* which sometimes have the addition of the names of the *aediles* and, in one case the *duoviri quinquennales* (pl 8; Clifford *1955* 69–70). These and the Bath tombstone, which refers to a decurion, allow the conclusion that Gloucester

Plate 8  A stamped brick from Hucclecote, near Gloucester, bearing the legend:  R(es) P(ublica) G(levensis) Q(uinquennalibus) Q(uinto) IVL(io) FLOR(O) ET CCRSM

had the corporate government and officials that might be expected in a city of its status.

The physical side of the colony's role as a promoter of Roman standards, which Tacitus describes in a well-known passage about Camulodunum (*Annals* 12. 32), is also becoming more evident. Parts of at least four public buildings have been found within the walled area and of one outside. There are signs of a monumentally laid-out civic centre with a forum-basilica and other public buildings in the insulae to the north-east and north-west of it (fig 10). The most extensive excavation in this area has been in part of the forum (Hurst *1972* 53–8). This was of the *principia* type, without a temple, and was in fact on the presumed site of the fortress *principia*. Two successive buildings of similar plan seem to have been constructed in quick succession, the first perhaps on the occasion of the *colonia* foundation. The little known of this suggests that, though at least partly of stone, it was not as substantial a structure as its successor. The second forum compares well in architectural detail with other Romano-British examples, though it was not exceptionally large. Its paved courtyard was flanked by limestone colonnades, with the basilica at the south end. This was constructed with its floor raised above the courtyard level, having an approach probably by triumphal steps and an open colonnaded side facing the courtyard, as at Caerwent. Remains probably of an equestrian statue base were found in the courtyard. Within the presumptive insula to the north-west of the forum, part of a colonnaded structure was found in 1894 (Medland *1895* 142), a hypocaust with lead water pipe in 1959 (Hunter *1968* 56) and a colonnade with metre-diameter columns in 1971 (Hurst *1972* 62–3). If the insula limits are correct, these discoveries suggest a public baths. The metre-diameter columns are the same size as those from the forum basilica nave. Columns of a similar size make up the Westgate colonnade, found in the nineteenth century on the sites of 28–40 Westgate Street (Fullbrook-Leggatt *1968* 42–3). A Corinthian capital now lost, but recorded in 1934, may have come from this (Gloucester Roman Research Committee *1934* 70–1). Another Corinthian capital of large dimensions was found in the nave wall of St Oswald's Priory and is now in the City Museum.

Gloucester's monumental buildings were clearly accompanied by the public services which might be expected. Wooden water mains at the sides of streets, a possible public fountain at the New Market Hall site and a private one at the Berkeley Street site all imply a municipal water supply brought to the city by aqueduct. Stone drains have been found in a number of streets, but so far nothing on a scale comparable to the Lincoln and York sewers.

## THE TERRITORIUM

Of equal importance in the colonial foundation is the land allocation made to the city and its inhabitants; *coloni*, after all, means literally 'tillers of the land'. We are no nearer to knowing what the *territorium* of Gloucester was than when Richmond wrote a generation ago, but it is worth posing his questions again. What size of land allotment could we expect for a *colonia* the size of Gloucester? For Lincoln, where the primary *colonia* is slightly smaller than Gloucester, Richmond suggested not less than 100 square miles, using north Italian evidence where centurial systems can be associated with particular cities (Richmond *1946* 66). An estimate of minimal needs could also be made from the number of colonists. If there were 720, each with the most common size of land allotment of 50 *iugera*, the total area required would be about 35 square miles. If the land allotment was 66⅔ *iugera*, then the total would be just under 47 square miles. Richmond pointed out that to the total of cultivated land can be added an allowance for *pascua* (public grazing land) and probably *silvas* (woodlands), which Frontinus says would have been included in the grant of *territorium.*

Although there is no direct evidence for a land allocation near Gloucester, the adjacent Severn valley is rich farming land with both heavy and light soils. The Cotswold scarp, which forms the eastern limit of this type of land, is on average six miles east of the river near Gloucester. If this was the eastern limit of the *territorium*, the valley contains ample space for any of the areas suggested above. Attention has been drawn to the distribution of the *RPG*-stamped tiles as a possible indicator of the *territorium* extent (Clifford *1955* 68). So far the distribution extends eastwards from Gloucester to the Cotswold edge at Ifold (Painswick) and probably Dry Hill and southwards to Frocester (Gracie *1970* 19), but it will not be a reliable guide until many more tiles are found. There is also a possibility that the *territorium* remained an intact unit into historically documented times. Finberg, for example, speculated on whether it might be the 300 *tributarii* mentioned as being attached to the *civitas* of Gloucester in the supposedly seventh-century charter of St Peter's Abbey (Finberg *1957* 55). Theoretically it could ultimately relate to parish or hundred boundaries. But to suggest this would always require the crucial assumption that the *territorium*

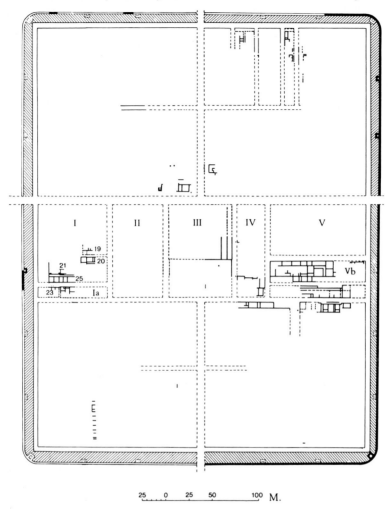

Fig 11   The *colonia* at Gloucester at the beginning of the third century

remained unaltered over many centuries, for which there is no evidence. A final answer, therefore, can be provided only by fieldwork. If there was a land allocation based on a centurial system, it should have left physical traces in the form of roads and field ditches or even centurial stones. Even if it is thought that fragments of such a system are fossilised in recent field and parish boundaries, the confirmation of evidence in the field will still be needed.

## Gloucester (Glevum): A Colonia in the West.Country

As a result of recent fieldwork near Gloucester, we now know that there was a high concentration of Roman sites in the area (Fowler and Walthew *1971*). Many of these must lie within the *territorium* and one of the most interesting problems of the future will be their relationship with the *colonia*. Some of the sites are evidently villas like Hucclecote. Do they represent a secondary stage in the occupation of the *colonia*, when the landowning population moved out to live on the land? The question seems to be posed as much by evidence in the town as by evidence in the country. At the Berkeley Street site, for example, the situation *c* AD 150 is that there were six buildings where there were an estimated twelve units in the *colonia* foundation (fig 10). By AD 200 there were only four (fig 11). A comparable development was found at 10 Eastgate Street, and in Insula Vb a single massive building, occupied from the late second century to the late fourth century, seems to cover an area of *c* 80m × 20m. This severe reduction in the density of building is evidently a general feature of the *colonia*, and the tendency towards fewer and larger buildings must mean that wealth was now being concentrated in fewer hands; the artificial order of the first *colonia* was evidently short-lived. In this respect – the low-density, spacious buildings – Gloucester comes to look like the more familiar Romano-British towns such as Silchester and the excavated parts of Verulamium.

Richmond concluded from his assessment of the evidence for the *colonia* that Glevum was a failed city. He drew particular attention to the poverty of art, especially in contrast with Lincoln, and the relative absence of evidence for spread or growth (Richmond *1946* 72–3). The latter point can surely be refuted by the new evidence for the city's size and character outside the defended area. Gloucester still presents a contrast to Lincoln in that the walled area was apparently not extended, but the possibility of outer Roman defences is far from being ruled out. The artistic argument also carries less conviction now that the Roman dating of the well-known limestone head, supposedly of a Celtic deity (Gloucester Roman Research Committee *1934* 78–9, pl viii), is seriously in doubt. Recent excavations at the New Market Hall site and at 10–36 Eastgate Street have yielded fragments of the high-quality mosaics which evidently existed throughout much of the city, while the peristyle courtyard house at Berkeley Street (Building I,18, fig 10) shows a higher level of architectural refinement than is usual for Romano-British town houses. Glevum was not, therefore, a failed city on these grounds, but its apparent depopulation after the initial *colonia* foundation renews the question. It has been seen that the result of this is to give the city an appearance like other Romano-British towns. So if the sprawling, generously spaced out third- and fourth-century buildings at Berkeley Street, the New Market Hall and Eastgate Street indicate urban failure, the failure is to be shared with Silchester, Verulamium, Cirencester and Wroxeter.

## GLOUCESTER IN THE FOURTH AND FIFTH CENTURIES

The final phases of Roman Gloucester so far follow lines that are familiar from elsewhere. With the possible exception of the forum, occupation on all the sites where evidence survives seems to continue in conventional Roman style until at least the late fourth century. This applies to sites both within and without the wall. The latest mosaic so far known (33 Southgate St) sealed a coin of Valens, but this may only be a rarity because levels of this period have so often been removed by later disturbance. A characteristically late fourth-century reinforcement of the city defences took place, with bastions being added apparently at the same time as the wall was strengthened (Hurst *1972* 32, 34–5). In the forum the final courtyard surface was overlain by a rubbish deposit containing a large number of bones and a small amount of pottery and two coins, none of which need be later than *c* AD 350 (*ibid* 58). Some of the courtyard paving slabs had already been robbed by the time this material, which was mixed with building rubble, was deposited. The evidence could therefore point to the disuse and dismantling of the forum in the mid fourth century but could equally fit its continued use and final abandonment a century and a half later.

A major change in the late fourth century or later can be seen in an occupation sequence at Berkeley Street. A small courtyard house (Ia,23) was demolished after the deposition of several *Fel Temp Reparatio* imitations. After this, rubble was heaped up on one side of a room in the ruined building as the packing behind the wall based on a timber sill. This bounded an incompletely excavated area containing a hearth. A large contemporary oven was found near-by in the former courtyard. This appears to have been followed by at least one, and probably two, more phases or periods when solid levels of stones and rubble associated with more ovens were laid down. The well in the former courtyard appeared to continue in use in the latest of these phases. The latest levels in this sequence, for which there was no dating evidence, were destroyed by early medieval disturbance. On the same site, just north of this, the latest coins associated with the timber building I,21 were similar to those ending the occupation of Ia,23 and, further north-east, a hoard of 653 coins in Building I,19 so far contains issues no later than the House of Valentinian but has yet to be fully examined. In both these areas there is unfortunately no evidence for the period after the deposition of the coins. The destruction layer of Building I,20 on the same site sealed two pits containing Arcadian and Honorian issues.

On the New Market Hall site a hoard containing Arcadian and Honorian issues was found among roof collapse. This had fallen on the floor of a room where there was evidence of bronze working and a valuable group of late Roman pottery and small finds. The excavators suggest that the hoard may have been hidden in the roof of the building and so may not give a true guide as to date. Make-ups of re-used building rubble similar to those which followed Building Ia,23 were noticed on this site and to the north of it at 10–36 Eastgate Street. These are clearly levels which occur widely and thus may contain many answers about the sub-Roman period. The effect of medieval disturbance is, however, such that their survival at all has so far been a rarity and even then has only been in small, isolated areas which are impossible to interpret. Because of a general lack of distinctive artifactual material, all evidence for or against occupation in this period is lost where the levels are disturbed. Up to now the only possible sub- or post-Roman finds of pottery have been a probable B(ii) imported amphora sherd from St Oswald's Priory and a few grass-tempered sherds, similar to those discussed by Fowler (Gracie *1970* 51–3). These have occurred, presumably residually, in late Saxon and early medieval contexts on the Berkeley Street and forum sites.

It is possible that the Germanic element, for which there is increasing evidence in other Roman towns, was also present in the population of late and sub-Roman Gloucester, as a buckle with zoomorphic decoration was found unstratified at the New Market Hall site. The grave goods from an inhumation at Kingsholm, probably of the fifth century, seem to belong to a high-ranking individual with sub-Roman, or British rather than Germanic associations, possibly one of the ruling class which preserved Gloucester's political independence until the battle of Dyrham in 577. Perhaps the last 'contemporary' reference to Roman Gloucester is that already mentioned, to a *civitas* with 300 *tributarii*, in the supposedly late seventh-century foundation charter of St Peter's Abbey.

# 5

# CIRENCESTER (CORINIUM):
# A CIVITAS CAPITAL IN THE WEST COUNTRY

During the military occupation at Cirencester (*supra* p 30), activity in
the pre-Roman *oppidum* of Bagendon, situated about four kilometres
north of Cirencester, seems to have declined (Clifford *1961* 21) and the
presence of early timber buildings north-west of an auxiliary fort at
Cirencester points to a movement of the native population to the sur-
rounds of the fort (Wacher *1962* 11). So far excavation has revealed no
evidence for pre-conquest occupation beneath the site of the later town
of Corinium, and the presence of buildings outside the fort marks the
beginning of civilian settlement at this spot. When the army was with-
drawn from Dobunnian territory during the late seventies the site
became a natural one for the capital of the *civitas Dobunnorum*. Not
only was there the nucleus of a settlement formed by the buildings outside the fort, but by the seventies the road pattern was established and
an important road junction existed.

## PUBLIC BUILDINGS AND THE DEFENCES

During the last quarter of the first century AD, streets were being laid
out and work started on the public buildings. Although not all the streets
have been positively dated by excavation, those which have suggest that
a considerable area was deliberately planned during the closing decades
of the first century.

The central insula (I on fig 12), containing the forum and basilica,
measured 168m × 105m and was second only to the corresponding
insula in London in size. On the south-eastern side of the forum stood
the basilica which spanned the width of the insula, 105m, and was 25m
wide (Wacher *1962* 5). Present evidence points to there being an apse
only at the south-western end. The basilica was built over the filled-in
ditches of the auxiliary fort and insufficient foundations were provided,
thus causing the basilica to subside and its walls to crack. Consequently,
reconstruction work was necessary by the middle part of the second

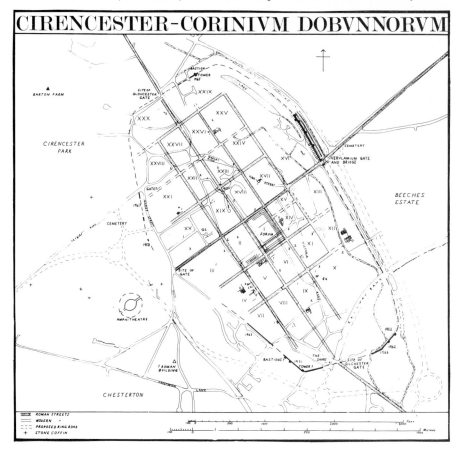

Fig 12   Cirencester. Plan of the Roman town

century AD. Architecturally the whole complex must have been most impressive and, although little can be said about the internal decor, some idea of its splendour can be gleaned from the mosaics found in the north-west range of the forum (Wacher *1964* 12) and from the marble veneers found in the basilica.

Adjacent to the forum and basilica stood an extra market hall built during the first quarter of the second century (Wacher *1962* 8) which may have served as additional space for a general market or have specialised in a particular commodity.

The only other certain public structure, other than the town wall and gates, is the amphitheatre. The oval arena, 50m × 40m, was surrounded by an earthen bank for seating, originally held in place by timber posts and dry-stone walling. During the middle of the second century these walls were rebuilt in mortared stone, and probably at the same time small dry-stone walls were built into the seating bank in order to terrace the bank and to provide a firmer base for seats. An estimate of the seating capacity suggests that between 5,000 and 7,000 people could be accommodated (Wacher *1963* 23; *1964* 17; Brown and McWhirr *1967* 185). The site chosen for the amphitheatre may at first have been a Roman quarry, for it is surrounded by evidence of quarrying which probably dates from the Roman period. It would indeed have been logical to utilise abandoned quarries when constructing the amphitheatre.

Other discoveries in the town suggest that the buildings found were in public rather than private use. In Insula XXX, two concentric curving walls about 2m wide and with a diameter of some 58m were found in 1966 (Brown and McWhirr *1967* 194) which it seems reasonable to identify as part of a theatre, although conclusive evidence is at present lacking. If this interpretation is correct, the position of the theatre so far from the centre of the town might imply that at least one other theatre awaits discovery nearer the heart of Corinium. An eighteenth-century discovery (Haverfield *1920* 179) of a tessellated pavement measuring 15m × 12m and with heating underneath might again, by its size, suggest a public building. From its position in the insula west of the forum it would not be out of place for the public baths.

There is no evidence for the construction of defences round the town until the very end of the second century AD when the town was ringed by an earth rampart and either one or two ditches. The fact that the monumental stone Verulamium Gate and two interval towers were built before this earth rampart has suggested to some that an original intention to build defences completely in stone was changed by some emergency during the course of construction which necessitated the remainder being left as an earth bank and ditch (Wacher *1971* 13). Sometime about the middle of the third century, the earth bank was cut back and a stone wall inserted. The thickness of the wall varies. Originally two thicknesses were recognised, a narrow wall 1.2m wide and a wider version 3m wide. Observations during reconstruction work in 1967–8 showed, however, that at least four distinct types of wall existed in a 48m stretch north of the Verulamium Gate (Cullen *1970* 235). The narrow wall was shown to be earlier than the various wider walls and it may have been that the entire circuit was, at first, a wall 1.2m wide. Conditions in particular parts of the town may have necessitated replacing this wall by a wider and perhaps more stable version. Only more work will provide the answer. Along with other towns of Britain, Cirencester was provided with external bastions during the fourth century.

## PRIVATE HOUSES (fig 13)

With the erection of public buildings and the laying out of streets, shops and houses began to appear during the last quarter of the first century. Shops have been identified in Insula V just south of the basilica and excavations in 1972 have shown that they extend along the entire frontage of Street II/V.

By the beginning of the second century houses were being built in stone, replacing earlier timber buildings. The internal decoration of these houses was impressive. Building XXIII, 1 had its walls plastered and painted (Wacher *1963* 19) and several second-century mosaic floors from elsewhere in the town have been noted (Smith *1974*).

There is surprisingly little upon which to base a discussion about the development of the private house in Cirencester. Despite the considerable number of mosaic floors from such houses that have been recorded (Haverfield *1920* 174) and the fine collection of architectural fragments, it is only in recent years that complete plans of town houses have been recovered and something of their development elucidated. Owing to the presence of large gardens in modern Cirencester, sizeable areas have remained undeveloped until the recent shortage of land has brought them on to the market. Consequently over the past fifteen years some big areas have been available for excavation, although at first there were insufficient funds and no organisation to deal with the problem. Consequently, between 1957 and 1959 several areas were developed in which, had money and labour been available, considerably more archaeological work could have been done. Dyer Court provided Webster with an opportunity of carrying out more extensive excavations, but even here only a limited area was examined. With the formation of the Cirencester Excavation Committee, however, more detailed planning could be formulated and a series of annual excavations carried out.

When the opportunity arose to excavate an area in Insula XII thought to contain Roman houses very close to the surface and free from later disturbances, the Excavation Committee planned a series of excavations between 1970 and 1973. These excavations have, for the first time in Cirencester, made it possible to uncover the complete plans of two Roman houses and to work out their development. In order that the results of these excavations can be put into their correct perspective it is worth reviewing the results of earlier excavations that have taken place on the houses of Corinium.

Rescue work in 1958/9 in Parsonage Field (Insula IV) revealed a series of buildings, the history of which could not be completely deduced from the limited excavations carried out. In 1958 Rennie had only seventeen days to examine the buildings beneath the Health Centre

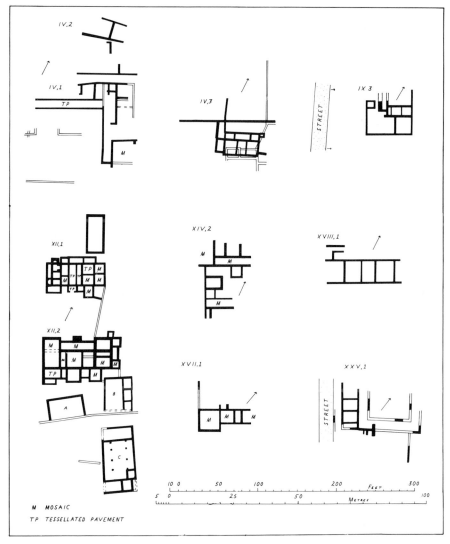

Fig 13   Cirencester. Plans of town houses

(Rennie *1972* 64), whilst in 1959 Richardson was able to spend six weeks disentangling the maze of walls found beneath Pater Noster House (Richardson *1962* 160). Observation work was done during the construction of the buildings by Grace and further excavations were conducted by Wacher in 1963 (Wacher *1964* 14). The numbering of the buildings as planned by Wacher after his excavations differs from that published recently by Rennie, and as the former has been adopted on the town plan it is intended to use that system in this chapter. Building I in Insula IV replaced an earlier timber building of Antonine date and seems to have been a house with at least two wings (Rennie *1972* 65). A corridor of one of these wings contained a tessellated pavement 2.5m wide and at least 25m long. In view of the nature of the excavations there is little firm dating evidence, but Rennie points out that of the nineteen unstratified coins, fifteen are later than AD 380. One coin, however, dated to AD 388–95, was discovered in the foundations of the latest floor in one of the rooms, and Miss Rennie suggests that, as a number of the rooms seem to be contemporary with this one, considerable rebuilding took place at some date after AD 388. It is also suggested that the mosaic floor discovered in Room 2 was laid at this time. Further north, Richardson was able to show (*1962* 163) that the first stone building in that area dated from the second half of the second century and that by the early third century the northern part was rebuilt and extended. Coins and pottery suggest that the building continued in use throughout the fourth century.

In 1963 Wacher found timber buildings dating from the early second century which during the same century were replaced by a stone structure (Building IV,4), itself drastically altered in the fourth century (Wacher *1964* 15). Little of the plan was recovered and so the true function of the building could not be determined. From the slender information that has come from the observations and excavations in this insula it is clear that timber buildings existed by the early second century and that the first building in stone appeared during the second century, and, with various modifications, continued in use until the end of the fourth century or later. A similar situation was found by Brown in the insula to the south where a stone house (VII,1) was built between AD 140 and AD 180 and continued in use until after AD 348 (Brown and McWhirr *1969* 230).

In Insula IX a building of some style (IX,3) was found in 1868–9 and observed again by Rennie in 1958 during hasty rescue work. She found an octagonal room with a hypocaust contemporary with a small

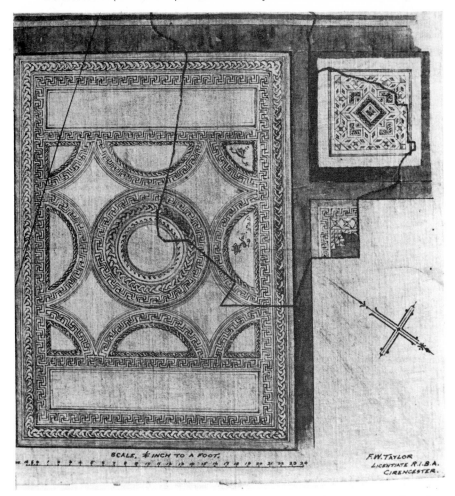

Plate 9   A drawing and reconstruction of a mosaic pavement found
in Victoria Road, Cirencester, in 1922

heated apse. Two small apses and a series of rooms were also found
at the same time. Rennie suggested that these rooms were part of a bath
building of fourth-century date (Wilson *1959* 127).

Other examples of houses in the south of the town have to be sought
in notes and drawings held at the museum and from the observations of
people in Cirencester. In 1922 various walls and mosaic floors discovered
in Victoria Road (pl 9) were planned by a local architect, F. W. Taylor.
Smith refers to the main mosaic as a 'nine-panel design' and, on stylistic

grounds, he assigns a second-century date to it. Other buildings have been recorded in Insula X, but little sense can be made of their plan. However, in 1960–1 Reece excavated part of a stone building (X,3) which he showed was constructed around the middle of the second century and which was having floors relaid in its rooms during the first third of the fourth century (Reece *1971* 11).

The houses so far discussed lie at some distance from the forum, but there is evidence to show that private houses were following similar patterns of development in insulae close to the centre of the town. Excavations in Insula XIV revealed part of a courtyard house which had mosaics dating from the second and fourth centuries (Brown and McWhirr *1969* 231).

The house which has produced the most remarkable collection of mosaics from any single Roman building in Cirencester, and perhaps even from any town house in Britain, was found beneath Dyer Street in Insula XVII. The discoveries concerning this house are described in chronological order:

1   Lysons illustrated (*1817* pl vii) a mosaic floor that was found in 1783, part of which has recently been located by Reece in the cellars of 60 Dyer Street (Reece *1971a* 175). This 'Marine Scene' has been described by Toynbee (*1964* 270) as 'one of the best drawn and most classical in style of all British mosaics'.

2   A pavement usually referred to as the 'Hunting Dog' mosaic (pl 10) was found in 1849 (Buckman and Newmarch *1850* 35 and pl 6). The central roundel, which is not complete, contains three hounds in pursuit of a quarry. The rest of the floor has the usual quota of motifs as well as two blue-and-red sea-beasts, the head of Medusa in a corner panel and in two of the interspaces a mask of Neptune/Oceanus. The floor, which is 4.61m square, is dated by Smith (*1974*) to the early part of the third century.

3   Found at the same time as the mosaic just described, this floor measures 7.69m square and is one of the series of octagonal designs (Buckman and Newmarch *1850* 38 and pl 2). It consists of nine octagonal panels arranged in three rows of three and framed by a continuous guilloche. These floors are characteristic of the second half of the second century and Smith (*1974*) suggests that this one dates from the late second or early third century. All that survives of the central roundel is a pair of horse's legs which might be those of a centaur. The four corner panels represent the seasons and those in between contain the

88

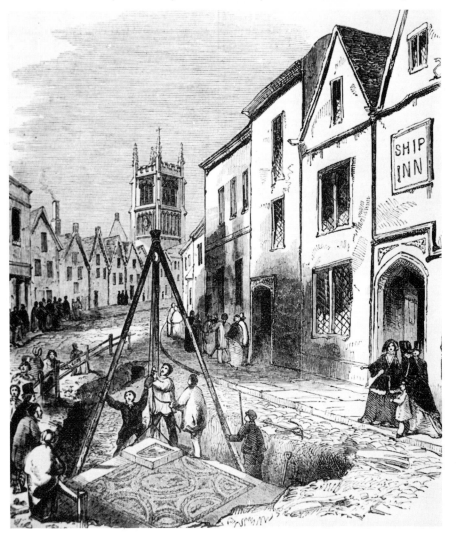

Plate 10  A drawing from the *Illustrated London News* showing the lifting of the 'Hunting Dog' mosaic pavement in Dyer Street, Cirencester, in 1849

metamorphosis of Actaeon, Silenus riding on a white ass, and the standing figure of Bacchus.

4  Beecham's *History of Cirencester* (*1886* 266) contains the only record of an Orpheus pavement, found at 93 Dyer Street (now

33 Dyer Street) in 1820. It is strange that Buckman and Newmarch *(1850)* do not refer to this. The central medallion includes Orpheus and a rather peculiar unidentifiable figure. Around this is a zone of birds moving in a clockwise direction and then a zone of animals moving the same way. This floor is undoubtedly the product of the same workshop that produced the Barton Farm Orpheus pavement discovered in 1837. The significance of these floors has already been discussed by Smith *(1965* 106).

5   During 1972 the Cirencester Excavation Committee was undertaking observation work on the site of a new supermarket in Dyer Street when a section of mosaic floor was noticed in the southwest corner of the site (McWhirr *1973*). As this was only about 18m from the house under discussion it seems likely that this floor also belongs to it. From the rather small portion of this floor that remains, it looks as though it is of an octagonal-panel design, similar to number 3 above and probably dating from the middle of the second century.

The Orpheus pavement stands out from the rest of the mosaic floors listed from Building XVII,1, for it clearly belongs to the fourth century Corinian School. The rest can be dated to the second or early third century. This need not cause any surprise, for we do not know of the relationship of the floors to each other. Experience elsewhere in the town has shown that second- and fourth-century mosaic floors can survive side by side from the same building, e.g. XIV,1 and XX,2. The plan of what survives probably represents one wing of a palatial town house which had heating under mosaics 3 and 4 and wall plaster in a number of the rooms.

In the adjacent insula to the one just referred to, both Webster and Wacher have conducted excavations. In 1957 Webster was unable to recover the complete plans of the buildings he was investigating (XVIII,2). He found a flourishing Claudian-Flavian occupation in the area followed by two stone building phases lasting until the end of the fourth century (Webster *1959* 51). Wacher, excavating in the north-west corner of the insula, found the clay wall of a timber building fronting Ermin Street, which was later replaced by a stone building (XVIII,1) of at least five rooms constructed at some time during the second century. At the beginning of the fourth century the building appears to have been levelled and replaced by a building with walls 1.52m wide, of which little of the plan was recovered (Wacher *1963* 16).

A number of houses have been examined in part from Insula XX.

90

Haverfield (*1920* 176) records at least three floors from this insula as well as a fine collection of sculptured stones from either Insula XX or XXI. The finder suggested that the sculpture came from a mason's workshop, but Haverfield preferred to assign them to a temple.

One of the mosaics recorded by Haverfield (number 21) probably came from Building XX,2, which was examined by Wacher in 1964 (*1965* 102). The house, if that is what it was, contained two fourth-century mosaics in the relatively small area investigated and one of an earlier date. To the north of Ashcroft Road in Insula XXI excavation has shown the presence of timber buildings during the period AD 60–75, with stone buildings replacing these in the middle of the second century (Wacher *1962* 11). The main building on the site appears to have been a large courtyard house of late second-century date containing a mosaic floor, probably dating from the second century, with a cantharus in the central medallion.

Two other buildings that have recently been investigated should be mentioned in this brief survey of houses from Corinium. The first was discovered during the excavations which revealed House XVIII,1 (*supra* p 90). Here, a building (XXIII,l) with stone outer walls, probably dating from the first century, was reconstructed in the second century to provide the house with an external portico along Ermin Street. Wall plaster from this period of rebuilding was found on the outer surface of these walls, protected by the portico (Wacher *1963* 19). The second was found during excavations of the Saxon and abbey churches whose foundations had caused considerable damage to the Roman levels in Insula XXV, but, even so, much of the plan of Building XXV,1 was recovered. It was a courtyard house of which two wings were traced and the beginnings of a third suspected. The outer wall of the veranda was made of large stylobate blocks which originally carried pillars on them at distances of 3m (Brown and McWhirr *1966* 244). Little can be said about the developmental history of this house.

## THE HOUSES IN INSULA XII

Excluding shops and public buildings, the above is an almost complete list of structures found in Cirencester up to 1970 that throw any light on the evolution of the private house in Corinium. Consequently the excavations between 1970 and 1973 on two Roman houses in Insula XII (pl 11) assumed considerable importance and are here discussed in some detail (McWhirr *1973*). These excavations were unable to prove

Plate 11  Air-photograph of the excavations in Insula XII, Cirencester, in 1973, showing the foundations of two houses just inside the
Roman town's defences which lie beneath the trees in the foreground

the existence of Street X/XII in the area and some doubt must now be
cast on whether it extends as far in a north-easterly direction as has
always been supposed. For this reason it is assumed that both buildings
are in Insula XII and they have been numbered accordingly.

The first house investigated was XII,1. From a preliminary examination of the finds it appears that construction first began on the site during the second half of the third century, although a detailed study of
the pottery from the pre-building levels may push this date into the
fourth century. The house started life as a simple rectangular building
measuring 15m × 10m, but additions were made on all four sides. To
the west was added a bath suite, most likely in the middle of the fourth
century if the mosaic floor in the changing room is contemporary with
these alterations. Service rooms were added to the north and living
rooms with simple, but poorly constructed, mosaic floors added to the
east of the original building. To the south, an entrance porch was
attached to lead into the main corridor, and a completely new room was
built to the east of the entrance. The floor of this room contained the

'hare' mosaic (pl 12) which on stylistic grounds can be dated to the second half of the fourth century. This was not the end to alterations in this room, for later in the fourth century (or in the fifth?) the floor was sacrificed for the benefits of central heating. Masonry blocks were laid on top of the mosaic to form a channelled hypocaust, and a new mosaic floor, none of which remained *in situ,* was laid on top of these blocks.

To the south of the house just described, a building (XII,2) with a most interesting plan was discovered (fig 14). It resembled that of a 'winged-corridor' villa and like XII,1 may date from the second half of the third century, although further work may cause this date to be

Plate 12   The 'Hare' mosaic pavement in Building XII,1, Cirencester, found in 1971 and dated to the second half of the fourth century AD (0.5m rule)

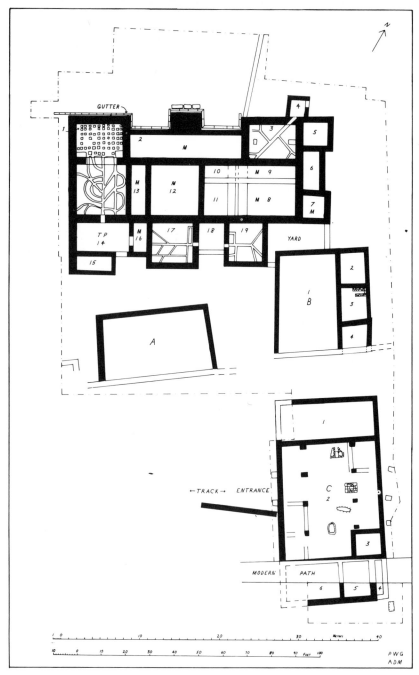

Fig 14    Cirencester.  Plan  of  Building  XII,2

revised. The first phase of building comprised a single range 30m × 12m with projecting rooms at the western and eastern ends. There may have been a corridor along the front of the house in its earlier phase, but this was not proved conclusively. Alterations to this basic plan were made to the south of the main range and at its eastern end. In its latest phase at least nine rooms contained mosaic floors and one other a plain white tessellated floor. Four rooms were heated, the western room of the main range containing a most elaborate system of underfloor heating (pl 13). To the south of the house, but obviously associated with it, were two barn-like structures. One seems to have been abandoned and the levelled walls covered by a roughly paved surface. The other at the south-east corner of the house measured 8.5m by at least 15.5m and to the east were three small rooms, one of which contained a structure similar to an oven or a copper. From within this 'barn-like' building came several pieces of iron slag from smithing furnaces. From disturbed levels, but from the area of this building, came an iron coulter and several bone plaques which may have been for tablet weaving.

Excavations late in 1973 located another structure south of the one just described. It was separated from XII,2 by a well-worn cobbled surface, which seems to have been an alleyway, and by a boundary wall. The newly discovered building was an aisled structure measuring *c* 10m across and containing four features which may have been connected with iron-working to judge by the quantities of slag that came from the building. There was an entrance on the west side. Whether this aisled building is to be connected with the house and outbuildings to the north (XII,2) is uncertain, but the evidence is accumulating to suggest that these buildings are to be associated with agriculture and that we are dealing with a farm inside the walls of Corinium.

Although the excavations of 1970–3 have done much to fill the gap that exists in our knowledge of private houses in Cirencester, these particular examples should not be taken as a true reflection of what was taking place in the rest of the town. In Insula XII we appear to have people acquiring land, close to the defences and previously unoccupied by houses, in the second half of the third or in the fourth century. They built substantial houses, well-appointed with mosaic floors and other internal fittings. Elsewhere in the town, from the meagre evidence reviewed above, the pattern seems to be one of continual rebuilding on the same site. Dating evidence points to stone houses first appearing in the first half of the second century. Some of these were quite elaborate (eg XVII,1), attesting to the wealth that was being attracted into

Plate 13   The channelled hypocaust under the floor of Building XII,2, Cirencester, showing the elaborate pattern of hot-air ducts beneath the town house (2m poles)

Cirencester at that time. That this wealth was based on an expanding agricultural economy in the *civitas* is suggested by the need to provide a market hall in Insula II by the Hadrianic period (Wacher *1962* 8).

## INDUSTRY

Evidence for industries centred on Cirencester is growing. Smith (*1965* 105) has shown the existence of probably the largest fourth-century mosaic workshop in Britain, the Corinian School, which he suggests was based in Cirencester. Some of its products have been referred to above, and those which have been found in recent years are being subjected to a study to see if the exact sources of the stone used can be identified and hence some idea gained of the scale of the stone-quarrying industry. During the lifting operations of some of the mosaic floors a careful watch has been kept for evidence of the mosaicists' techniques. When the floor from the changing room of the bath suite of Building XII,1 was lifted it was found that the all-over meander pattern of the floor itself had been traced out by the mosaicist on the bedding, prior to the laying of the floor.

Other industries, including a whole range of building materials (pl 14), must have been centred on Cirencester, but in many cases insufficient

96

research has been done to elucidate the details. There must have been local firms producing pottery for the considerable market that existed in the region, but as yet no single pottery kiln has been found within a ten-mile radius of Cirencester. That the local clays were exploited is clear from the considerable number of tiles found; in particular the distribution of stamped tiles suggests that Cirencester may have been the centre for one such tiler. The discovery of over forty stamped tiles from Buildings XII,1 and 2 during the excavations of 1970–3 has added considerably to the number of stamped tiles previously listed by Clifford (*1955* 68). One such group of stamps has a very limited distribution, the majority being found in Cirencester. They are stamped ARVERI and of the twenty or so known only about three or four have been noted outside Cirencester. Other stamps found include TPF, TPFA, TPLF and LHS and work is now under way analysing these stamps to see how many different dies were used. Later it is hoped to examine the tiles to see if the clays can be positively identified. Once this has been done it should be possible to say more about the tile industry in this part of Roman Britain. The techniques of locational analysis have already been applied to some industrial products that may have been distributed from Cirencester (Hodder *1972*) but at present the samples are too small to allow definite conclusions to be drawn.

Plate 14   A pile of sandstone roughouts for roofing tiles stacked against the outside face of the wall of Building XII,2, Cirencester (0.5m rule)

## CONCLUSION

The evidence accumulating from excavations points to a prosperous town. In the fourth century Cirencester almost certainly became the capital of *Britannia Prima*, one of the four provinces into which Britain was divided soon after 300. The distribution and quality of the villas in the Cirencester region at this time again reflects the prosperity of the area during the fourth century (Wacher *1971* 19; Goodburn *1972* 8; *infra* p 130).

There is increasing archaeological evidence for the continuation of life in the town well into the fifth century, but the difficulty of dating means that at present reliance has to be placed upon structural sequences for postulating fifth-century occupation of houses. The excavation of a cemetery west of the town is, however, beginning to throw light on this difficult period. The latest phases of burial are clearly to be dated to the fifth century, for one skeleton had a silver coin of Honorius sealed beneath the vertebrae. When the skeletons have been closely studied it should be possible to learn something about the people who were living in Corinium in the fourth and fifth centuries.

# 6

# THE VICI OF WESTERN ENGLAND

An earlier paper of mine (Todd *1970*) attempted to outline some of the general problems presented by the small townships and roadside villages of Roman Britain and to sketch the present state of our very patchy knowledge on this neglected subject. I was not intent on the construction of a deeply entrenched position, for the available evidence did not, and does not, allow anyone to do so. In so far as it seemed possible to draw conclusions from the slender evidence so far accessible to us, I argued that the 'small towns', to give them their common name, must be studied in close relation to their rural environment. These sites are commonly treated as though they were all minor urban settlements. In a few cases there is ample justification for this view, but this should not blind us to the fact that in all instances there were the strongest possible links with the land. As more information accumulates, it becomes clearer that the 'small towns' are more varied in character than has usually been supposed, and this variety will be apparent among the sites discussed in the following pages. They range from important townships like Kenchester to villages which scarcely differ in essentials from those discussed by Leech elsewhere in this volume.

## KENCHESTER (fig 15)

The largest and in some senses the most important of the small walled townships in the western regions of Roman Britain is Kenchester (Magna), in the upper valley of the Wye. Kenchester stands out among its fellows in several respects. In the first place, there are few other large nucleated settlements in these border lands and Kenchester's twenty-two acres within its walls leave it not so far behind the internal area of Caerwent, Caister by Norwich and Aldborough, all of them administrative centres of tribes. Further, the degree of Roman culture evinced in those parts of the interior which have been explored is appreciably higher than that of the common run of small townships, even in the more Romanised parts of the province. In seeking reasons for this

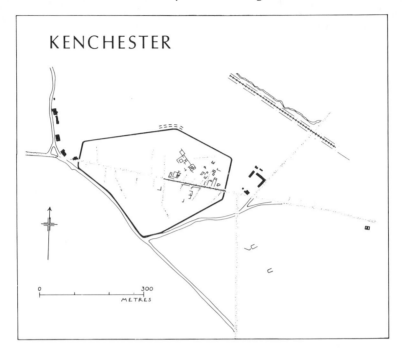

KENCHESTER

0                  300
METRES

Fig 15   Plan of Kenchester

striking development on the very fringe of the Welsh uplands, it is
tempting to seek at least part of the solution in the Roman administrative
order. The well-known milestone found at Kenchester (*RIB* 2250),
apparently re-used in the north wall (or more probably in the footings
of an external tower), makes it clear that in the later third century (the
milestone is dated to the reign of Numerian, AD 283–4) this part of
Herefordshire belonged to the territory of the Dobunni. Their tribal
*caput* Corinium, however, lay some forty-five miles away to the south-
east and it may have been found convenient to administer that part of
the tribe which occupied the Wye valley from a local centre. Kenchester
in its fertile vale may thus have become an independent community late
in the Roman period, perhaps as a self-governing *vicus* rather than
merely the centre of a *pagus,* if a guess is allowable. Elsewhere in the
western provinces of the empire there are several recorded cases of
prosperous villages which developed into autonomous communities,
receiving Latin or even Roman rights of citizenship. The case of the
Vocontii, a *civitas foederata* in Gallia Narbonensis, is a striking example

which may not be as isolated as our scanty records suggest (Pliny *Nat Hist* 3. 37).

The origins of the town at Kenchester are still obscure. A possible nucleus of pre-Roman Iron Age settlement is the nearby hillfort of Credenhill Camp, one of the largest Iron Age forts in this region. It continued to be occupied down to the Flavian period and its most recent excavator suggests that it was for a lengthy period a major centre for people living between the Wye and Severn (Stanford *1970*). Archaeology has as yet thrown no light on the first Roman occupation of the site at Kenchester. An early Roman fort here, at the meeting-place of the road along the Wye valley and the route from Wroxeter and Leintwardine to Abergavenny, makes good sense on the map, but there is still no appropriately early pottery from any part of the site. The only *terra firma* is thus the evidence from the civilian settlement which belongs mainly to the period from the second century to the fifth.

A prime source for the planning of the town is a series of air-photographs taken by St Joseph. These show beyond all doubt that the place had no rectilinear grid of streets, only a series of many lanes linked to both sides of a central roadway which crossed the town in a direct line from east to west. The arrangement of buildings and other structures in relation to the main east-west road and to the subsidiary lanes is rather haphazard – a fact underlined by the early excavations in the interior. There is no obvious focus to the place, no crossing of major streets, no apparent centre of social life. Buildings now crowd in upon each other, now stand apart from their neighbours. Those parts of the interior which have been sampled by excavation – albeit excavation of a pre-Wheelerian kind – are invested with a homely, almost backwoods, air.

But by no means all the buildings of Roman Kenchester were modest in character. In 1924–5, Jack excavated part of a large and complex dwelling on the north side of the main street and close to its frontage, a building which would not be out of place at Wroxeter or Cirencester. The various structural phases were evidently not fully understood at the time of excavation and they cannot now be separated one from another. There is about the plan, however, the suggestion of a porticoed house with projecting wings. Again, near the north-east angle of the town was a house which possessed a substantially built bath-suite, to which the niche (or 'chair') of early accounts may be attributed, as well as a tessellated floor found in the seventeenth century (Walters *1908* 178). Fragments of other buildings – probably two – lay between this bath-house and the main road. This little group of structures included four hypocausts, a small but competently executed mosaic panel, and a fragment of a very handsome geometric mosaic floor, 7.5m wide and originally some 9.1m long.

Other recorded buildings suggest that Kenchester was one of the more ambitious of the Romano-British small towns. Along the south frontage of the main street there ran a series of square piers, presumably the remains of a porticoed façade, as at Wroxeter, and sections of both frontages seem to have been flanked by rows of stone blocks with squared mortice-holes in them, apparently designed to take the timber uprights of a veranda (Jack and Hayter *1926* 21ff). Knowledge of the buildings outside the defences is not extensive, but many must have existed, judging by the number of lanes leading from the main road to the east of the town. They included at least a square Romano-Celtic temple about 500m outside the east gate (Baker *1966* fig 1, pl V). Buildings apart, there were other features unusual in a small town. The most striking is the large central drain in the main road.

I have left to the last the defences of Kenchester, for they are not particularly remarkable. They went through three familiar phases: an earthwork, to which a stone wall was later added, with later modification in the form of external towers and a wide ditch. The last-named changes should, by analogy, date from the late fourth century, but the date of the earlier phases has not yet been closely defined. The stone wall most probably belongs to the third century, the earthwork defence to the end of the second. The west gate has also been examined, its dual carriageway entrance and twin flanking guard chambers revealing it to be notably more ambitious than other known small-town gateways (Webster *1957*; Heys and Thomas *1959, 1963*). This feature has produced a little evidence of fifth-century occupation at Kenchester, in the form of modification and perhaps repairs to its structure at that date.

Kenchester remained a focus of settlement for long enough after AD 400 for its name to be adopted by the early medieval settlers in the region, the *Magonsaetan*. Archaeologically, however, these are not yet distinguishable. On the end of the town, Leland must still have the last word: 'To be short, of the decaye of Kenchestre, Herford rose and floryshed.'

## SEA MILLS (fig 16)

An unusual instance of a settlement overlooking the site of a harbour and presumably concerned with its functioning is provided by the site at

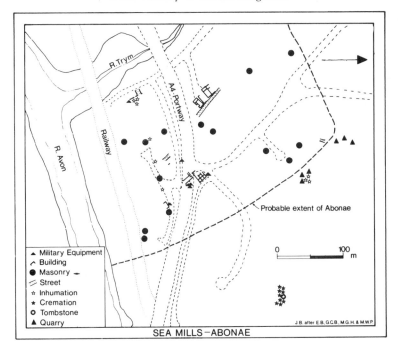

Fig 16   Plan of discoveries at Sea Mills

Sea Mills, Bristol, at the confluence of the Trym and the Avon. A considerable body of material evidence, including more than 100 Claudio-Neronian coins and 15 items of military equipment, makes it certain that a military force was resident here about the middle of the first century, but in the absence of definite structural evidence it is not clear whether the presumed military post was a garrison fort or an installation connected with the harbour. Where their find-spots have been recorded, the pieces of military gear have been found on the low ground close to the confluence, an area which is more likely to have been occupied by quays and storehouses than by a fort. The idea that Sea Mills was a stores or supply-depot served by a naval detachment operating in the Bristol Channel is an attractive one and it receives a certain measure of support. How long this base remained in commission is unknown, but a number of stamped tiles and a stamped brick of *Legio II Augusta* hint strongly that a unit was still here in the second century, as military tile-stamps of the first century in Britain are at the least very rare, if they exist at all (Boon *1945, 1949*).

The earliest recorded structures at Sea Mills are a series of timber-framed buildings and a cobbled street dating from the late first century. The earliest of the excavated stone buildings appear about a century later, but most of the known buildings are of the later third and fourth centuries. Little is known of the street-plan, except that the streets so far recorded appear to share the same alignment. A fire in the Hadrianic period seems to have destroyed a part of the settlement, but this setback did not inhibit the growth of the place. A continuing use of the harbour during the second century is suggested by the finding of two Antonine lead pigs from the Mendip mines in the river Frome near Wade Street, Bristol (*infra,* p 234). No trace of defences has ever been noted at Sea Mills, but their existence, though unlikely, has not yet been entirely precluded. If the place was defended, its exposed position will not have made it attractive to its surrounding population at the end of the fourth century. The coin series continues to Arcadius, but by that time its inhabitants will have been looking towards the safer refuges of sites like Congresbury, Portbury and possibly Gatcombe. The last-named site may be treated next.

## GATCOMBE (fig 17)

Of all the defended sites in this region which are commonly considered under the general heading of small towns, the oddest is the site at Gatcombe, four miles west of Bristol on the south side of the Failand Ridge. The massive late-Roman walls of this settlement (pl 15) are alone sufficient to mark it as an oddity (the wall measures nearly 5m in thickness), but still more anomalous is its situation. Unlike the great majority of walled settlements, it does not lie on or near a major route, or any other known Roman road. The setting of Gatcombe is not appropriate, then, to a small town as that term is commonly understood.

The area walled was an enclosure of at least eighteen acres. It may have been considerably greater than this, but the precise area cannot be established until the south side has been certainly located. The buildings within included at least two aisled halls – a building type which has been recorded at other nucleated settlements in Roman Britain but which so far does not appear to have been a common feature of them (Cunliffe *1967*). As yet no orderly planning of streets has been noted, although five buildings near the north-east angle were roughly arranged as though fronting on to a yard or a lane. Occupation began at Gatcombe in the mid first century, but structures and other material remains are sparse before the mid third. Thereafter, almost all the excavated buildings were

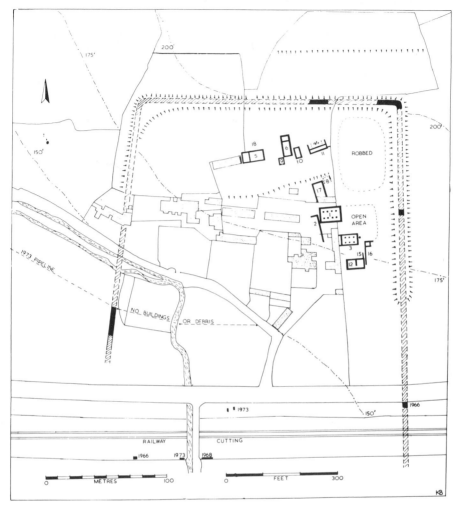

Fig 17    Plan of Gatcombe

erected in the following half-century and continued in use until the third quarter of the fourth century. After 367–9, it has been suggested, the place began to decline as a result of barbarian raids on its hinterland (Branigan *1968* 49). This point – if it can be established beyond question – is an important one, for we would expect defended sites like Gatcombe to achieve greater significance in the conditions of the late fourth century, and not to perish before the century's end.

The installations inside some of the buildings suggest certain functions for them. Building 9 was a small workshop containing a smelting

Plate 15   The outer face of the *c* 5m thick wall around the late-Roman site at Gatcombe, Somerset (1ft units on the pole)


furnace. The aisled hall 1 possessed two or more cooking or baking ovens and larger examples lay in Buiidings 12 and 16 (pl 16 and 17). Their excavator suggests that all three buildings were bakeries, but it is always a difficult matter to decide whether ovens and furnaces like these were operated by specialists who aimed to disperse their products widely or whether they were installations used by a single family or group of households. Unfortunately, the term 'industrial' is too freely and loosely used by writers on Roman Britain. Often a building or an installation is labelled 'industrial' when in reality it was no more than the work-place of a local craftsman who was serving a very limited market. Many 'industries' of the province should with greater accuracy be termed local crafts.

Perhaps the most interesting problem posed by Gatcombe concerns the kind of settlement it was. Why was it walled, but Camerton, for instance, not? If Gatcombe is considered to be a small walled town, there is no obvious answer to the question. But the position of the site suggests that this was not a small town at all. The rapid growth of the settlement in the later third century, after a very undistinguished existence in the preceding 200 years, suggests the wielding of capital by some wealthy landowner. If this was the case, and if Gatcombe could then be regarded as the headquarters of a large private estate, this site may be a humble Romano-British version of Mogorjelo (Dyggve and Vetters *1966*) or Pfalzel (Kutzbach *1935*).

## BOURTON-ON-THE-WATER

We turn now to two large unwalled settlements on the Fosse Way, at Bourton-on-the-Water, 20km north-west of Cirencester, and Camerton, 11km south-west of Bath. The extensive area of occupation near the crossing of the river Windrush at Bourton-on-the-Water, which extends eastwards for about a kilometer to include the older Iron Age settlement at

Plate 16   Typical masonry in Carboniferous limestone in Building 12 at Gatcombe, showing a fourth-century oven and a platform incorporating the inverted top of a rotary quern (1m rule)

Plate 17   One of four fourth-century ovens in Building 16 at Gatcombe. The stone slabs in the foreground formed the raking platform in front of the flue (1m rule)

Salmonsbury, does not easily fit into any category. Near the river crossing, however, the remains are plainly those of a roadside village straggling along both sides of the Fosse Way (Donovan *1933, 1934, 1935*). O'Neil's recent excavations (O'Neil *1968*) add to her earlier picture of fairly simple buildings mainly rectangular blocks without partitions. The only structure with any pretensions was a winged portico-house close to the river-crossing recorded in the late nineteenth century. Of the buildings recovered in the recent excavations, one contained two furnaces and is to be interpreted as a workshop. Another had an apse fronting on to the Fosse Way and has been interpreted as a shrine. A third contained two small ovens and on the strength of these has been termed a bakehouse. Next to this structure lay a house which has been identified as a place of refreshment. Although all these identifications are plausible, the Fosse Way and its traffic must not be allowed to dominate all our ideas of the functioning of the villages along its line. In particular, we must beware of a tendency to see these roadside villages as no more than halts and posting stations. The evidence from other parts of Britain and from other provinces is that they played a much more significant role in agrarian settlement.

One of the most striking features of the Bourton settlement is the fact that it extends so far to the east of the Fosse Way in an untidy huddle of buildings towards the Iron Age defended site of Salmonsbury. In this respect it differs from most of the other known settlements on the main roads. Few of these buildings have been studied, the exception being the 'Leadenwell villa', from a well inside which two lead tanks were recovered. The history and chronology of the entire settlement must await further excavation for their elucidation. For the moment, it may be remarked that the place was occupied down to the beginning of the fifth century at least.

As with all these sites, there are questions which our evidence simply cannot answer. What, for instance, was the relationship of the Bourton settlement to the contemporary village at Great Chessels, Lower Slaughter, rather more than a mile to the north? (O'Neil *1961*; O'Neil and Toynbee *1958*). And what kind of settlement was contained within the earthwork of Salmonsbury and what was its relation to Bourton (O'Neil *1966* 42; unpublished excavations by G. Dunning)?

## CAMERTON (fig 18)

One of the most extensively examined of all Romano-British open settle-

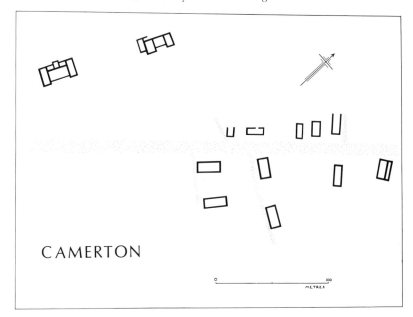

CAMERTON

Fig 18   Plan of Camerton (omitting Buildings XVI and XVIII)

ments is that at Camerton, and it has the further recommendation of including buildings which incorporate various installations connected with crafts (Wedlake *1958*). The origins of Camerton are still obscure. There appears to have been no late pre-Roman Iron Age progenitor, although an occupation site of the earlier Iron Age lay on its north-eastern margins. There is a strong hint of military occupation in the form of a fort, presumably of the mid first century AD, but this has not been verified. The sizeable unwalled settlement developed from the later first century onward, reaching its apogee in the late third and early fourth. In the layout of its streets there is a trace of regular planning, although the date at which this was effected has not been determined. The great majority of the recorded buildings date from the third and fourth centuries, in common with other 'small towns'.

Those buildings fall into two distinct groups. Close to the Fosse Way frontage there lay a group of twelve simple, rectangular structures without stone subdivisions. Of these, no less than eight contained the remains of substantial furnaces of various types and a further two furnaces were found to lie in the open. The second group of structures comprises a trio of more pretentious buildings set back at some distance from the western frontage of the Fosse Way. One of these had a familiar winged

109

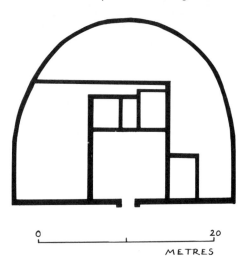

0                                    20

METRES

Fig 19   A shrine (?) excavated by Skinner, at Camerton

portico plan, but the other two, if credence is given to the early nine-
teenth-century record, were much less commonplace. One was essentially
a four-roomed block with projecting wings, but at the rear it was provided with a courtyard surrounded by a semi-circular wall (Bldg III). The
other house had a still more exotic plan (Wedlake *1958* 47ff). Even if we
agree with Haverfield and Lewis that a local shrine may here be under
consideration, the plan of this structure is either incomplete or too full,
and it must therefore remain under a cloud (fig 19, Bldg XVI).

The ten furnaces found in the area near the road margins are an
extremely interesting group. The functions of all are not immediately
apparent, although the smelting of iron and bronze will account for the
majority. Furnaces, ovens and hearths are among those features of
Romano-British settlement-sites which have not yet attracted the attention they deserve, so that the whole range of craft-activities carried on at
Camerton cannot be clearly defined. One installation, however, does
require special mention. This occupied a corner of Building VIII and
consisted of two chambers (fig 20), one a rectangle measuring 1.51m by
1.14m, the other a narrow flue 1.22m long. The latter was only 18cm
wide at the base but splayed out to more than 50cm at its surviving
height. It had not been used for any metalworking process and its
elaborate character seems ill-suited for cooking. More probably this was
either a corn-drying kiln or a kiln for the malting of barley. Beer was

110

so popular a drink in Celtic Europe that it is odd that malt-kilns seem so far to have gone unrecorded.

Activities such as those attested by the Camerton furnaces are no more than we should expect of a village community which in most respects must have been self-sufficient. Camerton, however, is one of the few *vici* of Roman Britain to have produced evidence of small-scale industrial working which must have involved some of its inhabitants in a wider world. One building near the Fosse Way frontage (Building XVII) yielded two moulds of Bath stone, designed for the casting of pewter vessels (*infra* p 196). One mould had produced a shallow bowl with a wide flange at the rim. The other, of which only part was recovered, was for handled skillets or *paterae* (Wedlake *1958* 82ff). Similar moulds for pewter tableware have been found in the recent excavations of the roadside village at Nettleton Shrub (Wedlake, *forthcoming*), some sixteen miles away to the north-east, so that it begins to look as though production of these vessels, which are familiar items in the domestic equipment of late Roman Britain, was dispersed over a number of small, local workshops. This view is supported by the finding of other moulds for pewter vessels as far afield as south Yorkshire and Cornwall (Langton: Goodall *1972* 34; St Just: Brown *1970* 107).

On the whole, Camerton presents a braver show than might have been

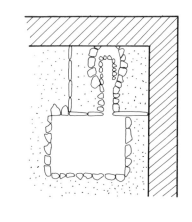

0                                            5

METRES

Fig 20   A malting oven (?) at Camerton

111

expected from an unwalled roadside settlement. It possessed buildings of some size, and a series of high-quality architectural mouldings suggests that they were not inhabited by a troupe of Tony Lumbkins. All this is revealing, but it does not reveal all. We are still very much in the dark about certain social matters. What kind of community was this? Was it an entirely independent village? Or did its growth reflect the interest and capital of some local landowner, resident perhaps in one of the villas on the fringe of the settlement? These are essential queries about the very fabric of Romano-British society with which our inarticulate evidence cannot assist us. A fifth-century problem, too, beckons. Where was the settlement with which the cemetery of that date must have been associated (but *cf* Fowler *1972a* 200)?

## WYCOMB AND DORN

A less well recorded but no less interesting site which was never walled is that at Wycomb, near Andoversford (Glos). Although extensively dug in the nineteenth century, the contemporary records permit us to distinguish some unusual features (Lawrence *1863, 1864*; O'Neil and Saunders *1959* 161). Wycomb was plainly a straggling roadside village in which most of the houses were single-roomed blocks. But the place also included a square Romano-Celtic temple within a *temenos*, and a large curved structure which, if it was accurately recorded, can best be interpreted as a rustic theatre associated with the cult-place. The prominence of the temple and the 'theatre' on the plan should indicate that the religious functions of this site had much to do with its growth in the Roman period. This is underlined by the fact that Wycomb lies well away from any major road and thus cannot have been concerned with large-scale commerce. Though not as striking a case as the cult-centres (presumably of *pagi*) at Springhead in Kent and the site at Nettleton Shrub in Wiltshire, the settlement at Wycomb is a reminder of the significant role which could be played by religious centres in the settlement-geography of Romano-Celtic lands.

The little walled settlement at Dorn (fig 21), near Moreton-in-the-Marsh (Glos), occupied an important position on a route leading through the central Cotswolds. Recognition that this actually was a walled site came only thirteen years ago (Taylor *1961* 132). The defences enclose a mere ten acres, but nevertheless a planned system of streets existed within them. This is by far the smallest settlement known to have received anything approximating to a grid-plan of streets, and the reasons for

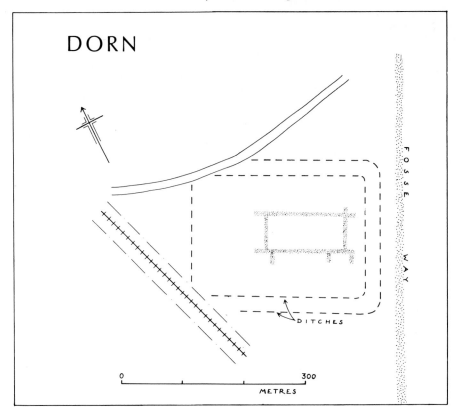

Fig 21   Plan of Dorn

this unusual treatment are not clear. Dorn is unusual in one other way. The walled enclosure lies entirely to the west of the Fosse Way and not, as normally, astride the main road. There has been no organised excavation here and we have therefore no secure information about the origins and character of the community. An official *mansio* or *mutatio* may well be the answer.

The site of Dorn long retained some local significance. In the third quarter of the eighth century, Ethelbald of Mercia awarded the estate of *Baecceshora* to the bishop of Worcester. This land lay mainly on a ridge to the west of the Fosse Way, but at the south-east corner its bounds included the walled site of Dorn. The very name 'Dorn' may be derived from the Celtic 'duro-', meaning gate, ie town with gates and thus with walls.

There are many other small walled settlements in Britain which can hardly have been wealthy enough or important enough to have defences provided for themselves alone. It is much more likely that such sites – in this region one might mention Mildenhall as well as Dorn – received defences because they were fulfilling one or more official functions. Literary evidence on this point is lacking for Britain, but, as I have indicated elsewhere, there is a little epigraphic evidence that here, and in Lower Germany, *beneficiarii consulares* were outstationed in certain small townships, for instance Catterick and Dorchester-on-Thames (*RIB* 235, 725, 726), presumably charged with the control of communications and the traffic using them. The collection of the *annona*, never an imposition lightly borne by the provincials, and the protection of this and other forms of tribute while in transit is another possible function. One might recall the remark of Ausonius on the fortified road-posts of Gallia Belgica: 'non castra, sed horrea Belgis' (*Mosella* 456–7).

## WORCESTER AND TEWKESBURY

There has been a steady accumulation of information from excavation and chance finds over the past twenty years at Worcester and Tewkesbury, the result being that we can now with some confidence speak of them as 'small towns' in the Roman period. Worcester now has more than a lengthy coin list and records of frequent pottery finds beneath the medieval city to support its claim. An Iron Age defended settlement apparently formed the nucleus of the early Roman civilian occupation, the latter receiving its own substantial defences in the middle of the Roman period, perhaps in the early third century (Barker *1969* 15ff). Those defences have been much denuded by later destructive agencies and only the great water-filled ditch, 27m wide and nearly 8m deep, has so far been defined. The role of an earlier defensive earthwork has not yet been clarified: its association with a possible first-century fort is still speculative. The existence of such a fort now seems highly likely. The mid-first-century coins and the Claudio-Neronian brooch from the Castle Mound have recently been supplemented by a small hoard of ten Claudian bronze coins, a group which is likely to have been concealed not much later than about AD 60 and certainly before about AD 65 (Sutherland *1963*). The coin list on its own does not prove the presence of a military unit, but it adds useful support to the argument based on topographical grounds. The area enclosed by the later Roman defences measured some 6.5 hectares. Outside the *enceinte*, however, there were extensive 'suburbs' to north and south. To the east, in the Broad Street area, there existed at least one substantial house decorated with ambitious wall-paintings. Craft or industrial installations are represented by an iron-smelting workshop, also in the Broad Street area, where four simple bowl-hearths were examined, while another iron-smelting site was long ago revealed in the Pitchcroft area near the bank of the Severn.

Demonstration in 1972–3 of the existence of a sizeable settlement at Tewkesbury is a timely reminder of how little co-ordinated work of survey, much less of planned excavation, has been carried out on many of our smaller historic towns (Miles and Fowler *1973* 9f). Stone buildings, a corn-drying oven, a cemetery containing stone sarcophagi, together with a marked nucleation of lesser chance discoveries beneath the northern parts of the medieval town, all these earlier finds told a reasonably coherent story, while the situation of the place, where the Roman road from Gloucester to Droitwich passes hard by the confluence of the Avon with the Severn, spoke further in favour of this site being a 'small town'. If we seek a name for it, the best candidate is the so far unidentified *Argistillum* of the Ravenna Cosmography, which plainly lay between Gloucester and Droitwich (Richmond and Crawford *1949* 23).

The nucleus of the Roman settlement now appears to have been that part of the town called Oldbury, a name which therefore assumes a fresh significance. Of possible Roman defences, however, there is as yet no positive trace. It is, all the same, clear from the recent excavations that well before the establishment of the late Saxon town this had been a site with modest urban pretensions. The most remarkable single find from Roman Tewkesbury may well be connected with the early Roman origins of the place. This is a 'well', found near the Gas Works in Oldbury in 1840. It contained the skeletons of animals and a human being, as well as a dozen or more urns which probably contained cremations. Other human remains lay near-by. This may have been a ritual shaft rather than a well, and if this is correct, it could plausibly be linked with a Celtic sanctuary at the confluence. Once more, we may be dealing with a 'small town', like Wycomb, Springhead or Nettleton Shrub, which was a religious focus for the surrounding population.

## MINING CENTRES

The region contains two extensive settlements which were associated with important mines. One is Weston-under-Penyard (Ariconium), the growth of which was linked with the local iron deposits. The site appears to have been straggling in its layout and excavation here has not yet

Plate 18  Air-photograph, from the north, of part of the Charterhouse area on top of Mendip, with the outlines of the street pattern of
the Roman mining town showing in the pasture

been on a large enough scale to deal with its problems (Jack *1923*). The
other mining centre was Charterhouse-on-Mendip, exploiting the famous
silver-lead veins of the Mendip hills (fig 46). Excavation has been limited
here, but air-photographs and field-survey permit the definition of
certain salient features in the local topography (Wilson *1971* 277). The
earliest in date is the site of a Roman fort, lying close to the mine-
workings of Blackmoor. On the slopes to the north of the fort, which
is likely to belong to the first and perhaps the early second century,
there lies a substantial settlement of at least thirty acres. The air-photographs (pl 18) reveal that this township had a much more regularly
planned system of streets than might have been expected. At the centre
of the settlement this system takes the form of a grid, with one row of
roughly square *insulae* lying on an east-west alignment and with less

116

regular blocks to north and south. The well-known amphitheatre lies further up the slope to the south-west (fig 47).

There is no sure evidence as to how the Mendip mines were administered, and thus we do not know what role this settlement played in their operation. Lead pigs from these workings bearing imperial stamps continue until the Antonine period, although a number also bear the marks of private firms and individuals, including C. Nipius Ascanius (*infra* p 186), also recorded as having interests in the Flintshire lead deposits. After this earlier period of imperial control, the operation of the mines may have passed to the municipal council or to private entrepreneurs, as happened in other parts of the empire. The Charterhouse settlement might, then, have begun its life under the auspices of the imperial administration, and later reached its peak of development under the direction of a group of businessmen, or perhaps of the tribal *curiales*. There are few settlements of this size in Roman Britain which can be so intimately associated with an industrial centre, and thus Charterhouse deserves especial remark.

## THE VICI IN THE FOURTH CENTURY (fig 22)

The settlements discussed in the foregoing pages are on the whole a miscellaneous gathering, but they have one thing in common. Like most of the other small towns of the province, they all (or at least those that have been excavated to any extent) appear to have been late developers. Not one seems to represent a sizeable community until after the second century, and some, including Camerton and Gatcombe for instance, did not begin their major development until the late third century. A major reason for the material advance made by the *vici* from the later third century is provided by the fact that this is the period when Romano-British agriculture entered its heyday. An access of prosperity in the countryside inevitably brought increasing benefit to the towns of all degree. Indeed, since the main economic basis of all the towns was agriculture, that access of prosperity could scarcely fail to be reflected in them. But there are other reasons why the smaller townships grew at a disproportionately faster rate than the cities in the later Roman period.

When *vici* prospered and became independent communities, they might expect to acquire some of the territory which belonged to their parent *civitas*. Thus the old municipalities could lose control of a good deal of land and other property. Still more land was taken away from the

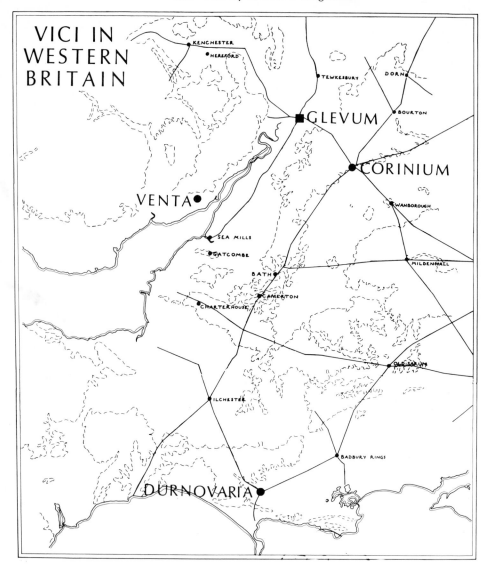

Fig 22   Map of the *vici* in western Britain

cities from the later second century onward by the rapid development
of private estates, and the patronage exercised by the owners of such
estates sometimes ensured that the land alienated from the city administration came under the control of the magistrates of a large *vicus*. A
rescript of Aurelian (*Cod Just* 11.59,1) reveals yet another way in which

118

land could pass from the cities to private owners and to *vici*, and gives us a sense of the increasing pressure upon the *curiales* in the late third century. This rescript made the entire curial order of a city responsible for the taxes on estates abandoned by their members, after a lapse of three years. If they could not support that burden, the land in question was to be distributed *among the neighbouring private estates and villages.*

These are only two of the factors which tended to favour the growth of the lesser towns and inhibit the development of the cities. There were others, chief among them the demoralisation of the municipal *curiales* by the imposition upon them of liturgies, both imperial and municipal. The Roman town could not thrive without a prosperous middle class and the shackling of the *curiales* which took place in the fourth century dealt that middle class a heavy blow, from which, in the western empire at least, it never recovered.

# VILLA SETTLEMENT IN THE WEST COUNTRY

There are nearly 250 Roman villas plotted on our map of south-west England and south Wales (fig 23), and no doubt others remain to be discovered. These villas form the most convincing evidence we have to support the concept of a highly Romanised West Country – a Roman, as opposed to a British or Celtic, west. For the most part, the villas are closely bound together culturally and historically, but, as the distribution map perhaps intimates, the villas of Devon and Cornwall and of south Wales do not really fall into the mainstream of villa development in the West Country. Partly for this reason, and partly because they are so few in number, the villas of these areas will receive little mention in the pages which follow. Our discussion will therefore be centred on a group of about 230 villas. It must be remembered that only about half of these have been even sampled by excavation, the rest having been identified mainly from surface scatters of characteristic debris – tesserae, wall plaster, flue tiles, and pottery. Amongst the excavated examples, both the extent and quality of the excavations have varied greatly, but we have a hard core of about 50 villas for which there are reasonably comprehensive reports and plans. Much, though not all, of what is written in this chapter is based on the evidence from these 50 villas.

## THE PATTERN OF VILLA SETTLEMENT

The villas of the West Country are found on a variety of soils, but the great majority are found in low-lying situations close to running water. In Wiltshire it was found that three-quarters of the villas were situated off the chalk on valley bottoms or lower hill-slopes (Bonney *1968*), in contrast to the distribution of both Iron Age settlements and 'native' settlements of the Roman period. The same pattern can be seen elsewhere in the West Country. In the Somerset valleys of both the northern and southern Yeo, the villas are strung along the edges of the flood-plain, overlooked by 'native' settlements on the higher hill-slopes. In the northern part of the region, the pattern is altered by the domination of

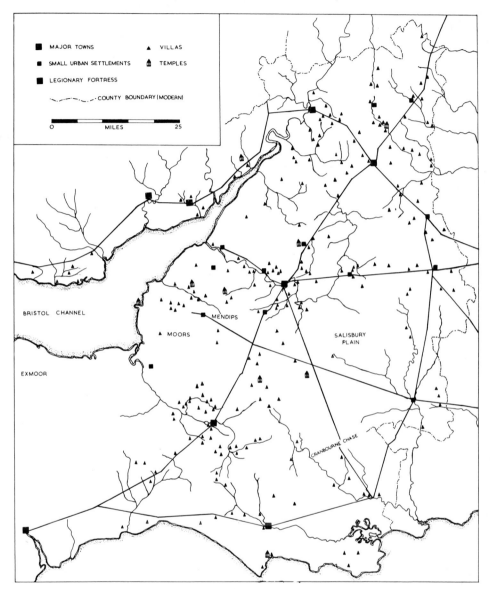

Fig 23   Villas in the West Country

the Cotswolds, though villas still stay close to the rivers, and therefore
in relatively low-lying situations. More surprising than the topographical
situation of the villas, however, and certainly more important for our
study of them as a social phenomenon, is their distribution in relation to

121

the major Roman towns of the south-west. Villas, as surplus-producing farms, needed accessible towns in which to market their produce, so that they must be expected to be concentrated within easy reach of towns, and close to roadways which lead to them. This economic factor is clearly evident in the south-west, and the importance of the Fosse Way as an economic corridor, for example, is emphasised by the fact that one in nine of the West Country villas lies within a mile of it. But the concentrations of villas around Cirencester, Gloucester, Bath, and Ilchester is greater than can be expected, or explained, in purely economic terms. Bath was a small town, with little room to spare for a resident population, yet within five miles of its walls there are twenty-three known or suspected villas. These villas were too densely concentrated around too small a market for them all to have been the centres of farming estates: some of them must have been the residences of those who earned their profits in Bath itself. Although Bath may have been exceptional, the attractions of the social amenities of a Romanised town are again illustrated at Ilchester, where fifteen villas lie within five miles of the town, and thirty-five within ten miles of it, and again at Cirencester where twenty are found within ten miles. Considering that Cirencester almost certainly acquired a *territorium*, which may have restricted the amount of villa-building close to the town, the concentration is high indeed. The same may be said for that around Gloucester, where eighteen villas are found within ten miles of the walls (*supra* p 76).

## THE DEVELOPMENT OF THE PATTERN

Not only is the size of these concentrations of villas unusual, but so too is the date at which they begin to appear. One might expect that the pattern of villa settlement began to develop during the second century, since by that time the towns in question were thriving, Romanised communities. In a similar situation in the south-east, we find that the majority of the villas were first built during the late first and early second centuries (Branigan *1973* 42–8). But second-century villas are difficult to find in the south-west. We must remember that we are speaking of villas, not of farms in the broader sense, and that first- and second-century pottery found on the site of a villa does not automatically imply that the villa itself was first constructed during that period. If we consider only excavated villas, we find that there are little more than a dozen whose foundation dates can confidently be placed before AD 200, and half of these lie at the extremes of our region. Thus Magor, Seaton and

Holcombe are second-century foundations, and so it seems are the Welsh villas at East Aberthaw, Ely and possibly Whitton. Some might include Llantwit Major too, though I am in sympathy with Webster's (*1969* 238) re-interpretation of the evidence there as pointing to a much later foundation date. The remaining villas include Witcombe, Eastington and possibly Hucclecote, all of which probably lay within the *territorium* of the colony at Gloucester, and further east Chedworth and possibly Cricklade, the latter in the territory of the Atrebates. Finally, in the centre of the area, there are Combe Down and Box. Of these Combe Down is well known as an exceptional case, to which we shall shortly return. The picture of second-century villa settlement which emerges is one of small-scale and unimpressive villa development in the territory of the Dumnonii and the Silures, and of none at all in the territory of the Durotriges, the western half of the canton of the Belgae, and the southern half of Dobunnic territory. The only exceptions are to be found in the *territorium* of Gloucester – presumably villas belonging to the veterans (and Roman citizens) of the colony – and in the isolated villas of Chedworth and Box. Others may yet emerge around both Gloucester and Bath, but it seems clear that, despite the splendours of Bath, Cirencester and Gloucester, and to a lesser extent of Ilchester and Dorchester, the western Belgae and the Durotriges did not, in general, build Romanised farmhouses in the second century.

This requires some explanation, for not only does the existence of Romanised urban populations lead one to expect the appearance of Romanised rural ones, but we have seen that the less Romanised Dumnonii and Silures were beginning to build villas in the second century, albeit that they were few in number and unpretentious in design. The most likely explanation is that this pattern of development was determined by Roman policy. It has long been argued that Salisbury Plain and Cranborne Chase were maintained as a great *saltus* or imperial estate by the Roman administration. Similarly, an imperial estate based on Charterhouse and related to the mining of lead has been recognised, whilst another agricultural *saltus* is generally agreed to have been focused on the villa site at Combe Down (Rivet *1966* 113). Here, fortunately, we have an inscription and a lead seal both of which suggest the nature of the site. I suggest that south Gloucestershire, Somerset, and most of Dorset were all treated in a similar way, and that the whole area was kept under government control as a series of estates.

The reasons would have been partly economic – control of Mendip lead, and the production of wheat, beef and hides for the garrison of

Wales – and initially partly political. The Durotriges and the southern Dobunni had opposed the Roman conquest fiercely, if unsuccessfully (*supra* p 16). Indeed, in this respect it is interesting to contrast the appearance of second-century villas in the eastern half of the canton of the Belgae with their absence in the western half. It was only the western half which was occupied by people of the Dobunni, who under Corio had opposed the Roman advance (Branigan *1974*). Unfortunately we cannot produce more inscriptions like that from Combe Down which would throw light on the situation, but one or two further points may be made. There is, for example, an altar from Bath which was set up by a *centurio regionarius* – a centurion in charge of the region (*RIB* 152). Here is a likely candidate for the overseer of one of our suggested *saltii*. One would like to know, too, what cuirass scales were doing in the native Romano-British farmstead at Butcombe, some fifteen miles to the west of Bath (Fowler *1968*). Another cuirass scale and bronze sheathing from the curious villa on Ham Hill (Bedmore Barn) one is tempted to regard as scrap collected from the site of the fort presumed to be near-by. But not only is the plan of this villa unusual (fig 39): so too is its situation, stuck atop the hill, high above a cluster of fourth-century villas in the valley of the Yeo. Its situation is more reminiscent of Combe Down, and I think it not unlikely that it fulfilled a similar function. Its proximity to the presumed fort may be significant in this respect, although it is possible that the military metalwork from Ham Hill was never associated with a fort at all but should be related to the administrative centre of a *saltus*, such as that we are proposing.

It is of course possible that no such *saltus*, or series of estates, existed and that the dearth of first- and second-century villas is due to other factors. If that is so, then they are certainly factors we cannot begin to comprehend. We cannot explain the situation in purely social or economic terms, since, as we have said earlier, the urban populations were already highly Romanised and the suitability of the reign for exploitation by farming cannot be in dispute. Whatever the truth of the situation, however, it may have begun to change in the early third century, at least in the southern half of the region, where four or five villas focused on Ilchester may have been founded in this period. The Mendip mines had passed into the hands of civilian lessees by the middle of the second century, so that the relinquishing of agricultural estates by this time is quite possible. The most dramatic change, however, falls within the last thirty years of the third century. Some forty villa sites in the south-west have provided satisfactory evidence of foundation during this period,

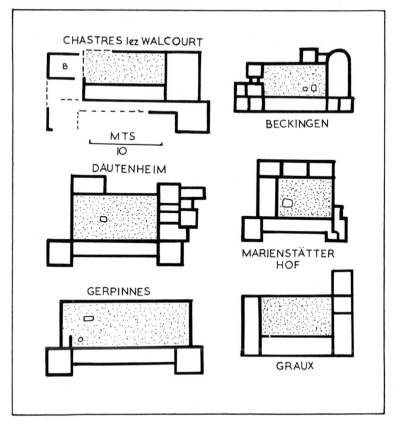

Fig 24   Plans of villas with intra-mural yards in Gaul

and another forty, where excavations and publication have been less rigorous, have produced little or no material earlier than the mid third century AD, so that they too are probably late-third-century foundations.

This remarkable surge in villa settlement in the south-west has been noticed by others, and they have suggested that the reason for it is to be sought in an influx of Gallic landowners at this time (Rivet *1969a* 207; Smith *1969* 113). This certainly seems to be the most plausible explanation yet offered, and it has the merit of fitting the situation very well indeed. In Gaul, the period *c* 260–76 was one of constant disruption as the barbarians swept across the frontier and plundered widely. The confidence of the rural population must have been badly shaken and they may well have looked for somewhere safer to invest their capital. Britain was near at hand, culturally akin, and a comparative haven of

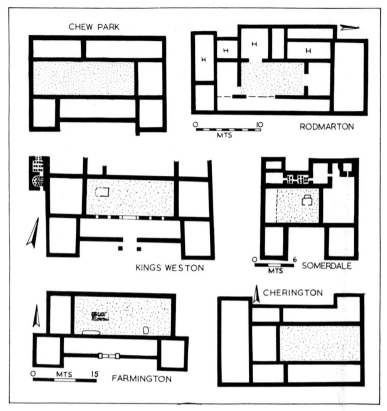

Fig 25   Plans of villas with intra-mural yards in the West Country

peace. The West Country was particularly inviting since it had extensive areas of farmland not yet exploited by villa estates, and it also possessed two of the most Romanised and civilised towns in the province – Cirencester and Bath. The latter in particular was already well known to Gallic tourists and pilgrims, some of whom dedicated altars in the temple there. Finally, in the financial difficulties and military uncertainties of the late third century, both the Gallic and British usurpers may have been inclined to dispose of remaining imperial estates for ready cash.

There is some evidence which can be brought to support the argument. In northern Gaul many villas were abandoned, and in some cases their previous owners certainly left the region altogether (Wightman *1970* 57–9; Parlasca *1959* 49). That some found their way to the West Country is partly suggested by altars dedicated to Gallic deities found in this region (Clifford *1938*), and partly by the sudden flowering of two major mosaic schools based on Cirencester and Dorchester (Smith *1969* 114). There is, too, an unusual concentration of small villas with an intra-mural yard, a design which is common among the smaller villas in northern Gaul (fig 24). In the south-west (fig 25) we have fifteen or sixteen examples (almost one in four of all the south-western villas for which plans are published), more than any other region in Britain (Branigan *1974a*). The distribution of other British examples is not with-out interest since it is largely along the fringes of the area in which first- and second-century villas are found. It is in this fringe zone that one finds most of the remaining great fourth-century villas, and the other fourth-century mosaic schools (Rivet *1969* fig 5–7). That is to say, the transformation which took place in the West Country in the late third century may have been repeated on a lesser scale, and slightly later (Smith *1969* 115), in other areas where there had also been little or no villa development in earlier times. Finally, the degree of Romanisation that we find in the fourth-century villas of the West Country far out-strips that of any other regional group of fourth-century British villas, and this too requires some explanation, such as the arrival of immigrant Gallic landowners might provide.

## ROMANISATION IN THE WEST COUNTRY VILLAS

Rivet has shown that about half of all the really sumptuous villas in Britain lie within the region with which we are concerned (Rivet *1969* 209). Just how Romanised these new houses were can best be expressed at present in terms of their architectural merit and their furnishings. Of the 200 villas about which we have *some* information, nearly half have produced evidence for mosaic floors. In the rest of the province the figure is about 70–80 villas out of a total of about 500 sites. Although figured mosaics may have cost no more than geometric ones, they do imply on the part of their owners a desire to decorate their homes with the trappings of classical civilisation. Again, therefore, it is significant that about two dozen West Country villas have produced figured mosaics – twice as many as are known from the rest of the province's villas (Smith *1969* 82). The Pitney 'Gods and Seasons' pavement (pl 19) epitomises the *Romanitas* of the West Country villa owners, just as the Low Ham 'Dido and Aeneas' mosaic takes the story a stage further by suggesting an acquaintance with classical literature. At Frampton some sort of ability in the Latin language is demonstrated by the mosaic with

Plate 19  The 'Gods and Seasons' mosaic pavement from the Pitney
villa, Somerset, as recorded by S. Hasell in 1829

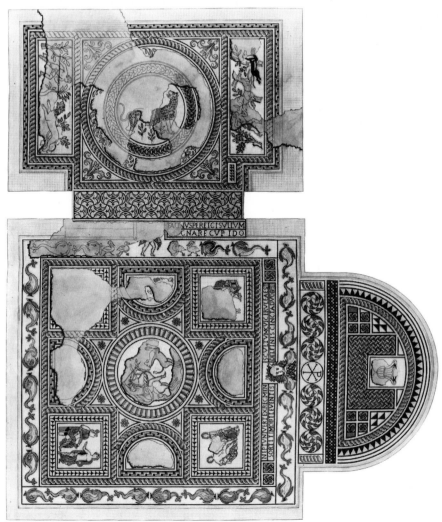

Plate 20  Mosaic pavements in the villa at Frampton, Dorset, showing classical scenes and Latin couplets, a fine symmetry and a prominent chi-rho

the couplets included (pl 20). Mosaics with inscriptions are rare in Romano-British villas – only eight are known, but four of them are in the south-west.

Statuary is also notoriously difficult to find in our British villas. Outside the West Country extant examples can probably be counted on the

129

Plate 21   A statue of Bacchus from the Spoonley Wood villa, Gloucestershire

Plate 22   A statue of Luna from the Woodchester villa, Gloucestershire

fingers of one hand. But a dozen West Country villas have produced fragmentary remains of stone sculptures and reliefs which, to judge from the best surviving pieces – the Spoonley Wood 'Bacchus' and the Woodchester 'Luna' – were of excellent quality (pl 21 and 22). Other stonework of note includes stone table tops (from twelve villas) and the veranda balustrade fragments from Witcombe and Chedworth. Furthermore, stone porticoes or colonnades are attested at nearly thirty villas. The general impression is one of buildings richly embellished, and the buildings themselves, of course, were often of exceptional size and

Fig 26   Plan of Room W in Keynsham villa

elaboration for Romano-British villas. Several of the West Country villas have more than thirty rooms, and the best of these are spacious and often clearly intended as show-pieces. Apsed *triclinia* (dining-rooms) and octagonal or hexagonal rooms and plunge baths are relatively common (eighteen examples), while the two great rooms at either end of the main wing at Keynsham show just how architecturally complex some rooms could be (fig 26). Buildings like this were clearly the homes of men of highly Romanised tastes, with the wealth to indulge them.

## VILLAS AND THE RURAL ECONOMY

We must not forget, however, that even buildings like these were in most cases the centres of farming estates whose principal purpose was to produce a surplus and show a profit. The rural economy on which the West Country villas were based is in most cases impossible to reconstruct: there is simply not sufficient evidence to sketch even the outlines of it.

131

The surviving evidence for agriculture is widely, if thinly, spread and reveals no obvious regional differences in the importance of grain production. The main crops seem to have been wheat and barley, which have been found in a carbonised state in twelve West Country villas, but vetch is also known to have been grown (Downton, Wilts). A thin scatter of agricultural ironmongery includes ploughshares from Chedworth, Gatcombe and Box, and the heavy coulter from Witcombe thought to indicate the use of the wheeled plough and the cultivation of long, narrow fields. Small reaping hooks are known from Brislington, Downton, Halstock and Portishead, a sickle came from East Grimstead, and from Barnsley Park are the great scythes found by Webster. The long, narrow fields postulated from Witcombe are indeed found accompanying the villas at Barnsley Park and Lye Hole (Webster *1967* 80; Fowler *1970* 178), and other traces of field systems are known at Seaton, Kingdon, and Lechlade. The hundred acres of surviving fields at Barnsley Park (fig 45) obviously imply that agriculture was of some importance here, and the same conclusion may be drawn where we can identify substantial granary buildings. The buttressed tower at Pitney is one such, and a similar one may have existed at Witcombe. In addition there are the 'granaries' and large barns at Yeovil, Halstock, Low Ham and Cromhall, and a wheat-processing building at Llantwit Major. Most of these seem to have been built as part of the original construction work, and in most cases that means in the late third or early fourth century.

Turning to stock-raising, in general there is little that can be said in default of adequate study. The usual range of domestic animals are represented in most of the villas where we have any details at all of animal remains (about one villa in every nine!). Cattle seem to have been predominantly Celtic short-horns, but a larger breed has been noted, in smaller numbers, at several villa sites. Applebaum has identified byres at several south-west villas (Applebaum *1972* 122–205). The number of villas where the horse is attested is almost as many as that where cattle are recorded, and I, at least, find this surprising. In the Chilterns, evidence for the horse has proved scarce, even where careful reports on faunal remains exist (Branigan *1972* 183). It seems likely that the horse really was used with greater frequency in the south-west, and this is perhaps underlined by the recognition of smithies on the villa estates at Barnsley Park, Frocester Court, and Low Ham. Anvils from Downton and Fifehead Neville suggest the existence of smithies there too. One is tempted to see the importance of the horse on these estates as related to the free-ranging of cattle, as suggested for Appleton and

132

Hambleden by Applebaum (*1966* 102). As for sheep, by and large we do not know enough about either the strains which were kept or their age at death to postulate confidently the main purpose for which they were kept. The shears from Chedworth and Whatley, and the shed for felting and fulling at Frocester, obviously point to wool production. On the other hand, barely a dozen villas are known to have produced spindle-whorls, and no certain examples of loomweights are recorded, so that if wool was produced in quantity by the West Country villas, it seems that it was taken elsewhere, presumably to the towns, for spinning and weaving.

In the West Country, where we have many villas with one or more enclosed yards, there may have been a third element of some importance in the villa economy – the market garden. At Frocester Court certainly there was a garden enclosure to the rear of the villa. One wonders if the rectangular enclosure around Lye Hole villa was used for orchards, vegetable plots and perhaps root crops too. Peas may have been a par-ticularly favoured vegetable in the south-west; apart from the peas found at Goathill villa, other known occurrences are at Caerwent and Wookey (Bean *1958* 97). Spade-irons from Chedworth, Combend and Woolaston presumably imply gardening on these estates, although at Chedworth at least they could have been used in the formal gardens which no doubt existed there. As for orchards, we have no direct evidence except perhaps a pruning knife from East Grimstead, but one would like to think that the walnuts, fruit stones and seeds found at

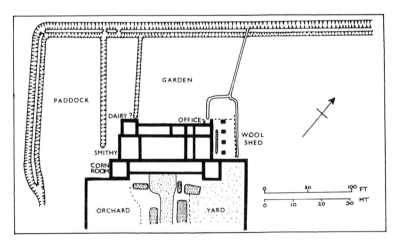

Fig 27   Frocester Court villa as a farm

133

Low Ham (Dewar *1955* 58) are the remains of fruit grown close to the house where it was consumed.

From these general observations we can move to a brief consideration of a few villas where there is just enough evidence to suggest the outlines of the economy practised there. Between them, these sites reveal the variety of ways in which the West Country farmers made the best use of available land resources. At Frocester Court (fig 27) wheat and barley were the principal crops, processed in a room at the west end of the villa. There may have been a dairy here too, as well as a smithy with access to a small paddock. Further paddocks have been found, and early reports on the animal bones suggest that horses were here being bred for sale rather than for a working life on the farm. The fulling and felting shed attests to sheep kept for their wool, as study of the bones has confirmed. Additional food (and perhaps profit) came from the gardens to the rear of the villa, from the orchards before it, and from chicken, duck and goose (Gracie *1970* and personal communication). A basically similar economy, though less diversified, seems to have operated at Downton, where wheat was identified as the main bread crop, supplemented by barley, and the predominance of cattle and the ample evidence for horse repeats the situation at Frocester. There was evidence here for the growing of vetch and possibly other pulse crops for winter fodder (Rahtz *1963* 328).

A different type of economy may be recognised in two of the villas

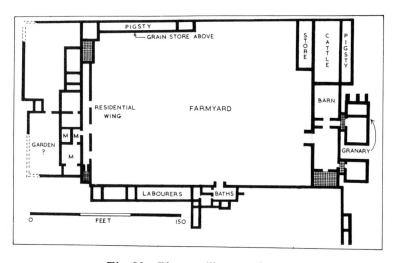

Fig 28   Pitney villa as a farm

focused on Ilchester. At Ilchester Mead corn was certainly grown (wheat grains, corn ovens, querns), but the faunal remains were predominantly pig and cattle; sheep were notably scarce. This ties in well with Applebaum's reconstruction of the Pitney villa economy (Applebaum *1966* 102), based on the architectural remains rather than the faunal ones (fig 28). His identification of two pigsties, a cattle shed, barn, granary tower and overhead grain store – if accepted – clearly point to an economy based on pig and cattle, with overwintering of cattle on hay and grain. Here, there were excellent summer pastures on the moors, and Ilchester Mead and Pitney might be representative of the typical villa economy in the vicinity of Ilchester.

Finally, moving north to Star in the Mendips, we find a different picture again. There is little evidence for agriculture here until the mid fourth century, and cattle and pigs are also poorly represented. Sheep predominate at Star, and the majority of them were killed off during their second year, suggesting that most were reared for mutton rather than wool. Presumably the farmer at Star was exploiting the extensive rough grazing above the villa on Mendip.

There are other aspects of the rural economy which limitations of space prevent us from discussing at any length. In particular one would like the opportunity to examine in detail the relationship between the villas and other types of settlement. On the one hand there are the small but significant concentrations of villas around some of the smaller urban centres. Andoversford, for example, has six villas within five miles of it, and Sandy Lane and Mildenhall each have seven. Such concentrations presumably reflect the value of such towns as markets for the produce of villa estates (*supra* p 117). Rivet has suggested (*1966* 126) that rural shrines could fulfil this function too, and again there are some notable villa concentrations around them: eleven within five miles of Henley Wood, Yatton, and seven within five miles of Bruton and of Pagan's Hill. A different relationship presumably existed between the villas and the 'native' rural settlements. Several of the villas in the Ilchester area are situated uncomfortably close to native settlements which seem to be contemporary with them. At Catsgore, the villa is only some 600 yards from a contemporary and thriving settlement (*infra* p 159). Here, and elsewhere in the same area, one feels there should be some tenurial relationship between the villas and the 'native' settlements. The same may be said for the villa at Lye Hole, and the settlements at Butcombe and Scar's Farm, and for Wraxall villa and the settlements nearby on Failand. Further north, the discovery of a wooden chest in a keep-safe at Frocester Court might imply the collection of rent from tenants by the owner of this comparatively modest villa. Here, one looks to the string of native-type settlements revealed by the M5 as likely tenant-held farms (Fowler and Walthew *1970*). A similar chest was found at Brislington.

Finally, one contribution of the villas to the rural economy which is often forgotten was probably particularly noteworthy in the south-west, and that is the stimulus they provided to rural-based industries. There is, for example, the impact on the stone quarries. Apart from columns, table-tops and balustrades, there was a great demand for pennant roof tiles, and extensive use of coping stones and finials. Surviving fragments of Kimmeridge Shale chairs and tables from the villas at Preston, Frampton and Upper Langridge no doubt represent widespread use of these pleasing items of furniture. In a similar way, fragmentary finds of pewter ware from West Country villas must be seen as the last traces of splendid dinner services long since melted down for scrap. Fortunately, seven vessels from such a service were preserved at Brislington (pl 33) and at Preshute the pewter plates from the villa may well have belonged to the same service as the hoard of twelve pieces found near-by. Whether or not any of the villas not only utilised these products but actually participated in their manufacture is uncertain. A plausible case has been made, however, for relating the villa at Creech to the Kimmeridge Shale industry (RCHM *1970* 522), and evidence for iron *smelting* from Brislington, Lansdown and Lechlade may have some economic significance.

## THE VILLAS IN AD 367 AND AFTER

If we are to believe Ammianus Marcellinus, the wealth of our West Country villas would have availed them little in AD 367 when Britain was invaded by Scots, Picts, Franks and Saxons, all at one and the same time. In recent years there has been a tendency to play down the importance of this interlude, largely perhaps because it is difficult to find unassailable archaeological evidence for it. But Ammianus leaves us in no doubt that, at the time, the attacks were extremely serious and widespread. In the south-west, with its long coastline extending in effect well inland up the Severn, the activities of the Irish pirates might be expected to have left some trace. Amongst the few villas which are widely agreed to provide some evidence for the events of 367 are Kings Weston and Brislington, with fire and violent demolition noted at the first, and fire, destruction and human bodies thrown into a well at the second. Both these villas stand on the Avon, which would provide a natural point of penetration to raiders sailing up the Bristol Channel, and it is reasonable therefore to see what evidence the other villas along the Avon can provide. At Keynsham the great room J seems to have been burnt down during the fourth century, and one victim of the event was found amongst the collapsed wall debris. At Combe Down and Wellow II there are undated destructions by fire, while to the north of Bath there are fourth-century destructions at North Wraxall and Box. At least three rooms at Box seem to have been fired, whilst at North Wraxall three skeletons in the well repeat the story of Brislington. Further along the Avon, at least two rooms in the villa at Atworth were fired between *c* AD 340 and 375. On the opposite, east, side of the Avon four other villas seem to complete the story, though the information on all four is inadequate. At West Park, burnt human bones are associated with coins down to the mid fourth century; at Nuthills the excavator claims that the villa was 'mercilessly raided' but gives no details – the coins here cease between AD 353 and 360. Then comes Bowood, where six skeletons were found with ash and charcoal deposits, and finally Calne where bones and ashes were again associated. At none of these sites is the dating evidence sufficiently close to place the destructions even within the decade *c* 360–70, and some sites produce no dating evidence at all. Yet taken together the evidence from this string of villas along the Avon does present a plausible case for identifying at least one of the attacks of which Ammianus speaks. Other isolated villas may be suggested as possible victims of the raiders: Tockington and Lye Hole, for example, are both in relatively exposed positions and both were partially or completely destroyed by fire, but in neither case is the catastrophe closely dated. At Ilchester Mead, on the other hand, there was partial destruction by fire in the mid fourth century (Richmond *1958* 147), and nearby at West Coker the excavators believed that the building was burnt down and looted in the same period (Haverfield *1906* 331). It is of course true that, in many cases, where fire destruction alone is attested without clear evidence for hostilities, the disaster may have been accidental. On the other hand it is also true that many villas may have been raided but not fired by the raiders, and if they were re-occupied there would be little or nothing in the archaeological record to attest the raid. On the present evidence one may fairly claim that the West Country villas did not escape unscathed from the events of 367, and it may be that more villas suffered attack than the archaeological record suggests (fig 29).

137

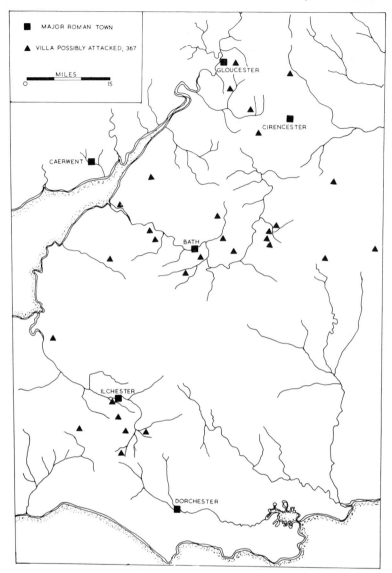

Fig 29   Map showing villas possibly attacked in AD 367

The remarkable thing is that so many villas survived and continued to function. This applies not only to villas where there is little or no evidence to suggest attack in 367, but even to those where the evidence is at its clearest. A careful re-examination of the evidence from Brisling-ton has recently shown that the remains in the well probably belong to a clearing operation in preparation for a re-occupation of the building (Branigan *1972a*). If that is true of Brislington, it may well have been the case at North Wraxall too. West Coker, Ilchester Mead, Atworth, and Kings Weston were all certainly occupied after 367, and Keynsham too saw re-occupation. It is perhaps significant, however, that in several cases the nature of the re-occupation is different from that of the occupation before 367. At Kings Weston and Keynsham large hearths were built in a main corridor, sitting on debris from the destruction which had not been cleared up. At Kings Weston occupation was restricted to the east wing, and at Keynsham room J at least was not cleared or rebuilt. Equally, at West Coker the re-occupation seems to have been in a poorly built structure made of burnt stones, presumably re-used from the original building. In these villas at least, the raid of 367 may have seen the permanent removal of the owners to town houses whilst the estates were run by bailiffs who lived in much reduced accommodation in, or over, the remains of the villa building.

Elsewhere the effects of the raid were felt more slowly, and in some cases, one might argue, not at all. At Whittington eight mosaics were laid no earlier than *c* 330–7, and much later in the opinion of the excavator (O'Neil *1952*). Comparisons with the post-367 mosaics of Lydney suggest that the excavator may well be right (Smith *1969* 81). At Low Ham, the 'Aeneid' mosaic was laid over a plunge-bath which was itself not built until after *c* AD 330, but there are no good pointers to a more precise date. To these somewhat dubious examples of post-367 mosaics one must add the more certain examples from Ilchester Mead, inserted between *c* 364 and 375, and Hucclecote, where the mosaic was laid over a coin of Theodosius (379–95). The evidence from these villas argues that villa life still flourished in the West Country in the twenty years following the barbarian conspiracy. One can support this view with a list of twenty villas where occupation after *c* AD 380 is attested by coins; almost all of these sites in fact produce coins of Arcadius or Honorius, carrying occupation beyond AD 395.

Taking all the evidence into account, however, the picture is not as hopeful as the coin list and Hucclecote might suggest. Hucclecote clearly points to a very late investment in villa property at this one villa, close to the walls of Gloucester, but the twenty villas with coin lists up to the beginning of the fifth century do not necessarily form part of the same picture. Occupation of the villas continued, but not necessarily occupation on the same, or even a higher, level of Romanisation than before. That the occupation was of a degraded kind is in fact quite clear in several cases. At Whittington, for example, where the coins end with two of Honorius, the latest material is associated with a hearth inserted into a room and using old roof rafters. At Witcombe the coins end with Theodosius, but in room 34a a rough floor of old roof slates and door-steps was associated with a corn-drying oven and coins of Valentinian I and Valens. Post-holes had been dug into the floor, suggesting that the original roof may have previously collapsed. Two other rooms here produced similar evidence. In the Dewlish villa hearths were built on the floors in two rooms, re-using material from the villa roof, and again it was with one of these hearths that the latest coin (of Honorius) was found. The impression created by these discoveries is one of villas which, while continuing to function as farmhouses, were coming to the end of their life as fashionable residences for the wealthy men who owned them. There is no reason to suppose that such men suddenly shed their pretensions to civilised living or lost their taste for the amenities of the Roman way of life. Rather we must suppose that they now sought these amenities exclusively in the towns, leaving the farms to be run by foremen or bailiffs who maintained the buildings as best they could, at little or no expense, but inevitably led an increasingly squalid existence.

Under such conditions, it may have become increasingly common for the villas to operate almost entirely outside the money-economy, with proceeds from the farm produce kept in the town where the market was situated and the owner of the estate lived. Coin lists may therefore provide little reliable evidence for the final abandonment of the villa-buildings (*supra* p 58). Certainly many villas where the coin list ends before the 390s reveal very similar evidence to that just described from Whittington, Witcombe and Dewlish. The hearths at Whittington and Dewlish are paralleled by others inserted into corridors at Frocester Court and Lufton, and the use of corridors as living rooms or kitchens is of course seen also, as we noted above, in the re-occupation of Kings Weston and Keynsham. Whether or not a blocking built across the corridor at Spoonley Wood points to the same usage is uncertain but likely. At Spoonley Wood the existing kitchen floor was mended with re-used stone steps, whilst at Frocester the patching of the corridor floor, first with mortar and then with irregular paving of re-used roof tiles, neatly underlines the progressive decline of standards. Elsewhere rough floor surfaces were introduced over worn tessellated and mortar floors. At Lufton the new floors were of stone slabs, whilst at Bratton Seymour they were of cobbles. In both cases, the new floors were associated with new partition walls. Those at Bratton Seymour were, significantly, made

140

of wattle and daub.

In some cases alterations and additions can be related not only to changing fortunes in the villa buildings but even changing functions. We noted the very late insertion of a corn-drying oven into a living room at Witcombe, and rooms at Atworth, Painswick and Frocester were also adapted for farm purposes. At Painswick a rough cobble floor was laid over the remains of a mosaic, and bounded by upright stones, suggesting to the excavator that it was perhaps used as some sort of stall for live-stock. In room I at Frocester it was possible to identify its last function as a stable, with dung preserved on the rammed stone floor and a manger built in one corner. Here, too, late repairs were carried out in wattle and daub rather than masonry.

How long the villas were occupied in such circumstances we do not know, but in the south-west there was no reason why the estates should cease to be farmed, and the buildings inhabited, until at least the fifth century and possibly later. Some buildings may have fallen into rapid decay which made them unsafe to live in, and some may have succumbed to accidental fires – such as seems to be the case at Frocester Court. But others may have continued to provide shelter for many decades into the fifth century, with a small number of rooms maintained by cannibal-ising the rest of the building. At Barnsley Park, for example, the bath house was robbed of material at a date which cannot be earlier than the last decade of the fourth century and is probably considerably later (Webster *1967* 77). In some cases the buildings, and presumably part of the land which went with them, may have been acquired by members of the auxiliary forces which now garrisoned many British towns. Their buckles have been found at Chedworth, Spoonley Wood, North Wraxall and Barnsley Park. Some of them were probably of Germanic origin, and this would apply to North Wraxall, which produced characteristic boar's-tusk pendants in addition to a buckle. Similarly, both the style of the buckle and the appearance of grass-tempered pottery at Barnsley Park suggest the arrival here of a Germanic soldier and his family, and the same must be considered for Frocester Court where this distinctive pottery has also been found. It may be that several of our West Country villas which were originally founded and built by continental immigrants were finally occupied by more of them, albeit of a different social class and calling.

# 8

# LARGER AGRICULTURAL SETTLEMENTS
# IN THE WEST COUNTRY

The economy of Roman Britain was centred upon agriculture. The majority of the population dwelt in the countryside and the problem of exactly how and where this population lived is perhaps worth considering in a general survey of the West Country in the Roman period. For the purposes of this chapter the area to be studied is restricted to the 'Roman West' – that is, the area in which a villa economy can be seen to have operated – and will include east Devon, Dorset west of the chalk uplands, Somerset and Gloucestershire. To the east of this area, on the chalk uplands of Wessex, there are few villas to be found, but a large number of agricultural settlements varying in size from single-family communities to villages consisting of over forty possible dwellings (Bowen and Fowler *1966*). This chapter will suggest that while villas may have played a more important role in the rural economy of the Romanised West Country in the late third and fourth centuries than they did on the Wessex uplands, the majority of the population may have lived in settlements varying in size from under one acre to over forty acres, separate from, and in some cases independent of, villas (*cf infra* p 120). This chapter confines itself to the evidence for larger agricultural settlements in the Romanised West. Sites occupying less than one acre have been excluded, as probably indicating smaller agricultural settlements associated with single-family communities. Sites showing evidence of industrial activity, considerable wealth, or urbanisation have also been excluded, though it should be pointed out that the distinction between larger agricultural settlements and small towns is often blurred and difficult to make. Rural sites without any evident special function have been regarded as agricultural. Again, it must be emphasised that few settlements have been examined, even partially, in the course of properly recorded excavations. This makes it difficult to generalise about the agricultural functions of the settlements with which we are concerned.

142

## THE DISTRIBUTION AND SIZE OF THE SETTLEMENTS

We may begin by summarising the evidence for large agricultural settlements in the region. Romano-British agricultural settlements of more than one acre in extent are to be found throughout most of the region. One notable exception is the area embraced by east Devon, west Somerset and south-west Dorset. Although there are a number of villas here, such as Holcombe and Uplyme (Devon), Seavington St Mary, South Chard, Whitestaunton and Wadeford (Som), and Rampisham (Dorset), there are no obvious Romano-British sites of 'non-villa' type except for one settlement of uncertain extent at Holway near Taunton. It is possible that the scarcity of settlement sites in this area may simply reflect inadequate fieldwork.

In north Dorset and south Somerset, particularly the area around Ilchester, a large number of settlement sites are to be found in an area that also includes many villas. Settlement sites in this area of north Dorset include those at Goathill, Pinford Lane, Castleton, extending over 40 acres, Chorlock Hill, Sherborne, spread over a distance of *c* 500m, and two separate sites at Bradford Abbas. In south Somerset there are similar settlement sites at Sutton, Ditcheat, at Podimore extending over several acres, and at Charlton Mackrell extending over 5 acres. At Montacute a settlement covers a distance of 1,000m inside the Iron Age hillfort on Ham Hill. Further sites in the area are at Catsgore extending over 10 acres, at Littleton spread over at least 30 acres, at Wearne, Huish Episcopi, stretching over 500m, and at Upton extending over at least an acre. There are settlements at Bancombe Hill, Somerton, extending over 5 acres, and at Stoodham, South Petherton, extending over 24 acres.

Further to the north-west in Somerset, extensive settlement sites have been found along the line of the M5 motorway. These sites include East Brent covering a distance of 100m, Cricket Field, Puriton, extending over 100m, Bush Marsh, Bawdrip, spread over 300m, Clapton in Gordano and Hutton. Further to the east in north Somerset other recorded extensive settlement sites include Monk Moor, Cheddar, where occupation debris has been found over a distance of *c* 100m, and Herriot's Bridge extending over 15 acres. In the Chew valley are Chew Park occupying over 20 acres and Golds Cross where buildings and debris dating from the second to the fourth century and including a corn-drier stretched over a distance of 70m. In the very east of the county at St Algars, West Woodlands, building and occupation debris including tesserae have been found over a wide area.

Northwards into Gloucestershire the work of the M5 Committee has revealed a number of settlement sites over an acre in extent. These include Whitminster, Eastington, where occupation covered more than an acre, Elmstone Hardwicke where an extensive settlement is indicated by fourteen 'Stanborough' field names, and Tredington Rise, Stoke Orchard, where occupation debris and floors have been found over an area of 20 acres. All these sites are situated in the vale between the Severn and the Cotswolds.

Further to the east in the Gloucestershire Cotswolds the recent work of the Royal Commission on Historical Monuments has revealed a number of possible large agricultural settlements. South-west of Cirencester the largest of these settlements is at Kingscote, covering an area of about 200 acres. With paved roads and covering such an area this settlement might be considered to be more than rural. Other sites in this area include those at Long Newton with occupation debris spreading over an acre and at Uley extending over at least 7 acres and including buildings with tessellated floors. North-west of Cirencester are extensive settlement sites at Duntisbourne Rouse, where there is evidence for a settlement occupying over 5 acres with possible building platforms terraced into the hillside, at Elkstone extending over 2 acres, and at North Cerney where a settlement of uncertain size is to be found inside an Iron Age hillfort.

South-east of Cirencester extensive settlements are found at Poulton, spread over at least $2\frac{1}{2}$ acres, and at Siddington, only 1.5km from Cirencester, where two separate settlements extend over at least 5 acres and 30 acres respectively. North-east of Cirencester are a large number of settlements of over one acre, including those at Temple Guiting covering at least 3 acres, at Coln St Aldwyns extending for a distance of *c* 300m along Akeman Street, and at Northleach, where a settlement of over 5 acres lies inside an Iron Age hillfort. Further sites are at Quenington, stretching alongside Akeman Street, Sherborne, covering at least 10 acres, Barrington spread over 7 acres and Yanworth extending over a distance of at least 100m. At Bourton-on-the-Water a settlement extending over *c* 500m is to be found on the hillside to the north of the roadside settlement at the Windrush crossing (*supra* p 107). Other sites are found at Farmington, extending over at least $2\frac{1}{2}$ acres, and at Winson extending at least 2 acres. (All the above Cotswold sites have been abstracted from the records of the Royal Commission on Historical Monuments.)

Throughout the region under discussion are a large number of settlement sites of uncertain size which, in many cases, are unlikely to be villas. Even on present evidence the above list of larger agricultural settlements cannot claim to be exhaustive. Many are known only from very limited excavation or fieldwork. There are no sites in the region preserved as earthworks in a state comparable to that of some of the settlement sites on the chalk uplands of Wessex. Only in a few instances is it possible to look at these larger settlements in the Roman West in some detail, and what is now attempted is a closer examination of a few selected sites.

## CATSGORE

The settlement at Catsgore (Som) has probably been more extensively examined than any similar site in the region, and for that reason will be discussed in greater detail (fig 30). Situated on a Romanised road 4km north-west of Ilchester, the site was first examined in 1950 (Radford *1951*). Fieldwork and excavation in 1970–2 (Leech *1970, 1971, 1972*) have shown that Catsgore was a Romano-British settlement extending over 10 acres. The settlement seems to have been established *c* AD 80. Both rectangular and circular structures and one possible boundary ditch belonging to this period have been found at the southern end of the site. In the mid second century the settlement was substantially extended and the areas of existing buildings were replanned (fig 30). At the northern end of the settlement the extension of the occupied area included the laying out of three separate properties, all defined by boundary ditches (fig 30, 1–4). In the northernmost property two buildings of this date were identified. One (fig 30, 5) was evidenced only by the fragmentary remains of stone foundations, all other features having been totally robbed by later building and ploughing. The other (fig 30, 6) had also been much robbed, but there is sufficient evidence for internal partitions, an oven and a storage bin. The next property to the south included two buildings, one totally robbed except for its foundations, the other (fig 30, 7) similarly eroded but with evidence for two ovens and an earth floor in an extension to the original building. Still further to the south, again separated from the former by a boundary ditch, was a third property, not as yet completely examined. It appears that here were at least two second-century buildings (fig 30, 8,9), one with an apsidal north end. Still further to the south, again separated from the former by a boundary ditch, was an open space (fig 30, 10) completely free of structures or even pits for burials. Further south an area including at least one build-

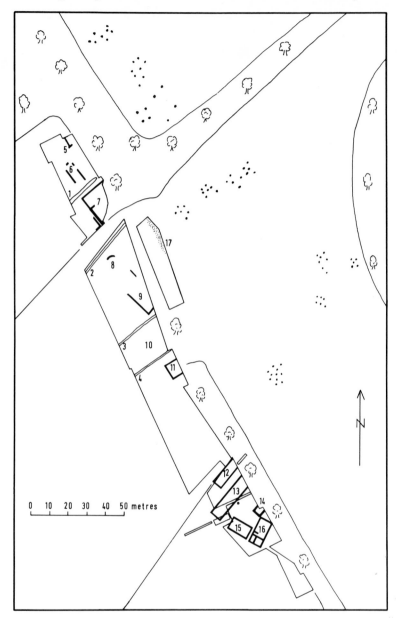

Fig 30   Plan of Catsgore settlement, *c* AD 150–300

ing (fig 30, 11) has not yet been completely examined. In the south-west part of the settlement a fourth property included five buildings of which four were grouped round a courtyard. These consisted of a probable byre or stable (fig 30, 12; fig 31) with a well-defined system of drains and possible stall divisions and storage bins, and a much larger building (fig 30, 13; fig 32) measuring 7m by at least 25m and containing several hearths, a rectangular storage bin, several drains and two ovens. An entrance on the south side led past a well into a courtyard bounded by two buildings to the south and west (fig 30, 15, 16). These, both excavated in 1950 and 1973, and one with a paved floor and internal partitions, were probably dwelling houses. A fifth building (fig 30, 14) has not yet been completely examined.

All the parts of the settlement excavated so far have indicated that a period of major rebuilding took place towards the end of the third century AD (fig 33). In several instances buildings were erected over second-century structures. At the same time the property boundaries laid out in the second century remained in use. The northernmost property excavated was divided into two by a new boundary ditch (fig 33, 1) and in the southern half was erected a new timber building (fig 33, 2) with an extension at the north end and facing directly on to the presumed road. In the property to the south, the two second-century buildings were replaced by buildings occupying roughly similar sites. One of these (fig 33, 3) faced directly on to the road (fig 33, 15) and internal features included three infant burials, an oven and a stone drain. The second building (fig 33, 4; fig 34) was set further back from the road. Including a later addition, there were six small rooms, three of which contained ovens or hearths. To the south, separated from the former by a boundary wall (fig 33, 10) built on the filling of the earlier boundary ditch, was another property not as yet completely examined. Here would appear to have been at least five buildings of late third or fourth century date. Three of these (fig 33, 5,6,7) fronted on to the road running through the settlement, but have not yet been fully examined. The other two buildings lay further back from the road. One (fig 33, 8; pl 23) with an apsidal south end, and replacing the earlier building with an apsidal north end referred to above, contained a Y-shaped corn-drier, and was approached by a cobbled roadway and courtyard. The other, initially with a T-shaped corn-drier (fig 33, 9), was later rebuilt to include both granary space and an H-shaped corn-drier. Further to the south was the open space referred to above, separated from the former property by a boundary wall built on the filling of the earlier boundary ditch. A build-

147

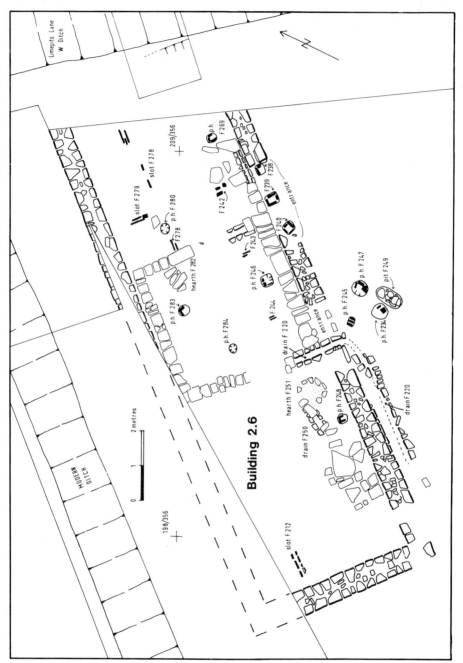

Fig 31  Catsgore. A byre, c AD 150–300

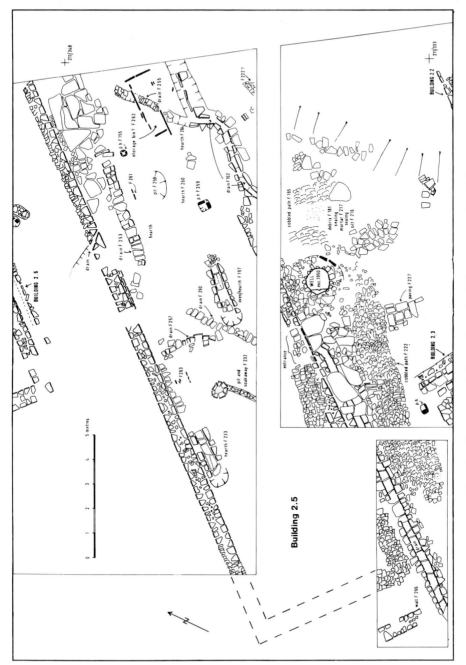

Fig 32   Catsgore. A long farm building, c AD 150–300

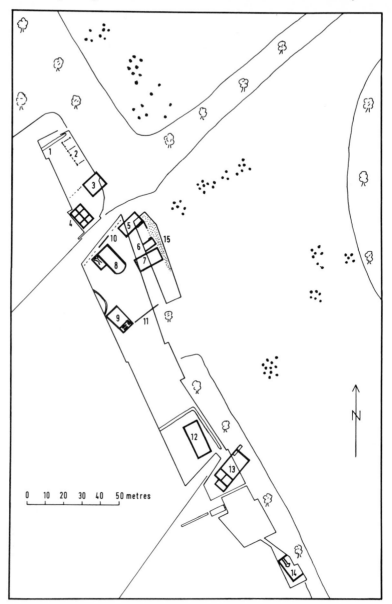

Fig 33  Plan of Catsgore settlement, *c* AD 300–70

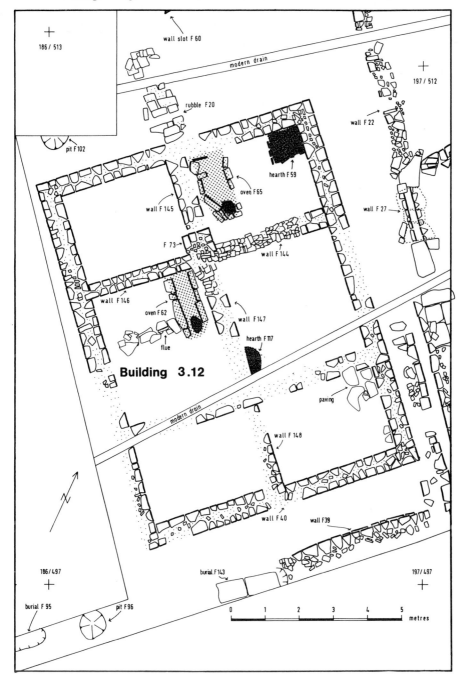

186 / 513

wall slot F 60

modern drain

197 / 512

rubble F 20

wall F 22

pit F 102

hearth F 59

oven F 65

wall F 145

wall F 27

F 73→

wall F 144

wall F 146

oven F 62

wall F 147

hearth F 117

flue

**Building 3.12**

paving

modern drain

wall F 148

186/497

pit F 96

burial F 95

burial F 143

wall F 148

wall F 40

wall F 39

197/497

0    1    2    3    4    5
metres

Fig 34   Catsgore. Plan of a small fourth-century building

Plate 23 Part of the excavations at Catsgore, Somerset, in 1972, showing a fourth-century building with an apsidal end, a courtyard beyond and a Y-shaped corn-drier in the foreground. Along the left-hand edge a tumbled wall is on top of an earlier ditch, apparently a property division (2m poles)

ing at the southern end of this area (fig 33, 12) has not yet been fully examined.

In the south-west part of the settlement the four earlier buildings were all demolished by $c$ AD 315. Two buildings which replaced those demolished have been examined. The first (fig 33, 13) overlay two of the earlier buildings. To begin with there were no internal walls, and features belonging to this phase included a rectangular storage bin built against the south wall. Later, the building was divided into three rooms, two of which were paved. The second building lay at the south end of the settlement, and features in the small part excavated (fig 33, 14) include a corn-drier (pl 24) and associated storage bin.

It would seem that the settlement at Catsgore was abandoned about the time of the disaster of AD 367. Out of a total of about 480 coins, of which 450 belong to the period AD 268–364, only five postdate AD 364 and only two of these need be later than AD 367.

Apart from infants and children, only three burials have so far been recorded, all in the northern part of the settlement. There are at present no indications of the location of the main cemetery.

As indicated by its farm buildings and corn-driers, the general economic development of Catsgore is likely to have been based upon agriculture. The settlement's origins are obscure, but it seems to date from the second half of the first century AD, possibly following the depopulation of near-by hillforts (Alcock *1972* 171). The abandonment of the settlement *c* AD 367 cannot be explained merely by the ensuing dislocation of trade if Catsgore was an agricultural community of some size, particularly when other rural sites in the area such as Low Ham and Bradley Hill (Leech *1972*) continued to be occupied into the fifth century. Nor is there any evidence of sudden, violent destruction at Catsgore. Perhaps the inhabitants joined in the disruptions of AD 367. If so it would be possible to regard the depopulation of Catsgore as a political act and part of the Theodosian restoration of order.

The changing plan of the site is of interest. It seems that the settlement expanded northwards from a first-century nucleus. Fieldwork and excavations have not revealed any traces of boundaries or defences surrounding the settlement at any time in its history. Within the settlement, second-century property boundaries remained in use until its abandonment, and it can be suggested that Catsgore consisted of several

Plate 24   A T-shaped corn-drier with a stone-lined storage-bin beside it in the corner of a fourth-century building at Catsgore, Somerset (2m pole)

separate farm holdings, each renting or owning its land, and all bene-
fiting from a massive injection of capital in the late third or early fourth
centuries AD.

## OTHER EXCAVATED SETTLEMENTS IN SOMERSET AND GLOUCESTERSHIRE

Other sites in the region which have been partly examined by fieldwork
and excavation have revealed both similarities to Catsgore and
differences.

The settlement at Pinford Lane, Castleton (Dorset) has been shown to
cover about 40 acres along the north side of the river Yeo. Some of the
buildings have been partly excavated, and were usually of stone construction varying in length from 13m to 17m. One was 13m square, and
another interesting building had an open end apparently closed by
wooden shutters. One building had inside it a T-shaped corn-drier. Outside the buildings were areas of cobbling, and it is thought that a road
ran through the settlement. The site was probably occupied from the
first century to the fourth. An unpublished plan of the site is in the
County Museum, Dorchester.

At Charlton Mackrell (Som) the settlement extends over a distance of

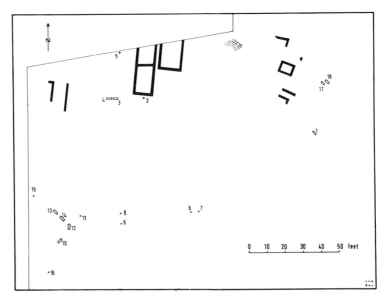

Fig 35  Plan of the settlement at Charlton Mackrell

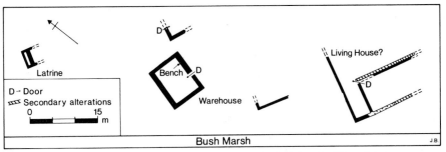

Fig 36   Plan of the settlement at Bush Marsh (Bawdrip)

at least 500m. A plan of part of the site (fig 35), observed and partly excavated in quarrying operations, shows buildings of unsophisticated construction and a wide scatter of burials. A stream runs through the settlement which is pleasantly situated in a shallow valley.

The settlement at Bush Marsh, Bawdrip, has been partly examined in a rescue excavation (fig 36). Although it was initially suggested that the site may have been a port, this may now be questioned since it has been argued recently that there was no marine transgression in late Roman Somerset (Hawkins *1973*). If this was so, then the settlement at Bush Marsh could have been some distance from the nearest navigable water. The following is an extract from the published interim report on the excavations:

The occupation recorded extended over a distance of *c* 300m, although the area examined by partial excavation was only 110m long by 20m wide. It is thought that the site extended southwards and northwards from the line of the excavated remains. In the time available for rescue excavation the stone bases of ten structures were partly excavated and their plans recorded. All were rectangular and fairly closely aligned on the same north/south axis up and down the south falling slope. None were definitely domestic buildings, and while the smallest can be said with some certainty to have been a lavatory, some at least of the others seem best interpreted as storage buildings. In particular the latest corridor type structures examined in some detail at the eastern end of the excavation seem best interpreted in this light. All the structures exposed at the highest level seem to belong to the late Roman period or later; but from the eastern end of the site where, below present water table, the earliest structures were timber buildings associated with Durotrigan pottery, it was shown that the occupation had spanned the Roman period from the first century onwards. The material from the site was considerable but lacking in variety, domestic items being conspicuous by their scarcity. The 129 coins ranged from Nerva to Valens with the majority dating from the fourth century.

Two extensive settlements at Herriot's Bridge and Chew Park in the Chew Valley have both been examined in detail, and the definitive report is now published (Rahtz *1976*). At Herriot's Bridge settlement extended over 15 acres and was evidenced by 'scattered hearths, a few small groups of post-holes and a complex of ditches containing several querns and much pottery dating from the mid first century AD to the end of the third'. At Chew Park occupation extended over 20 acres, but only $2\frac{1}{2}$ acres were examined in detail. As at Herriot's Bridge, there was a system of ditches dating from the mid first century AD. In the third century small-scale iron-smelting took place and at the end of that century a villa was built on the site. A corn-drier was constructed 300m south-west of the villa.

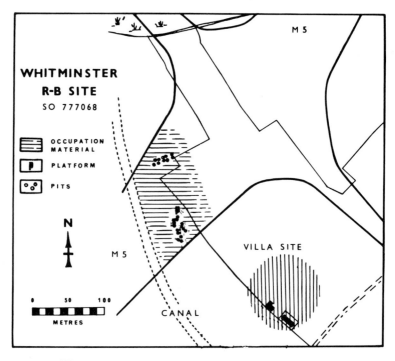

Fig 37   Plan of the settlement at Whitminster

In Gloucestershire the work of the M5 Committee has resulted in the production of outline plans of two possible extensive settlements. At Whitminster, Eastington (fig 37), settlement extended over an area at least *c* 100m by *c* 70m. Over two dozen rubbish pits containing material from the first century AD onwards were examined, and building debris was found associated with fourth-century material. A possible villa lay *c* 150m to the south-east. Further north at Tredington Rise, Stoke Orchard, a settlement extended over an area of 200 acres. Although no buildings were actually recognised, their former presence was evidenced by building debris and possible gravel floors. Other features included several hearths, two ditches and a well. Finds from the site ranged from the first to fourth centuries AD. The excavators concluded that 'farming was probably the main economic activity with perhaps sheep-grazing and weaving of particular significance'.

## THE HISTORY AND SIGNIFICANCE OF THE LARGER AGRICULTURAL SETTLEMENTS

In the area of Ilchester in south Somerset (fig 38) it is possible to glimpse the place occupied by these larger settlements in the Romano-British countryside. Settlement in this area is densest on the calcareous uplands around Langport and Somerton, and in the Yeo valley around Sherborne. In both areas settlements of varying size are found, in several instances less than *c* 2km apart.

The settlements at Catsgore, Pinford Lane, Goathill, Podimore and Stoodham all appear to have been founded in the first century AD, in all cases the evidence being the presence of Durotrigan pottery. At Catsgore the settlement is likely to have been created before *c* AD 80 and was possibly for the dispossessed occupants of nearby hillforts such as South Cadbury (Alcock *1972* 171). The same could be true of the other sites mentioned. At the same time, major changes in land ownership may have caused the abandonment of some undefended Iron Age settlement sites, such as Bradley Hill (fig 43) and possibly Westwood, Somerton (OS Record Cards). It is possible, then, that the larger agricultural settlements were Roman foundations, though further excavations will be necessary to clarify this. Of the second century, one can say very little except that at Catsgore rebuilding and an extension of the settled area took place. Until the late third century at least, the rural economy may have centred round the larger agricultural settlements, for none of the numerous villas in the Ilchester area, except possibly Littleton, can be

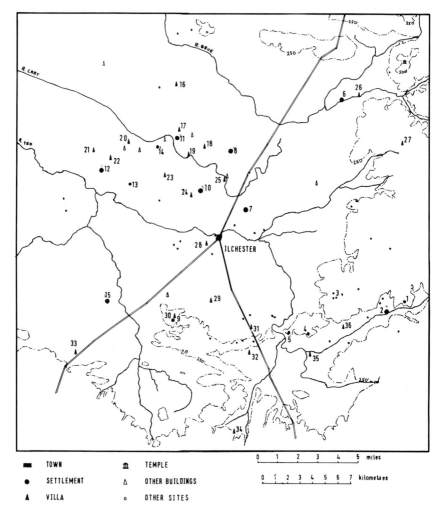

Fig 38  Distribution of the settlements around Ilchester

| SETTLEMENTS | | | |
|---|---|---|---|
| 1 | Goathill | 13 | Upton | 24 | Catsgore |

SETTLEMENTS
1  Goathill
2  Pinford Lane,
     Castleton
3  Chorlock Hill
4  Bradford Abbas
5  Bradford Abbas
6  Sutton Ditcheat
7  Podimore
8  Charlton Mackrell
9  Ham Hill
10  Catsgore
11  Littleton
12  Wearne

13  Upton
14  Bancombe Hill
15  Stoodham

VILLAS
16  Butleigh Wootton
17  Littleton
18  Hurcot
19  Hurcot
20  Pitney
21  High Ham
        (Bedmore Barn)
22  Low Ham
23  Melbury

24  Catsgore
25  Kingsdon
26  Castle Cary
27  Bratton Seymour
28  Ilchester Mead
29  Lufton
30  Ham Hill
31  Westland
32  West Coker
33  Kingston
34  Halstock
35  Thornford
36  Lenthay

158

shown certainly to have existed before that date. A comparison of the plans of these villas (fig 39) with that of the settlement at Catsgore shows planning on a grand scale owing little to earlier developments, and also the great difference between the larger agricultural settlement and the villa. As has been pointed out (*supra* p 125), the building of these numerous villas must have reflected a considerable injection of capital into the rural economy, and many of the larger agricultural settlements may have benefited from this process in that their lands may have been partly bought up by new, richer landowners. At Catsgore, where a substantial rebuilding took place in the late third and fourth centuries, a villa is to be found only *c* 600m from the settlement. Surface finds indicate that the villa complex may be too small to have included farm buildings, and this raises the possibility that there may now have been a connection between the villa and the settlement. At Wearne and Littleton settlements are also found in close proximity to the villa at Low Ham and Littleton respectively. A study of the plans of some of the partly excavated villas in the area (fig 39) reveals that some, for instance at Westland, Low Ham, Pitney and Ilchester Mead, possess possible farm buildings. On the other hand, the evidence at Catsgore for the third and fourth centuries points to the existence of several separate farms, and it would be difficult to reconcile this with the phenomena of newly arrived wealthy immigrants buying up estates (*supra* p 126). Far more research is needed to solve this problem. At Catsgore the problem is further complicated by the apparent abandonment of the settlement *c* AD 367.

In the Ilchester area, then, the evidence points to the larger agricultural settlements as being the main centres of population, apart from the one town at Ilchester. The relatively sudden building of a large number of villas may represent the arrival of an alien element in the countryside rather than, as has been suggested in the past, the gradual enrichment of a native aristocracy.

Little more can be said about the history of the larger settlements. The settlement at Cricket Field, Puriton, may date from the pre-conquest period. At Ham Hill and at Northleach and North Cerney (Glos) Romano-British settlements are found inside Iron Age hillforts, but this need not necessarily imply continuity between the two periods. As in the Ilchester area, few villas in the region as a whole date from before the late third century (*supra* p 124); in several instances, such as Whitminster and East Brent, they appear to have been built close to existing settlements. Throughout the Roman West Country the history of the larger

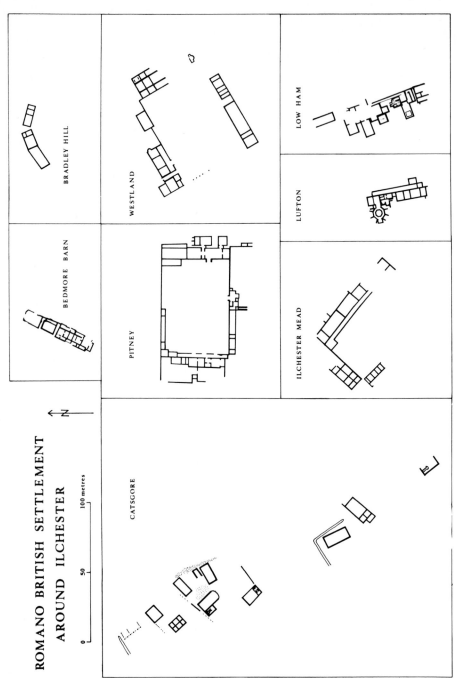

Fig 39  Plans of Romano-British villas and settlements around Ilchester

settlements in the late fourth and fifth centuries is obscure. In Gloucester-shire the settlements at Quenington and Coln St Aldwyns may have been abandoned *c* AD 367 as at Catsgore. Other settlements continued to be occupied into the fifth century as has been argued at Bush Marsh, Gatcombe and Whitminster. The still later history of the larger settlements is beyond the scope of this chapter.

# 9

## FARMS AND FIELDS
## IN THE ROMAN WEST COUNTRY

*Colonia, civitas* capital, small town, villa, village – and at the bottom of
the settlement hierarchy, hamlets, farms and isolated dwellings. It is all
too easy to disregard these last simply because they are morphologically
small, socially lowly, and archaeologically unimpressive as visible sites
and excavated remains. Yet, particularly in the West Country perhaps,
more people lived in such superficially insignificant settlements than in
any other type of site. If, just as a guess, there was a population of about
a million people west of a line from Tewkesbury to Southampton in AD
300, at least half a million can be envisaged as living in the smaller types
of rural settlement. In quantitative terms alone, then, they deserve at
least a footnote to history, despite the more obvious attractions of
military, monumental and more Romanised aspects of the Roman West
Country.

The rural, peasant base of society and economy in the West Country
in the first few hundred years AD cannot seriously be doubted; the
problem is to identify it archaeologically, and then to translate the
unappealing evidence – the scatter of potsherds, the area of ploughed-up
stones – into an understanding of people living on and working a geologi-
cally varied landscape 1,500–2,000 years ago. The problem is not con-
fined to the Roman period alone; it exists in prehistoric and post-Roman
centuries, too, when one seeks to study that anonymous and 'submerged'
part of the population whose unconscious memorial is the man-made
landscape rather than any deliberate monument.

The fundamental nature of some of the as yet unanswered questions
about peasant farming (a phrase which itself raises a query or two) and
the landscape in the first five hundred years of our era needs to be
emphasised at the outset. What did the landscape itself look like – was
much of it forested, for example? – and did it change, and if so how,
during the Roman centuries? We can guess that there were thousands
of minor settlements from the hundreds that we know existed; but what
do they represent in social and tenurial terms and how long were they

occupied? To what degree do these 'RB sites' of so many maps represent a continuum from the pre-Roman centuries and, if any at all, in what sense? Similarly, is there any relationship between the rural settlement pattern of AD 400 and that of today? – is not at least an element of rural continuity to be expected in an area of delayed Saxon conquest and surviving 'Celtic' undertones? Within the Roman period, how many of the farms which we can now allow to have existed represent permanent settlement over four centuries? Is there any evidence amongst their number of deliberate 'Roman plantation' or of transhumance? And what about their internal development? – what is the history of their buildings, their growth and decay? Indeed, in studying the abandoned sites, located now in open countryside, are we by any chance just looking at the *failed* (and perhaps untypical) settlements, the successful ones remaining buried elsewhere, possibly under the medieval farms of the present landscape? Are we justified in looking for pattern, of distribution, of chronology, of economy, over regions, counties or districts; or were such matters determined by local factors alone? The list of questions is formidable and few answers are available, in large part because the questions have seldom been asked. The standard of reportage of the smaller 'RB sites' is dreadful: familiarity really has bred contempt.

## THE PRE-ROMAN BACKGROUND

The archaeology of the West Country in the last centuries before the conquest tends to be dominated by the hillforts (pl 25), but, it can be argued, their existence itself presupposes a large number of farms and other extra-mural settlements within their catchment areas. Furthermore, 'hillfort' is an umbrella term covering a multitude of varied sites, the size of which alone ranges from 50 acres plus down to an enclosure of an acre or two. Certainly some, both in Wessex and further west, are little more than single enclosed farmsteads probably used, in Devon and Cornwall especially, as much in the Roman period as earlier. The main point initially is that the very small settlement, recognised because it is enclosed, is a common type of site long before the Roman period. Nor is it always enclosed: from Bodmin Moor and Dartmoor back in the second millennium BC come many examples of small open settlements, morphologically if in no other sense the predecessors of the similar sites of the Roman period. Disregarding such differences as the shape of buildings and the types of pottery present, the basic farmstead of dwelling, one or two farm buildings, yards or closes, and several

Plate 25 Air-photograph of Old Sodbury hillfort, Gloucestershire, typically situated on the edge of the Cotswold escarpment, here dropping bottom left. Though the defences are well preserved, typically too the interior is ploughed flat. Medieval and later earthworks lie on the slope

adjacent arable plots and grazing area, is archaeologically recognisable for at least two thousand years before the conquest and is not fundamentally different after it. Significant changes, certainly in terms of day-to-day life and standards of living, are products of influences not so archaeologically obvious, such as climate, economic forces and tenurial relationships, rather than because any particular farm was occupied in AD 100 rather than 100 BC.

Such generalisations are, however, difficult to substantiate from firm evidence in this area. If for comparison we include in it the Chalk bounding the east of the region, Berwick Down, Tollard Royal, in south-west Wiltshire, provides a classic example of a 'family farm' in the decades just before the Roman conquest (Wainwright 1968): a ditched enclosure of less than an acre contained one round timber house 4.25m in diameter, four small rectangular structures, probably raised granaries, and thirty-three pits. (This site, now destroyed, is shown in outline only at the bottom of fig 40.) Here we see the basic furniture of the late Iron Age farmyard – with plenty of space left over in it for actually working and for penning animals. Actually an outer bank and ditch, some 30m from the farmyard boundary on all sides except the north, provided much more semi-enclosed space which hurdles could easily have shut off completely (*cf* Holcombe *infra* p 172).

This particular farm is actually one of at least three on the same spur of downland and, though it alone has been excavated, the field evidence is good enough to suggest a sequence of occupation. First, an open Iron Age settlement, perhaps later enclosed by dykes, contained at least two circular buildings surrounded by pits; then came the immediately pre-Roman farm already described; and finally, lying between these two sites, the farm or hamlet of the Roman period developed, initially sur-rounded by a small ditch forming the oval enclosure about 125m × 100m but subsequently spreading outside it. These three physically separate settlements, each characteristic of its own time, were spread over *c* 500m of downland; but surely here we are looking at basically the same farm, possibly the same small community, moving around within its land as time passed. The example is particularly instructive, since normally this is the sort of sequence in which the elements lie on top of one another on the same spot, whereas on Berwick Down the parts are laid out side by side. It is also a warning not to jump too readily to population estimates on the basis of site counts alone: the three settlements here are really the same site at different periods, and it could be argued that not more than a dozen people or so were ever living here at any one time.

Unfortunately, no similarly revealing sequence or clearly demonstrated late pre-Roman farm can be quoted from Somerset or Gloucestershire. The latter in particular, apart from its hillforts and Bagendon (Clifford *1961*), is notably deficient in evidence of Iron Age settlements of any sort, so it is difficult to identify the late pre-Roman farmers unless, as has been rather improbably argued for the opposite bank of the Severn, they were living entirely in the hillforts (Stanford *1974* 230–1). In fact, the hints are already there that, as elsewhere, at least some small Iron Age farms lay along the valley gravels, eg along the Warwickshire Avon and under Tewkesbury itself (Hannan *1973*; Miles and Fowler *1973*); stray finds and air-photographic sites in the Upper Thames area east of

# BERWICK DOWN, TOLLARD ROYAL, WILTS.

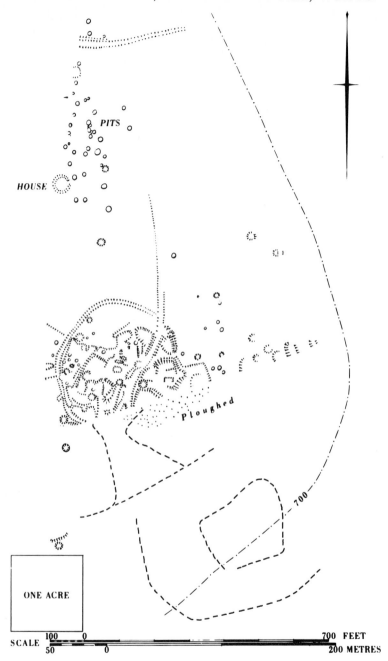

Fig 40  Durotrigan farm at Berwick Down, Tollard Royal, Wilts

Cirencester (Gingell *1971*; Smith *1972*). Nevertheless, the M5 motorway, so productive of Roman sites (*infra* p 177), produced not a single Iron Age one in the length of Berkeley Vale. On the Cotswolds themselves, the Royal Commission's recent fieldwork has, however, produced a number of candidates for small Iron Age settlements, again hinting that the whole population was not contained within the hillforts.

In Somerset, too, hillforts have dominated thought about Iron Age settlement, with Glastonbury and Meare 'lake-villages' tending to be regarded as wonderful anomalies rather than as representatives of lowland occupation: their unusualness in fact lies in their preservation rather than in the type of settlement they were (Tratman *1970*). Now that Glastonbury has been interpreted as a small, 'family unit' site (Clarke *1973*), it can be seen more objectively as a waterlogged version of a type of small settlement known elsewhere in the south-west; and *c* 20km further south, related settlement evidence from Weston Zoyland provides a glimpse of what was happening just before and during the Roman period on the Somerset Levels (Miles and Miles *1969*).

North of the Levels, an equally unusual habitat provides further settlement evidence: some of the Mendip caves were certainly being inhabited either side of AD 43, though the nature of their occupation is not altogether clear. Caves could have been used by refugees, outlaws or the very poor; alternatively, they could have been the summer quarters of transhuming stock-farmers or the homes of miners and metal-workers, none of whom need have been social or economic outcasts. On the top of Mendip, all the known Iron Age settlements are enclosed (which is why they have been found), except for one overlooking the Lox Yeo valley. This site, near the village of Christon, was discovered, and destroyed after archaeological rescue excavation, by the building of the M5 motorway. Its importance was threefold: it was not indicated beforehand by earthworks, thereby hinting that other buried pre-Roman settlements are yet to be found; it appeared to be a small farming type of settlement, similar to Berwick Down (*supra* p 164) though without any enclosure; and it was associated with an inhumation cemetery, a rare instance in the region of Iron Age burial evidence.

Devon and Cornwall contain, on the whole, much more revealing evidence about the Iron Age background to farms and farming in the Roman period. On many sites, AD 43 is meaningless: nowhere in England more than in the south-western peninsula is it clearer that the conquest was a military event and not a settlers' invasion. Settlements existing in AD 1 tend to be still in use a century later, probably continuing to use the same sorts of 'native' pottery. Amongst the small settlements of the Roman period in Cornwall are the 'rounds', circular, oval and even rectangular banked and ditched enclosures, often on locally high or sloping ground and seldom more than two acres in extent. Despite their characteristic siting, such settlements are not hillforts in any usual sense of that term, even where they originate in the first century BC; basically, they are enclosed homesteads, consisting of one or more buildings related to a yard. Though stemming from pre-Roman origins as a type, their use spans the Roman period and indeed continues at least well into the fifth century: AD 410 is no more meaningful in the south-west than AD 43.

## SMALL SETTLEMENTS IN ROMAN DUMNONIA

This point is made by the two most recent excavations of rounds. At Grambla, Wendron, an enclosure *c* 60m square was surrounded by a bank 6m wide by 1.5m high and a V-shaped ditch 6m wide by 3m deep. The gateway was 2.6m wide, possibly beneath a wooden tower. Inside, two buildings were excavated; two other probable building platforms exist. One building 18m long and up to 9m wide was of 'boat-shaped' plan. The other was apparently similar in form and 20m long. Occupation of the site probably began in the second century and continued until the late fifth or sixth century (Saunders *1972*).

Another round, at Trethurgy, near St Austell, has been completely excavated (fig 41). This example was oval, 48m × 55m, surrounded by a stone-revetted bank 4–5m broad by *c* 2m high with an external ditch 1.5m deep. As at Grambla, there was a single entrance, with double-leafed gates which had left scratches on the granite-slab paving. Construction and occupation of the enclosure began in the third century, the internal arrangements being simply of buildings backing against the bank and surrounding an open, central yard. At the fullest occupation in the later fourth century there were five such buildings, all apparently domestic; three smaller buildings were later. In addition, there were other structures including a byre, an open-air grinding area, a four-posted timber structure, perhaps a watch-tower, and a semi-circular stone-paved structure walled with orthostats, possibly a shrine. Imported Mediterranean pottery of later fifth or sixth century date, as at Grambla, indicated that life continued here apparently unaffected by the 'end' of Roman Britain.

Reviewing earlier and partial excavations of similar-looking sites in the light of Grambla and Trethurgy, the rounds are now firmly established as the characteristic small settlement unit in Roman Dumnonia – perhaps

168

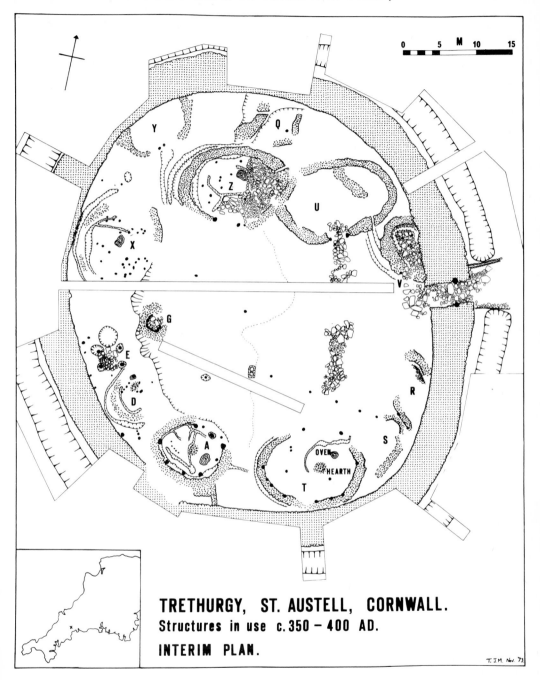

0  5  M  10  15

Y

Q

Z

U

X

V

G

E

D

R

A

OVEN

HEARTH

S

T

**TRETHURGY, ST. AUSTELL, CORNWALL.**
Structures in use c. 350 — 400 AD.

**INTERIM PLAN.**

T. J. M. Nov. 73

Fig 41   The round at Trethurgy, Cornwall

the main type irrespective of size. Of course they can be variously interpreted in social terms as housing several families or an extended family; either way, judging by Trethurgy in particular, a population of two to three dozen would seem a maximum (*cf* Thomas *1966* 95). Whatever the number, there can be little doubt that the sites were basically farms mixing arable cultivation and stock-raising, with other activities like tin-streaming, metal-working and stone-cutting as sidelines of varying importance.

Rounds, however, were not the only type of small settlement in the Roman south-west. The Isles of Scilly contained open settlements with courtyard houses, like Halangy Down on St Mary's (Ashbee *1970*). In West Penwith are the so-called 'courtyard house villages' like Chysauster, with or without their fogous, though these will be mentioned only in passing because their reassessment must now await the publication of the significant new evidence from Carn Euny, Sancreed (Christie *1970*; *Current Archaeology* 44 *1974* 262–8). In any case, as rural settlements they are clearly not amongst the smallest settlement units, which are our concern here. Courtyard houses can, however, occur singly and also in complexes within an enclosure. The most recent excavation at one such, Goldherring, Sancreed, showed that it had first been fortified with rampart and ditch and occupied by probable immigrants in the century preceding the conquest (Guthrie *1969*). It was abandoned in the first century AD, perhaps even before AD 43. In the third century it was re-occupied and saw several phases and many structural changes before another abandonment probably *c* AD 500 (its subsequent uses do not concern us here, but see *infra* p 181). Despite the structural complexities, the settlement in late Roman times seems basically to have consisted of one house with several rooms and various adjacent areas for specific tasks like drying grain and metal-working. In other words, though the site looks somewhat different from an 'earthen' round, functionally and probably socially it was similar. The apparent differences are the result of its position on granite rather than of cultural or economic factors.

Three other small sites in Cornwall can nevertheless serve to suggest the variety amongst the small settlements which further fieldwork and excavation will doubtless illustrate. At Trevinnick, St Kew, in the north of the county, one of several rectilinear enclosures listed in Cornwall as possible Roman (military?) sites was recently briefly examined (Fox *1969b*). Its non-military nature was satisfactorily established, but the excavation raised new problems for it showed parts of two sub-circular, gated features *c* 8m in diameter and other settlement evidence inside the enclosure. Even if the sub-circular features were stock-pens, the rest of the unexcavated interior could well contain other occupation evidence and place the site firmly as a variant of the small-farm type of settlement in the later first or second century.

Even smaller was the single-house settlement on the cliff-top overlooking Porth Godrevy in St Ives Bay near Gwithian (Fowler *1962*). This also was enclosed but only by a stone-faced bank surrounding an oval area 40m × 15m. Occupied from the first or second century to the fourth, and possibly a little later, the site contained only one sub-rectangular domestic hut and presumably represents the smallest enclosed settlement unit. While cereal cultivation was probably part of the inhabitants' livelihood, sea-food played a significant part too; and though a few coins and bits of samian pottery were found on the site, most of the surviving artefacts were of stone – an eloquent commentary on what 'Romanisation' meant in the daily life of west Cornwall and a far cry indeed from contemporary life at the southern end of the 'villa belt' *c* 160km to the east.

In fact just 5km inland from Porth Godrevy was Cornwall's nearest approach to a 'villa', perhaps a 'sunset home', in Thomas's (*1966* 92) evocative phrase, of a retired Dumnonian official. Villas proper are the concern of another chapter (*supra* p 122): the example of Magor, near Camborne, is merely mentioned, since its size puts it in the small-settlement category, to give the other extreme to Porth Godrevy in the range of sites from 'Roman' Cornwall. It is remarkable that another such has not been found since Magor's excavation forty years ago: perhaps it really is an isolated example.

In Devon, 'native-style agricultural settlements (of the Roman period) are unattested with the exception of one at Stoke Gabriel on the lower Dart' (Fox *1969a* 148). While this may seem incredible and is certainly regrettable, it is nevertheless the case. Particularly in view of the recent surveys of what is known of the county in Roman times (Thomas *1966*; Fox *1969, 1974*; but *cf* now, 'Exeter', *Current Archaeology* 39 *1973* 102–10), only two points need be mentioned here. First the similarity between the Trevinnick rectilinear enclosure (*supra* p 170) and that on Milber Down, Devon, is supported by another at Clanacombe, Thurlestone, which also seems to be a small second-century farming settlement (Greene and Greene *1970*). Second, what could well be a predecessor of this emergent type of small farmstead in the Roman south-west has recently been excavated at Holcombe just on the Devon side of the county boundary with Dorset (Fox and Pollard *1973*).

There, beneath a villa (one of only two known in Devon, the other being 8km west at Seaton, also with a hint of earlier timber buildings: Fowler *1969* 35), the main building of which 'began in the 2nd century as a single-roomed timber-framed aisled structure with stone foundations', a small settlement of the first half of the first century AD was found. Initially it consisted of one, possibly two, roughly circular timber huts. Then an area *c* 30m square was enclosed by a V-shaped ditch *c* 1.5m deep which cut through one hut; an accompanying internal bank would have overlain the other. Screening the entrance was a shallow ditch linked at one end by a shallow palisade trench back to the corner of the main enclosure. Inside and approximately at the centre were two more (presumably successive) huts some 7.5m in diameter. All the huts were built with a double facing of timber uprights, probably outside a turf wall and covered with wattle and daub. One of the earlier and one of the later huts each had a porch opening northwards. In a contemporary pit was a fine decorated bronze mirror.

This site is of great interest for several reasons other than its mirror – though that itself could be taken to indicate a certain social status for the inhabitants. As a settlement, it can be seen as a link between the Berwick Down late Iron Age chalkland farm (*supra* p 164) and the small, south-western rectangular enclosed settlement which is now beginning to be recognised in Roman Dumnonia. The way in which the Holcombe site develops over three centuries from such an Iron Age farm into a large corridor-type villa with octagonal bath-house speaks volumes about social and economic trends during the *pax Romana* in this frontier region; though, in view of the absence of comparable evidence further west, its inhabitants were arguably Durotrigan rather than Dumnonian. Nevertheless, are similar Iron Age farms to be found under at least some of the villa complexes only 40km to the north-east around Ilchester? Conversely, what were the factors which converted an Iron Age farm into a Roman villa and left others as lowly Romano-British farms? The question has particular point in Somerset where, compared to Devon, settlement evidence from the Roman period is overwhelming.

## SMALL SETTLEMENTS IN SOMERSET AND GLOUCESTERSHIRE

All the same, we have to look hard in Somerset for the ordinary farmer and the rural labourer: as other chapters here display, most attention has naturally been given to the towns and villas with, recently,

Plate 26 Air-photograph of the earthworks near Scars Farm,
Wrington, Somerset, representing a small settlement among contemporary fields in the Roman period

a major step forward in the recognition and study of the larger rural
settlements (*supra* p 142). Small settlements, the potential farms, with
associated fields have been identified on the Failand Ridge (the Clevedon
Hills) west from Bristol but not on the similar Carboniferous Limestone
of Mendip (Thomas *1974*). An exception is represented by a complex
of well-preserved earthworks on South Hill, Bleadon, a southerly outlier
of Mendip, while to the north, across the Vale of Wrington, a similar
settlement with building sites, enclosures, tracks and adjacent fields
survives near Scars Farm, Wrington (pl 26). A scatter of what were
probably comparable settlements have been identified in, around and on
top of the alluvium of lowland coastal Somerset (Cunliffe *1966*; Lilly
and Usher *1972*; Hawkins *1973*), but none has been reliably excavated
and published. Inland, the density of small rural settlements is not in
doubt, but information other than that they existed is scarce. Fortunately,
two have recently been excavated and can be quoted in the hope that
they are representative.

Plate 27  Air-photograph of the Roman period farm and its surround-
ings on Row of Ashes Farm, Butcombe, Somerset, showing an early
stage of the excavations and the traces of fields and tracks showing
up in low evening light

One lies on the southern edge of the Carboniferous limestone of
Broadfield Down in Butcombe (pl 27), one of the long north/south
parishes related to the Vale of Wrington (Fowler *1968, 1970*). The site,
almost uniquely (with Bleadon Hill and Scars Farm) still represented by
'earthworks', superficially looks complex (and is on excavation) but
basically consisted of a house (and byre?) set amongst a dozen or so
stone-walled enclosures, ie a farmhouse with surrounding yards, animal
pens etc, beyond which were arable fields (fig 42). This essentially simple
arrangement was laid out *c* AD 270, persisted for about a century, and
then became semi-ruinous although occupation continued. Before the
later third century, the visible plan was preceded by different arrangements, including another building (farmhouse?), during the later first and
second centuries. As at Holcombe, the Roman farm developed on top
of an Iron Age settlement, the extent of which has not yet been defined.
Its first phase included at least two timber buildings, one an impressive
circular structure with a rock-cut foundation trench and a central hearth;

174

later, and certainly including the conquest period, iron-smelting and probably bronze-working were proceeding on the site. The late-Roman farm of *c* AD 300 was then the successor to a long and varied history. It would be interesting to know whether another similar-looking settlement, 700m to the west at Scars Farm, has a similar history (Fowler *1970*, fig 26), not least because the other farm which has recently been excavated produced a rather different story.

On Bradley Hill, Somerton (Fowler *1972* 39–41), the whole settlement has been examined. Apart from an isolated Iron Age pit, the site had not been occupied when three buildings were constructed in the middle decades of the fourth century. The farm was inhabited until the early fifth century. It consisted of two dwelling-houses, each of three rooms, and a byre which was soon used for metal-working, and for burying infants (fig 43). In fact, forty-nine inhumation burials were found altogether, giving this site especial interest since seldom are settlement

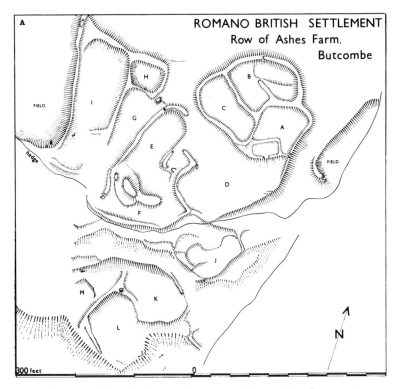

ROMANO BRITISH SETTLEMENT
Row of Ashes Farm,
Butcombe

Fig 42   Plan of the settlement at Butcombe, Somerset

175

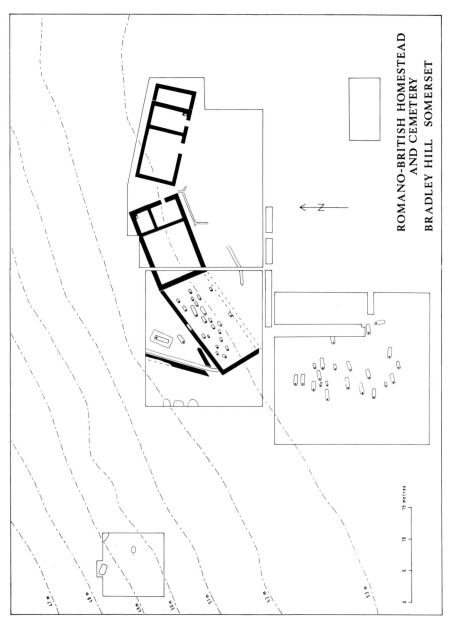

Fig 43   The farmstead on Bradley Hill, Somerton, Somerset

and cemetery associated, particularly at this level of Romano-British society. Apart from one burial in each of the two houses (a characteristic practice), twenty-two infant and child inhumations lay in the former byre, with all the adult burials outside, sixteen of them (plus six child burials) forming a definite cemetery south of the farm buildings. In this cemetery, all the burials but one were aligned east-west, with the head to the west – apparently Christian, but not later than second half of the fourth century.

It would clearly be both difficult and unwise to attempt to generalise on the basis of two excavations, particularly when their results are so different. We are further handicapped in Somerset by the scarcity of good field surveys, and by the fact that, where a potential farm-site has been recorded from casual finds of pottery, the characteristic early ('Durotrigan') and late wares tend to be noted to the exclusion of second and third-century material. We can only ask whether the landscape filled up with new farms on the Bradley Hill model during the Roman period (and if so, why? – where did the people come from?) or whether the multiplicity of sites, masking their earlier history through lack of excavation, are to be explained on the Butcombe model. And are the questions mutually exclusive?

That both types of settlement existed has been further suggested by recent results from the archaeological surveillance of the M5 motorway in Somerset and Gloucestershire. The first point to stress about this project, however, is the amount of Romano-British material that has been recorded from a strip, on average only *c* 50m wide, mechanically dug through the landscape. Along some stretches, 'RB sites' have occurred about every 4km (fig 44). Opportunity to excavate more than a few has been lacking, but from such examination as has been possible most of these sites appear to have been small farmsteads. Evidence of villa status, as at Brookthorpe, Glos, or of extensive communal settlement, as at Bawdrip, Somerset (fig 36), has been rare, and for the most part the structural remains have been represented by walls, ditches, gulleys, spreads of stones, hearths and post-holes, usually in a less than cohesive pattern. One such site, at Tredington, Glos, seemed to have a strong interest in weaving; another, at Wick, Glos, contained a small kiln; while a third, at Falfield, Glos, was involved in iron-smelting. In Somerset, one at Parker's Field, North Petherton, was involved in some as yet unidentified activity involving a trough-like pit, organic material and water; while at Holway, just east of Taunton, another contained a corn-drying oven. None of these sites was completely excavated, but together

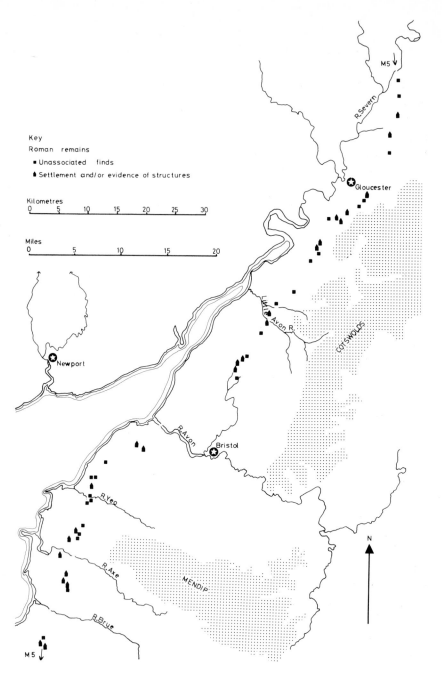

Fig 44 Romano-British sites on the route of the M5 in Gloucestershire and North Somerset

178

they seem to give some idea of the range of economic activities at the base of the social pyramid. They also indicate how difficult it is to generalise about the smaller settlements when, within the general pattern of farming, many may well have developed a particular activity in response to particular local circumstances.

Reverting to the origins of this farmstead class of settlement in the light of this M5 evidence, in sum it would seem that many were 'new' sites taking root in the peaceful Roman countryside. By definition, however, the fact that these sites were discovered in open countryside could suggest that the circumstances in which they were created had changed during the Roman period. It must be suspected, though it is not proved on the M5 evidence, that their appearance and disappearance was connected in some way with that other phenomenon of the Roman countryside, the villa, particularly in Somerset and Gloucestershire. None of the

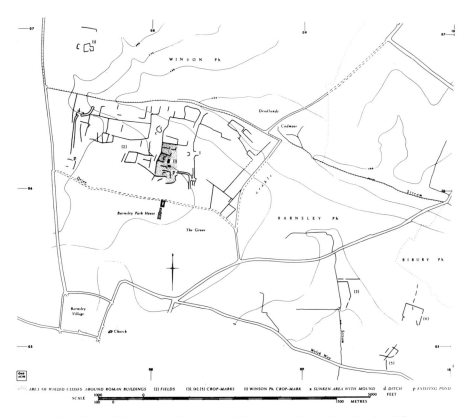

Fig 45  Villa and adjacent field system, Barnsley Park, Glos

179

Plate 28 Air-photograph looking down into the Valley of Stones in west Dorset, showing the pattern of small rectangular fields surviving from prehistoric and/or Roman times between the modern arable in the foreground and the valley floor

M5 sites was unequivocally on top of or beside a settlement of the first centuries BC/AD up to the conquest, though at both Tredington and Holway there were hints that immediately earlier occupation had been adjacent. Overwhelmingly, however, the sites were 'new', apparently more akin to Bradley Hill than Butcombe in type. In terms of date, however, some like Wick and Falfield were late first or second century, hinting perhaps at a fragmentation and regrouping after the conquest of a previously hillfort-orientated settlement pattern; others, like Parker's Field, were predominantly of the third and fourth centuries, perhaps reflecting a filling up of the landscape by secondary settlements. Yet others, like Tredington, lasted through much of the Roman period. Despite the unsatisfactory nature of much of the evidence behind this briefest of summaries, it underlines the importance of recognising that the Romano-British countryside was far from static. It saw an ebb and flow of settlement pattern, perhaps as dramatic as that a thousand years later during the four centuries after the Norman Conquest. In such circumstances, it is precisely the single farm, particularly if newly founded, which is most susceptible to the general fluctuation – witness the many farms in the West Country abandoned in the fourteenth century and again in the nineteenth century. Once the dynamic nature of the Roman countryside is appreciated, it is clearly no longer adequate merely to identify sites as 'RB': we need to know, minimally, in which centuries they started and ended, and the evidence on which that dating is based. Particularly for the ending, it is no longer adequate merely to say 'late-Roman' or 'late fourth century' when such an opinion is based on pottery which, as is now quite clear for certain types, could well have continued in use until the mid fifth century.

Another great lack in present study of the Roman countryside is the exact context into which the smaller settlements fit. While it is always going to be difficult to demonstrate a social or tenurial relationship with other settlements, it should be possible to recover at least some aspects of the immediate physical and agrarian situation. Some settlements, for example, have been related to adjacent field systems: Sancreed and Porth Godrevy in the far west, Butcombe in Somerset (pl 27), and numerous sites on the Wessex chalk (Guthrie *1969*; Fowler *1962*; Fowler and Thomas *1962*; Fowler *1970*; Bowen and Fowler *1966*). From such instances, the impression is conveyed that, apart from villa field systems like that at Barnsley Park, Glos (fig 45), the 'native' system of small, squarish fields was ubiquitous throughout the Roman West Country wherever cereal cultivation was practised (pl 28). We see, too, specifically associated with villas but also occurring on high ground apparently in non-villa contexts (Bowen and Fowler *1966* figs 4 and 9; Grimes *1960* fig 95), an innovation of the Roman period in the form of blocks of more regular, long, narrow fields (Bowen *1966*, *1969*; Fowler *1975* and *forthcoming*).

A field system on Brean Down, Somerset (pl 29), with elements of both the prehistoric and Roman types, represents the sort of challenge further fieldwork must tackle: whose are these fields, and where is the associated settlement? when were they cultivated? what crops did they support? why are there fields at all on this isolated, shallow-soiled, wind swept promontory?

An indication of the range of plants likely to be present in such fields, at least in lowland Gloucestershire, was provided by the contents of a corn-drier uncovered on the M5 at Upton St Leonards: with the wheat were thirty-five distinct species of weeds! Overall, however, palaeo-botany – and, indeed, environmental evidence generally – has barely

Plate 29 Air-photograph from the south-east of Brean Down, Somerset, a peninsula of Carboniferous limestone jutting out into the Severn estuary. Around its highest point, towards its western end, is a well-defined field system, undated but certainly pre-medieval

begun to make an impact on our understanding of the Romano-British farm in the West Country. Similarly, the study of animal bones is hardly yet on a systematic basis – though at least there is the excuse that frequently bones do not survive in the south-west – so the pastoral side of farming, and the diet of the farmers, remain to be explored. If this essay has done nothing else, it should at least, in summarising our present ignorance, have exposed that most dangerous of myths, the fable that the 'RB period' is fully explored. This is certainly not so in the West Country as far as the landscape is concerned, for in many respects the questions are only just beginning to be asked.

# 10

# THE MENDIP LEAD INDUSTRY

The Mendip lead industry was already in existence by the time of the Roman invasion of AD 43, for pre-Roman netsinkers made of lead have been discovered in the Mendip area. This industry was probably small and inefficient, yet it attracted the invaders. Within six years at the latest they were operating the mines under imperial control, and producing pigs (ingots) of lead which can be dated to AD 49. Two such pigs are recorded; one (1)* found in 1544 at Wookey Hole bore the inscription:

[product] of Tiberius Claudius Caesar Augustus, Pontifex Maximus, in the ninth year of his tribunician power, and sixteen times acclaimed Imperator, from the British lead-silver works.

This pig of lead, thought by both Camden and Leland to have been a commemorative trophy, has since been lost but another (5) found in 1853 at Blagdon, Somerset, and now in the British Museum, bears two inscriptions. The main one, moulded on the face of the pig, reads:

[product] of Britannicus, true son of Augustus

and on the front, a second inscription which is incuse, or stamped on when the lead was cold, reads:

in the consulship of Veranius and Pompeius.

Quintus Veranius and Caius Pompeius were the consuls in Rome in AD 49, and the former subsequently became governor of Britain from c 57–8.

The Romans were already well-versed in the techniques of lead-mining, for mines were controlled by them in several provinces, particularly in Spain. It is no surprise therefore that the Mendips and other mining areas in Britain were quickly taken over by the Romans. Soon after the conquest of the territory, lead mines were opened in the west

*Numbers in bold type in brackets after a reference to a pig relates to the number in the catalogue, Appendix 4. Inscriptions on pigs are given in translation in the text and in the original Latin in the catalogue.

of Shropshire, in Flintshire, Derbyshire, and in Yorkshire. There were smaller workings, too, on Alston Moor in Cumberland, and at Lower Machen in south Wales, where at Cefn-pwll-du a gallery of Roman date reveals evidence of fire-setting (Boon *1971* 461).

The Mendip mines were under military control for some time, for another pig of lead (**7**) bearing the inscription:

[product] of Nero Augustus, British [lead] – the Second Legion [produced this]

was discovered in 1883 at St-Valéry-sur-Somme, near Boulogne. It was moulded between AD 54 and 68, when Legion II was in the West Country. This evidence of military control of mines is supported by another Legion II stamp, taking more the form of a pottery-stamp and reading:

[product of] the Second Legion Augusta

which appears on a fragment of a pig found at Caerwent. This probably originates from the mines at Cefn-pwll-du, and suggests that the mining experts of Legion II moved there from the Mendips.


## CHARTERHOUSE (fig 46; pl 18)

On the Mendips, Charterhouse appears to have been the centre of the mining area. Here, eleven pigs of lead have been discovered. Aerial photographs have revealed the street pattern of a Roman town, and in an adjacent field there is an amphitheatre (*supra* p 116; fig 47). The amphitheatre is only 31.5m × 24.25m, with two entrances and grass banks upon which wooden benches would have accommodated the inhabitants of the town and the soldiers of the detachment of Legion II from their fort near-by. The amphitheatre was excavated in 1908, but the other fields containing the probable town, the fort and other earthworks still await full excavation.

Blackmoor itself, Velvet Bottom, into which it runs, and most of the Charterhouse area were extensively worked by lead miners up until the beginning of the present century, and so evidence of Roman workings has been destroyed; but sherds and other evidence of Roman occupation are often found at Charterhouse and in Blackmoor, where in 1968 the water which eventually flooded Cheddar Gorge first washed away the causeway just below the fort, exposing a great deal of pottery and other evidence, some of which was recorded but much of which was lost to indiscriminate treasure-hunters (Fowler *1969*).

The fort at Charterhouse will have held the soldiers whose duty it was to supervise and guard the whole of the mining settlement, the mine-workers, the slaves and prisoners of war, and it may also have been a control point through which the lead manufactured on the Mendips had to pass and be checked. A similar control point must have existed at Verterae (Brough under Stainmore), for the lead workings on Alston Moor and at Navio (Brough-on-Noe) for the Derbyshire mines. Caersws and Forden Gaer may have been the control forts for the Shropshire

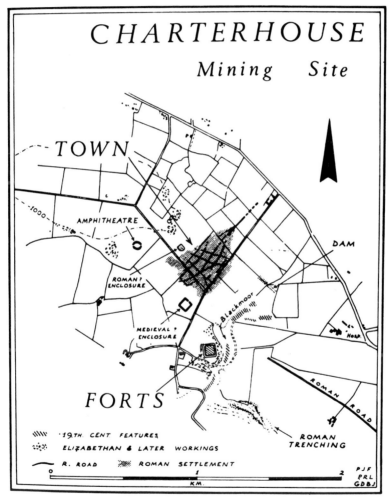

Fig 46 Charterhouse. General plan of the area

185

mines and Cardiff or Caerphilly for Cefn-pwll-du. At Dolaucothi, where the Romans mined gold, a fort was also situated close by the mining area.

## CIVILIAN LESSEES

During the reign of Nero, production continued on the Mendips, as is attested by the pig of Legion II from St-Valéry-sur-Somme, and by a pig of lead (6) discovered in 1783 at Bossington, Stockbridge, Hants, which bears the inscription:

> [product] of Nero Augustus from the first of January in his fourth consulship, British [lead]

This pig has also an incuse stamp on the back which reads:

> from the lead-silver works of Gaius Nipius Ascanius. '30'.

This pig, dated to AD 60, is a product of the emperor, as the inscription on the face tells us, mines being an imperial monopoly. Gaius Nipius Ascanius, a freedman, was probably the imperial agent, or procurator's official, through whose hands all the lead produced on the Mendips would have to pass. The mines may only recently have ceased to be under the military control of Legion II, and Ascanius may now have been in control of production for the emperor. His duty on the Mendips appears to have served as an apprenticeship, for on another, undated, pig from the Flintshire mines, discovered at Carmel, Flintshire, his name appears in the moulded panel on the face of the pig. It would seem that Ascanius left his post on the Mendips to take out a lease on the Flintshire mines, and produced lead there under his own name. The practice of leasing was common, particularly in Derbyshire, where most of the lead pigs so far discovered bear the names of lessees moulded on the face, rather than that of the emperor. Unfortunately, once again, none of these can be dated, and it is not possible to determine precisely whether leasing preceded or succeeded the closer supervision of the imperial procuratorial agents. It would be logical to assume that mines were run first by the army, then by procuratorial agents, and subsequently leased when circumstances permitted, though still under imperial control. On the Mendips, however, pigs bearing the names of lessees moulded on the face are not known. Besides the name of Ascanius, the names of two other officials are known. Like Ascanius, these are probably the names of procuratorial agents. Gaius Publius C—— had his name impressed five times into the end of a Vespasianic pig (**8**) discovered at Syde, Glos. In 1956, at the former Rookery farm, Green Ore, now aptly renamed Vespasian Farm, the farmer discovered under a stone cairn four pigs of Vespasianic date, three of which bear the incuse stamp of Tiberius Claudius Trifer(na) (**14–17**). Like Ascanius, Triferna may have become a lessee in his own right, for five pigs are recorded from the Derbyshire mines which bear the inscription:

[product of] Tiberius Claudius Tr ... British [lead] from the Lutadaron [mine], from the lead-silver works.

With this abbreviated name, positive identification with Triferna of the Mendips is not possible, but these may well have been the same man.

Leasing of mines to partners or *societates* was also practised in this province, and we have evidence of this both from Derbyshire and from the Mendips. In the Derbyshire area, known as Lutudaron, mines were leased to the *Socii Lutudarenses*, the Lutadaron partners, and on the Mendips to the *Novaec. Societas*, the Novaec. company. The incuse stamp of the *Novaec. Societas* appears on the Vespasianic pig from Syde (**8**) which was also stamped by the 'Imperial agent' Caius Publius C——, and also on two pigs of lead (**9–10**) discovered at Clausentum (Bitterne) on Southampton Water. The one surviving pig from Clausentum, which is also of Vespasian's reign, bears a further incuse stamp LRΛD. This stamp, which cannot be interpreted, also occurs on one of the four pigs from Green Ore, but, like the IMP stamp found on another of the Green Ore examples, probably indicated that the pig had passed through the official control point.

## THE EXPORT OF MENDIP LEAD

Ten pigs so far discovered from the Mendips date from Vespasian's reign (AD 69–79). Only four have been discovered that come from the preceding period of Roman occupation, and there are no further examples until the reign of Hadrian. The large number of Vespasianic pigs is interesting, for Pliny tells us that lead occurred in Britain so abundantly that there was actually a law limiting the output. We presume that this law was introduced following a complaint to Vespasian by the mining concessionaires from Spain who must have been hard hit by the amount of lead being produced from the new province. Until then, Spain had enjoyed the position of being the largest lead-producing province in the empire, and it is again interesting to observe that no pigs of lead from Spain have been found which can confidently be dated to any period following Vespasian's reign.

Evidence for the export of lead from the Mendips has been afforded by the pig made by Legion II from St Valéry **(7)** and by another pig found at Lillebonne, Normandy **(27)**. It was probably transported there from the Mendips via Sorviodunum (Old Sarum) and Clausentum. Further evidence of export comes from Pompeii, where samples from a lead cistern, buried in the eruption of Vesuvius in AD 79, contain an isotope composition of a type found in Britain (Brill and Wampler *1967* 70). It seems probable that the lead used at Pompeii was exported from the Mendips, where lead had been mined by the Romans for at least thirty years.

## THE ORGANISATION OF THE MINES

It is from the Spanish mines that we are able to deduce much of the information about mines, mining and processing techniques of the Romans, and the legal position of the mine-owners and the workers. Strabo, for example, records Polybius as saying that the mines of Cartagena in south-east Spain were very large, and embraced an area of 400 stades. Forty thousand workmen were employed there, who brought into the Roman *fiscus* (exchequer) a daily revenue of 25,000 drachmae. Strabo went on to say that silver mines were still being worked in Augustus' time, though they were no longer state property at Cartagena, but had been transferred into private ownership.

From another mining area of Spain have come two bronze tablets of Hadrian's reign, commonly called the Aljustrel tablet and the *Lex Vipasca*. Although incomplete, they give us precise information about the ownership of the mine. The whole of the mining settlement was under the control of the *fiscus,* and lessees, in paying their rent for their lease, accepted strict control under the administration of the procurator – the man responsible to the emperor for all the mines of the province. In addition to the rent, one half of the ore extracted had to be given to the *fiscus.* Partners, or *socii*, were allowed, and each partner had to undertake expenses in proportion to the amount of his share in the mine. In the pithead settlement, we are told that auctioneers, cobblers, launderers, bakers and others paid a fee to the *fiscus* for the right of the monopoly for their trade. The welfare of the mineworkers' families was ensured in part by exempting schoolmasters from taxation, and by providing facilities such as baths. Here special entry times were arranged for families. The baths were also held by a lessee who had to adhere to strict rules. He had, for example, to provide water 'up to the highest mark, and at least once every thirty days wash, dry, and coat with fresh grease all bronze fitments'. A fine of 200 sesterces was imposed by the procurator on the lessee who failed to open his baths for the service he advertised.

The procurator had under him a staff of civil servants, registrars, finance officers, revenue controllers, examiners and superintendents of mines, as well as a staff of technicians, foremen and engineers who supervised the mines and saw that they were being worked to their best advantage. As for the miners themselves, their lot was a hard one. Slaves and prisoners of war were used. We are reminded of the words which Tacitus attributed to the British leader Calgacus before the battle of Mons Graupius in AD 84:

Behind us are the tribute, the mines, and all the other whips to scourge slaves. Whether you are to endure this for ever, or take summary vengeance, this field must decide.

Criminals were also used in mines: those who had committed robbery with violence, or highway robbery, or the like, were sentenced to the mines, the *damnatio ad metalla*. The death rate was high – 12 per cent is thought to have been a likely figure – no doubt aggravated by the fact that it was cheaper to buy new slaves than to look after those already owned. In some mines, chains have been found which were used to keep the prisoners underground. In 103 BC at the silver mines of Laurion, Attica, in Greece, the slaves rebelled and killed all the guards.

Besides slaves, prisoners of war, and criminals, paid labourers were also employed, but most of the mine labour was unskilled. Expert guidance therefore was required to work the mines, and to comply with the requirements of the laws. A school of mining engineers may have existed at Rio Tinto in Spain, where the workings are strikingly uniform.

## THE EXTRACTIVE PROCESSES

In Britain, most of the work was opencast, which was the great attraction of the province as a source of minerals. Elsewhere vertical shafts had to be sunk or adits driven horizontally into the hillsides. This of course increased the expense involved, and for every 100ft driven underground the cost is thought to have doubled. Adits of over 3,000ft in length are known in Spain. In Britain, Roman adits have been identified at Cefn-pwll-du, and at Dolaucothi. Inside the adits and galleries, light was provided by lamps set in niches about three feet apart. Reconstructions have determined that the lamps would burn for about ten hours, and it is therefore reasonable to assume that ten hours was the length of the mineworker's shift.

On the surface – and surface working was probably the main method used on the Mendips, where deep pitting or digging can be seen in several places – besides the use of the pick, hushing and fire-setting could have been used. Hushing was a process thought to have been used in Yorkshire, where water was stored in reservoirs above the ore field, and then undammed so that it poured down over the hillside, stripping the soil from the surface and laying bare the ore-bearing rock beneath. The Reverend James Skinner, Rector of Camerton from 1800 to 1839 and an antiquary of no mean achievement, believed that fire-setting had been used by the Romans on the Mendips. By this method, rock was heated by fire, and then cold water, or vinegar, was poured on top, which cracked the rock.

In many mines water was a problem, and various methods were used to extract it from shafts and adits. One method was the kaduff – a bucket on the end of a long pole which was lowered by an operator into the shaft, and then levered out, using a tall, forked pole as a fulcrum. The *cochlea*, or Egyptian or Archimedean screw was another method. This was a device resembling a long corkscrew encased in a wooden cylinder. The lower end was placed in the water and the outer casing rotated by a slave. The water was then drawn up through the cylinder and emptied out at the upper end. Double-action pumps were also used, worked by alternating plungers raised and lowered by a rocking beam. A further method was the water wheel. These are known to have been used at the gold mines at Dolaucothi, and at Rio Tinto eight pairs of wheels, rotating in opposite directions, raised the water a total height of 120ft.

On the Mendips where complicated series of shafts and galleries are not known, drainage cannot have been so great a problem. For the same reason ventilation cannot have been a difficulty, whereas in other provinces this too caused great trouble.

An interesting discovery was made in Spain at Linares when a washerwoman was found to be scrubbing her linen on a bas-relief of Roman date. This relief, duly rescued, shows a group of five miners. The leader is holding a bell or lantern in one hand, and a pair of double tongs, which would have been used for raking in the ore or for tackling hot rock. Another miner carries a pick, and a third a lamp. Each miner has sandalled feet and wears a *tunica* round his waist.

Several examples of the tools that the miners used have been found. Before the Roman era miners used picks of stone, wood and horn. The Romans used iron picks, and their shape differs little from the picks used today. The ore was shovelled by wooden spades, which were sometimes bound with iron. Examples of these have been found in Shropshire, Yorkshire and on the Mendips, although the authenticity of the latter is in doubt. Hoes were used to gather in the ore, and this was loaded on to wooden trays which were dragged along the ground. Buckets were also used, made of leather or goatskin or even esparto grass.

The galena (lead ore) was taken from the mine to a smelting furnace. Here, in a hearth surrounded by a stone wall, the lead ore was subjected to a heat of about 300°C produced by wood and coal, assisted where possible by an air blast effected naturally or by means of bellows. Primitive hearths have been reconstructed and show that it is indeed possible, though rather wasteful, to smelt lead under these conditions. The slag that remains still contains quite a high proportion of lead, and it was this slag left by the Romans and later workers that encouraged miners at Priddy on the Mendips to re-smelt the slag which still contained 5–10 per cent lead and 3oz/ton (0.009 per cent) silver. The lead was smelted at several sites on the Mendips. Besides Charterhouse, hearths have been found at Herriot's Bridge, in the Chew valley, at Green Ore (Ashworth *1970*), and at Priddy where there must also have been a sizeable settlement to the west of St Cuthbert lead works.

The lead, once smelted, was then cupelled in order to separate the silver from the lead. The lead was heated in a shallow hearth to a temperature of approximately 1100°C, when the lead forms litharge and the silver is recovered. Traces of cupelling hearths have been found at Green Ore by the road leading from Charterhouse to the Fosse Way. Cupellation was an expensive process and it was only the richest ores that were worth cupelling.

The ores of Yorkshire, Shropshire and Derbyshire are not high in silver content, and the Romans may well have decided not to extract the silver. In Flintshire, however, they do appear to have cupelled the lead, and on the Mendips the lead was richer in silver content, containing up to 0.4 per cent silver. Nevertheless, the silver content of Mendip lead was still well below the standard of the ore from Laurion in Greece, where the content was 1.8 per cent.

After the silver had been extracted, the lead litharge was re-smelted and the lead recovered. This was then cast into moulds to produce the pigs.

## LEAD PIGS

Spanish pigs are of approximately 100 *librae* (32.74kg or 72.1 lb) in weight, and they were cast in semi-cylindrical moulds designed to produce pigs of this weight. British pigs have a far wider weight distribution, extending from 58kg to 90kg (127–223lb) with no significant number of pigs at any one weight, although from the evidence inscribed on some of the pigs it seems that 200 *librae* (65.48kg; 144.2lb) may well have been a more usual weight for the British pigs. On some of the Mendip examples there are numerals which have been stamped into the side or end of the pig when cold. There is the possibility that these numerals are an indication of the weight of the pig. On some pigs the numerals correspond closely with the present-day weight, in *librae,* of the pig. On one from Derbyshire the figures CCX have been scratched, and the present weight of the pig is 200 *librae.* Since a standard weight of 100 *librae* appears to have been used for pigs of lead from Spain, it is not unreasonable to assume that a standard weight was also used in Britain, but here the standard may have been intended to be 200 *librae.* (Perhaps thefts of lead pigs forced the Romans to increase their weight to act as a deterrent to the thief.) If this theory is correct, then the numerals stamped on other pigs of lead – all from the Mendips – can be identified, in all but two instances, as the weights of the pig in excess of the standard weight of 200 *librae.* The pig of lead from Bossington (**6**) bears the numerals **XXX**, and its weight in *librae* is 230: this example corresponds exactly with the theory. There are also inscribed numerals on three of the four Green Ore pigs. The one (**14**) inscribed LXV weighs 259 *librae*, the second example (**16**) inscribed LXIIX weighs 262 *librae*, and the third (**15**) with LXXIIX (pl 30) weighs 273 *librae.* The three pigs weigh just five or six *librae* short of the inscribed weight if added to the standard weight of 200 *librae* suggested above. However, there are two pigs of lead, those from Bitterne, which do not support the theory. On the one which is still in existence (**9**), the numeral IIVI is stamped on so clearly that a mistake cannot be possible. The weight of the pig is 240 *librae.* The other pig, which is now lost (**10**), bore the inscription VIII and was said to weigh the equivalent of 223 *librae.*

Thefts of these pigs must have occurred, and it is interesting to note that the four pigs from Green Ore of Tiberius Claudius Triferna were

Plate 30   Detail of front moulded inscription and incuse end inscription of a lead pig (no 15, *see* p 232) from Green Ore on Mendip

buried under a cairn of stones, perhaps deliberately placed there to be recovered at a later date (Palmer and Ashworth *1957*). On this occasion four pigs were discovered together, and this number may well have made up a convenient cartload. At Pulborough in Sussex in 1824 four pigs were also found together. Surprisingly, these four were the products of the Tiberius Claudius Tr—— from Derbyshire mentioned earlier. If these two names are the inscriptions of the same man, as seems likely, then doubts about his honesty gain support. Of the four Green Ore pigs, three contain virtually no silver at all, as one would expect after the cupelling process. The fourth, however, contains 0.056 per cent silver (over 18oz per ton) which is a far higher silver content than is recorded for any other British pig. This example had obviously not been subjected to the cupelling process. Tiberius Claudius Triferna had his name inscribed four times on this pig, and Boon (*1971* 467 f) has suggested that this was done deliberately so that the pig could easily be identified later.

Four pigs of lead have also been discovered together at Petuaria (Brough-on-Humber), which was the usual port by which Derbyshire lead was transported. Most of the pigs discovered in Britain have been found by the side of roads or rivers, and this has enabled us to deduce the main routes taken from the mines to the ports of embarkation. The Flintshire mines used Deva (Chester), and pigs of Mendip lead were taken to Bristol, or to Clausentum by way of Sorviodunum (Old Sarum). It has been suggested that the road leading westwards along the Mendip Hills was also used to transport lead to a port at Uphill, but while there is certainly evidence of a road, there is no record of any lead discovered west of Charterhouse, and it seems that all the lead went either east or north.

Although there were several mining areas in Britain, the pigs do not always carry an inscription indicating their origin. In Spain, the pigs often bore a moulded dolphin, or an anchor, or a swan, or the like. This probably indicated the producer, the mine or even the *officina* of origin. Three Shropshire pigs and one Mendip example (**20**) have moulded palm branches on their surfaces, though of different designs, and on two of these pigs there is a hammer mark of a reticulated pattern and a circle – all official marks no doubt, but of obscure meaning. Whittick has suggested (*1931* 264), by analogy with gold ingots from North Africa, that a palm branch may have indicated that the pig was destined for the Imperial Mint.

However, the exact provenance of the lead is recorded on some pigs. The name of the Derbyshire mining area, Lutudaron, identifies many of the Derbyshire pigs. The inscription BRIG for *Brigantes* occurs on some of the Yorkshire examples. *DECEA(N)GLI* appears on some Flintshire pigs and on several of the Mendip pigs are moulded the words:

BRIT·EX ARG·VEB
British [lead] from the Veb. lead-silver works [pl 30]

*Veb* is the abbreviation for the Mendip mining area, or possibly Charterhouse, but the expanded word is not known. The suggestion that the name survives in Ubley, the parish adjoining Charterhouse to the northeast, is attractive.

*EX ARG.* was formerly thought to have meant that the pig so inscribed had been de-silvered, but when two pigs from Petuaria were found with pieces of galena adhering to their bases, the translation 'from the lead-silver works' was found to be more accurate. Galena could not possibly survive the intense heat involved in the cupellation process for extracting the silver, although it is perfectly possible for lumps to remain intact after being in the smelting furnace (Smythe *1940* 142 f).

Plate 31   Lead pig (no 21) found in the river Frome at Bristol

The moulds into which the molten lead was poured have not survived, but they were probably made of clay and formed from wooden patterns. They were able to withstand at least five castings. Two of the Green Ore pigs were cast from the same mould, as can be seen by comparing flaws round the inscriptions on the face, and two pigs found in the river Frome at Bristol (21–22) also bear identical flaws (pl 31).

The striations which are observed on many Roman pigs (pl 32) are the natural result of cooling lead. Some have thought that this was caused when ladles of lead were poured into the mould and then cooled slightly before the next ladle was poured in. Experiments using ladles, however (Whittick *1961* 105 f), have shown that pigs so made have more pronounced laminations. The Romans cast their pigs from a single tapping operation, and this gives an indication of the large smelting furnaces that must have existed on the Mendips and elsewhere capable of smelting over 100kg (225lb) of lead.

## LEAD AND PEWTER IN THE THIRD AND FOURTH CENTURIES

The Mendip mines continued with the production of lead throughout the second century. Pigs of lead of Hadrianic and of Antonine date have been found, and one pig of lead (27) discovered at Lillebonne, near the mouth of the Seine, bears a Severan inscription and probably also came from the Mendips.

Lead was used by the Romans in the manufacture of coffins, weights, water-pipes and cisterns, and for roofs, and great sheets of it were used for lining the Great Bath at Bath. It was needed throughout the Roman occupation, as was silver, and during the third century, when coinage was being debased throughout the Empire, very successful coins of good

Plate 32   Lead pig (no 11) from Charterhouse on Mendip

quality were being minted at several sites on the Polden Hills south of Mendip.

During the third and fourth centuries lead was used in the manufacture of pewter. This metal is an alloy of tin and lead. The Romans would manufacture pewter containing a proportion of approximately 20–30 per cent lead to tin. Some pewter, however, had well over this proportion – in some cases more than 50 per cent lead, as in the case of a cup from Brislington, Bristol, and of a coffin from Ilchester, Somerset. There was at the time an increased need for tin, and this led to the re-opening of the tin mines in Cornwall, following the closure of those in Spain. The Romans had tried to exploit the mineral much earlier – between AD 60 and AD 70 – but had abandoned the attempt since production in Spain was much more economic. Now, with the use of *antoniniani*, tin was needed in increasing quantities. Roads in the mining districts of Cornwall were built or repaired and mineral was transported from the south-west.

Coincident with the increased activity in Cornwall, the small town at Camerton began to flourish. Camerton is on the Fosse Way between the Mendips and Bath. It was here, as well as at Lansdown near Bath, and at Nettleton Shrub, Wilts, that pewter was manufactured in the West Country. This metal occurs frequently in hoards in East Anglia, and although there is some evidence for pewter manufacture in the Fens, it seems that most of the pewter in Britain was manufactured in the west, where the metal was also in great demand. Camerton, Lansdown, and Nettleton Shrub were all on the Fosse Way, by which tin was transported from Cornwall, and were within easy reach of the Mendips. A number of stone moulds in which the pewter vessels were cast have been found at these sites. Bath stone was used, and so was a local white lias, oolite, which was smoother and more easily cut. The moulds were in two parts

196

Plate 33    Three flagons from the group of seven pewter vessels found
in the well of the Brislington villa near Bristol

and were held together by an iron clamp.

The large number of villas in the West Country meant that there was a good market locally for the pewter tableware manufactured along the Fosse. The many finds of pewter in north Somerset (pl 33) give some indication of the popularity of the metal in this part of the country.

Towards the end of the fourth century conditions in Britain had deteriorated to such an extent that the owners of many villas left them and took refuge in the towns (*supra* p 140). Near the Mendips this was true and we find that the villas on the estates which had formerly supplied the mining settlement with farm produce were occupied by bailiffs or even by the labourers. In these circumstances, it is uncertain how long the mines continued to operate, and how far into the fifth century the lead and pewter industries continued.

# 11

# THE END OF THE ROMAN SOUTH-WEST

It is doubtful whether we are yet ready to structure a full discussion of the evidence for the end of the Roman West, in the sense in which that term has been used in this book. I therefore confine myself to the great south-west peninsula, from the western edge of Mendip down to Land's End. No clear-cut solutions to all the problems herein stated should be expected; the most I can do is to set out the evidence, and the inferences, that I regard as helpful and relevant, and – using these – draw the general outline of what at the moment I believe may have taken place. If this does no more than narrow the front upon which future work might proceed, then at least the reader's time will not be wholly wasted.

We begin by recognising that there are two distinct historical situations – the Roman south-west, in the late fourth century AD, and the south-west of early English history at the time of the rise of the Wessex dynasty. Three or four centuries yawn between these entirely different situtations, and it is the task of the archaeologists, as well as of the historians, to explain how the first was transmuted to the second. There has, of course, been a great deal of attention paid in recent years to problems of the end of Roman Britain – archaeologically, because the old belief that all sub-Roman and post-Roman levels in historic urban settlements had been dug away in the Middle Ages now proves (happily) to be ill-founded; historically, I judge, because a new generation of British students has turned a corporate mind towards British proto-history. If any moral or lesson can be drawn from the first-fruits of such work, it is that no one standard set of circumstances, no truly universal model of fifth-century decay or of fragile continuity from *magistrati* to *ealdormenn*, can be used. Behind all our tenuous shreds of evidence, we glimpse the rich diversity of the individual cantons of Roman Britain, as diverse indeed as the Iron Age regional cultures in which they were largely rooted; we recognise, too, that where the cantonal capitals pro-cessed to later English cityhood, they cannot have done so in precisely similar fashion.

The south-western *civitas*, or canton, of the Dumnonii embraced Scilly,

Cornwall, Devon, and at least a large part of Somerset. Where the *civitas* (which we can call 'Dumnonia') ended, and the next two *civitates* (of the Durotriges Lindinenses, with Ilchester, and the primary Durotriges, with Dorchester) began, remains a matter of interpretation. Rivet's well-known map (*1966* 161) is described by its cautious author as showing 'largely hypothetical' boundaries. Frere (*1967* 16) has shunted the Dumnonian frontier some *millia* to the east. I have, earlier, suggested (Thomas *1966a* 83–4) that a natural bound was employed in the Somerset Levels – the river Parret seems to be the most probable; and that, in the higher and irregular countryside south of the levels, the Dorset/Devon river Axe is just as likely.

Politically, this was a *civitas* of Roman Britain, subjected in the first century to some degree of military conquest (Fox and Ravenhill *1972*), and later defined as the territory of the Dumnonii, with its centre at Isca Dumnoniorum (Exeter). Here was the regional version of a fiscal and political administration, now being provided with an appropriate tangible presence by the current series of rescue excavations near the cathedral (Fox *1971*). But – outside Exeter – how Roman was 'Roman' here? How far in relation to this very considerable peninsula, would we be justified in talking about 'the end of the *Roman* south-west'? How uniform, both before and after the Roman conquest, was the life-style within Dumnonia, the western extremity of which is as far from Exeter as Nottingham is from London? As we shall see, the bare existence of the area-label 'Cornwall' in its pre-Norman guises raises the argument that the generic word 'Dumnonii' included at least a submerged *Cornouii* – for whom I have previously tried to provide an archaeological setting (Thomas *1966a*). This divisive tendency can be taken still further, in itself; for there is reason to suspect that the six ancient so-called 'hundreds' originate in pre-English days, in territorial units of the late Roman period; *pagi*, in fact, smaller than (but reminiscent of) the territories of such sub-cantonal peoples as the Gangani, Setantii and Gabrantovices (Thomas *1964*).

The implication, long realised by many of the archaeologists working in the region, is that – native ways and *romanitas* being at some stage in the balance – the native mode, drawn from the pre-Roman Iron Age, was the more conspicuous in the material culture of most of the rural south-west during the Roman centuries. This is important in a world of pots and pans, knives and brooches, but (as Stevens *1966*, and others, have shown) it is potentially rather more important when we look at the obscure histories of settlement-patterns, land tenure, place-name elements and formation, and social and legal customs. That Dumnonia stood somewhat apart, in a poverty-stricken sense, from much of the cultural heritage of late pre-Roman Iron Age southern Britain can be and has been demonstrated (Thomas *1966a* 76). We can see this for ourselves, in the Roman period, by turning to two recent Roman villa distributions – of all Roman villas in Britain, and of such villas known to be of the third and fourth centuries (Rivet *1969* 211, 213). They stop just short of what is broadly agreed to be the eastern frontier of Dumnonia; and they stop emphatically, because the late Roman fashion for villas was so well marked in western Wessex, in the Cotswolds, and in the southern Marches. (I discount the isolated pseudo-villa at Magor, in west Cornwall, and stress that the Holcombe villa near Uplyme, with its magnificent mirror (Fox and Pollard *1973*), is presumably just inside Durotrigan territory.)

I wish that we could, in 1974, speak with greater certainty about our settlement-history. This is at the moment well explored, where it *is* explored; but it is unevenly known, because so much of it comes out hard on the heels of the great parish-by-parish survey begun in Cornwall (Thomas *1972*), now so ably followed around Bristol, and already begun in south Devon and central Somerset.

The archaeological evidence for a regional tradition of seeing cattle and domestic herds, rather than conventional coinage or other bullion, as the basis of personal wealth starts, perhaps, with the stock enclosures of the local hillfort manifestations (Thomas *1966a*). This is but one argument for suggesting that, like early historic Wales and Ireland, where surviving literature forms a surer guide, Dumnonian society was characterised by some hierarchy of chieftaincies, and was frankly non-egalitarian in its content. Given its broader Iron Age, Celtic-speaking, background, and the powerful arguments from analogy elsewhere, it would be surprising to find that it was anything else. But may we posit, between major and minor princes, and a subsistence-level peasantry, the existence of groups loosely describable as a free land-holding class? I persuade myself, if not everyone else, that this may have been the case; and that the existence of this social element is mirrored, not by hillfort occupation (which both preceded and succeeded the Roman centuries proper), but by the numerous small-to-middling and normally univallate enclosures known as 'rounds'. These occur very widely in almost all parts of Cornwall so far examined, with a rough average density of one per square mile (or perhaps a little less), and an estimate of about 700 for the modern county (Thomas *1966a* 89–90). Most known forms of the rounds (which are not necessarily all circular, or even curvilinear) are gradually being identified in Devon as well. While no one should suppose that *all* rounds were in occupation at the same time, the evidence so far shows that they constitute by far the largest settlement-type attributable to this period (roughly first century BC to fourth (or later) AD). Are these not, like the raths and cashels of Ireland, the enclosed homesteads of a stock-owning middle class or its proto-historic equivalent? Had Dumnonia been more urbanised, more Romanised, or more efficiently exploited, one could have hoped to recover substantial late Roman villas, symbol of the wealthiest and most ambitious faction of Romano-British society. But villas, appropriate systems of real Roman roads, recognisable tracts of Romano-British farmland with correct ancillary structures, and the extensive small change of *romanitas*, have all failed to appear in virtually all of Dumnonia. The reason for this lacuna cannot be, entirely, the relative poverty of the province and its lack of Romanisation; some of it, as in Wales, must be attributed to the retention (albeit in an evolving form) of alternative, and older, systems and cultures.

Again, it is perfectly likely that, in post-Roman if not in Roman times, Dumnonian society threw up a genuine ruling element – the analogy would be the petty territorial kinglets of early Ireland. We have, with one exception (Charles in North Devon, earlier *Carn Lis*, Gover *et al 1931–2* 61), lost the Devon place-names that portray this, but we still have the restricted occurrences of the Cornish onomastic element *les*, *lis*, to be translated approximately as 'chieftain's enclosure, important seat, court, palace'. It is found in the names of several rounds – Leswidden, in the Land's End (1302 *Leswen*, 'the white, or fair, L.'), Lestowder in St Keverne, which contains the personal name Teudar, that of a traditional king in medieval Cornish legends, Arallas in mid-Cornwall (from *argant, arghans,* 'the silver L.'). It also survives in the names of a few of the oldest towns and boroughs, like Liskeard, Lostwithiel, site of the ancient duchy palace, and Helston which, like the other Helston(e) in north Cornwall, is really *hen lis* ('the old, or obsolete, L.') with the English suffix *-ton*. The post-Roman phase of Castle Dore, near Fowey, though it lacks such a name, is perhaps a sound depiction of a pre-Norman *lis* (Rahtz *1972*).

One may continue, archaeologically, to underline this heavy native element from the most important group of data: inferences drawn from a study of the domestic pottery of the period. There does exist a fascinating field for advanced socio-economic enquiry into the question of the presence, or absence, of a native pottery tradition in the various regions of late Roman Britain. Why its virtual absence from most of Wales? Why is this native tradition so patchily distributed around the areas of the Lowland Zone, being neither exclusively urban nor rural? In the south-west, decades of productive excavation (with which the present rate of publication appears to be unable to keep pace) show clearly that the widespread ceramic group we once called 'South-Western B', in all its better-known manifestations, was maintained in a developing form for domestic use up to at least the fourth century AD; and this seems to be so wherever one looks. I am generalising, but not too much beyond the evidence, when I point out some of its characteristics – very localised production from indigenous, often poor-quality, clays; some specialist kilns like Trebarveth in the Lizard (Peacock *1969*), possibly linked to such special needs as briquetage and salt-containers; a heavy emphasis on basic functional forms (jars, bowls, platters); progressive loss of the fancier pre-Roman Iron Age repertoire of ornament; and evidence of imitation of Roman coarse wares, brought irregularly into the province. A steady trickle of samian and other well-known wares can be found, right down to Land's End and indeed to Scilly. There are also small scatters of Roman buff amphoras, and some mortaria, with copying of the latter in local soft stones (Hirst *1936*).

If, in strict pottery terms, we take 'sub-Roman' to mean 'the continued production into the 5th century AD, possibly later, of local types of pottery current during the Roman period proper', then again the south-west stands out in this respect. A well-fired, if typologically devolved, west Cornish group of sub-Roman pottery in this sense was isolated two decades ago and named 'Gwithian style' from its type site (Thomas *1958*). I detect traces of a similar, very localised (and parallel, rather than related) pottery in north-east Cornwall, appearing, presumably not before the late fifth century, among the Tintagel finds. Now the excavations at Exeter, under Michael Griffiths' direction, yield what I take to be an *urban* sub-Roman pottery group, with both coarse hard, and finer burnished, wares, conceivably spanning both the fourth and fifth centuries, but on his sequential evidence of the urban structures certainly going well into the fifth (Griffiths *1972*). This state of affairs is becoming commonplace in many late Roman towns, and my point is that here, in Exeter, we may have but one facet of a much wider phenomenon. Nor does this exhaust the list. There is a least one sherd of this kind, with the late fifth and sixth century imported wares, from Bantham Ham, on the south Devon coast (Fox *1955*). I leave aside for the moment the well-known 'grass-marked' pottery (Thomas *1968*) which is not part of this episode; but, as for the sub-Roman wares, there is at present a distributional gap until one moves outside Dumnonia, into the Mendips, the Cotswolds, and Wessex, where another and totally different sub-Roman or post-Roman native style, the pre-Saxon grass-*tempered* ware, emerges (Fowler *1970b*).

But of course it would be wrong, and misleading, to imply that the Roman south-west, when its history reached that point in time indicated by my chapter-heading, was still an entirely un-Romanised province. I mentioned the occurrence of actual Roman factory-made wares, like samian – less common in Dumnonia than in the Midlands,' but a little more frequent than in Scotland north of the Antonine Wall. There is the coin evidence, particularly in the pattern of late third and fourth-century hoards in Cornwall (*supra* p. 62), even if the coins did not actually circulate as money in the conventional sense. In my 1966 map of these (Thomas *1966a*), I drew attention to the existence, viewed only in the light of its long coin-sequence, of some mysterious settlement at Plymouth, and Fox *(1973)* has pointed similarly to Sidmouth. Time and chance may clarify these particular mysteries. We can now see that at Exeter, as elsewhere, it was unwise to equate the end of true urban occupation with the end of the recorded coin list in AD 388. We can go on redressing any over-emphasis on the native side by referring to the third (1956) edition of the Ordnance Survey's period map of Roman Britain. Some vestigial road system, it must now be suspected, traversed Dumnonia west of the Exe. There is a natural, major, spine route down the length of Cornwall, superimposed in large part on older ridgeways. I have argued (Thomas *1966a*) that, from the Ravenna Cosmography, one can detect an itinerary heading for the north coast by the Camel estuary, and some of the five late third or fourth-century Roman milestones in Cornwall must indicate minor routes to and from the coast, doubtless linked to embarkation points in the alluvial tin trade, among other purposes.

Again, though in local settlement-archaeology we may use the term 'round' as a portmanteau word for all the univallate homestead enclosures of this period, few are true circles, most are ovoid or 'curvilinear', and some are distinctly rectilinear. Stoke Gabriel in Devon (Masson-Philips *1965*), Carvossa in mid-Cornwall (Douch and Beard *1970*), and Grambla in the Lizard area (Saunders *1972*) are excavated instances, the extraordinary range of finds from Carvossa suggesting perhaps that it was an early *lis,* or some form of mercantile centre. One can suggest further that these, and a good few more known only from the ground (Dudley *1954*), may owe their shape and even their rough proportions to the influence of Roman models. The occasional appearance of mortared masonry must be likewise attributed.

We cannot know how widely, outside Isca and a few minor centres, spoken British Latin was current. The evidence, from those loan-words that we can trace in the British languages when we later encounter them in written form, or argue backwards to earlier stages, is not necessarily specific (beyond a few centuries) as to exactly when, still less where, the loans took place. On the other hand, it is a safe guess that loans relating to basic technology – as when *pont*, from *pontem*, replaced a Celtic word for 'bridge', or Latin *fenestra*, 'window', gave rise to the ancestor of Welsh *ffenestr* and Cornish *fenester* – took place as much in the south-west as elsewhere. It is curious, parenthetically, to note that apart from a few purely native words for 'lane', 'track', the oldest Cornish term for a 'road', *forth*, is, like the Welsh *ffordd*, a borrowing from English; and that there is doubt as to whether the Latin *stratum* gave rise to a south-west British loan.

The fifth and sixth centuries AD saw the end of an era, possibly by way of spasmodic and far-reaching changes at all levels of society; but how Romanised was the fourth-century situation? To my mind, and I stress that this is only one man's view, the crux of the problem lies in the realities of political control, even in the loosely knit, disorganised rural setting with which we deal. Can we penetrate the fog and glimpse the mere shape of those realities? There will be suspicions, if no more, that power in the fifth century grew out of the portals of some re-occupied hillfort.

I am not convinced that, in south-west Britain, change at the end of the Roman period was primarily initiated by the weight of external threats. Dumnonia is too far to the south, and on the wrong side of Britain, to have any meaningful connection with the Picts, even if we have, nationally, undervalued the maritime prowess of these vigorous northerners. Saxon pirates in the Channel cannot be excluded entirely but apart fom the Exe, leading to Exeter, and such putative settlements as those at Plymouth, Topsham, Sidmouth, and Seaton, there are few obvious targets for sea-raiders and a long, mostly inhospitable, coast. Irish settlements on the north coast of the peninsula certainly took place, but were, I think (Thomas *1973*), numerically weak. If we take as a current estimate – an estimate, not a guess – a figure of the order of 10,000 for the population of late Roman Cornwall alone (perhaps a quarter in the land-holding category, the rest as a peasantry in a variety of unenclosed settlements), we must note that Devon, and the Somerset Levels, constitute together an area of much greater size than Cornwall; subtracting the great belts of swamp, and moorland, and even supposing a population three or four times that put forward for Cornwall, we still have for the whole region a very low figure of people per square mile. There is no evidence that all available land had been taken up at this stage, and certainly not such as to make the presence of, at the outside, a few hundred Irish settler-families immediately intolerable.

The dim reality that we encounter, at a rather late stage, sketched for us in the early medieval recensions of Welsh annalistic and genealogical sources, is a quite acceptable model of the region in the middle of the first millennium AD. Dumnonia had become a native British kingdom, one of many. The degree of credibility that one may choose to place on these sources, the approach, the critical evaluation, are all matters open to continuous discussion (*cf* Pearce *1971*; Morris *1973*); but it is permissible to construct the outlines of a native dynasty, anchored in the usual pseudo-historical fashion to great Romanised heroes of the fourth century.

By no means the first Dumnonian ruler (he appears to be about the fourth, and not necessarily in a direct line of descent) was Cunomorus or Conomorus, who may be the man whose son is named on the inscribed stone near Castle Dore, in mid-Cornwall (Macalister *1945*, 465). The inscription is referred to the mid sixth century (Radford *1951a*): it might even be closer to 500. This dating propels the beginnings of native kings back into the fifth century, where the line begins with a semi-legendary Conan Meriadocus. After Cunomorus it is possible to find occasional, and independent, references to other rulers. Constantine, the medieval Welsh 'Custennin Corneu', may be the man categorised by Gildas about 540, and also the man converted in his old age (589) and subsequently sanctified. His son was called Erbin; and Erbin's son Gereint, perhaps a local hero of the sixth century, is conceivably – though far from certainly – the *Gereint hael*, 'generous Gereint', who raised his battle-cry in front of the men of the south at the battle of Catraeth, about the year 600. A subsequent figure, Cado (or Cadwy or Catovius) the son of Gereint, whose brothers Iestin and Selyf and nephew Kebi (or Cuby) were all three saints, occurs in the milieu of seventh-century monasticism.

A second Gereint can, with greater confidence, be dated to the early eighth century; he was the recipient, about 705, of a letter from Aldhelm of Sherborne, and in 710 fought against Ine of Wessex. He is also perhaps the heroic Gereint who was slain in a cavalry engagement at Llongborth, 'Ship Harbour', sometimes identified as Langport in Somerset on the eastern frontier of the kingdom. But after this person, there are great gaps. The *Dumnarth rex cerniu* whose drowning is recorded under the notional year 875 in the *Annales Cambriae* could well be the same person as the Doniert whose name appears on a surviving stone cross-shaft at St Cleer in east Cornwall (as a benefactor?), the ornament of which is consistent with this date.

It is vital to emphasise that these are only just historical figures. We omit mention of 'Arthur', who is not central to this theme, and whose later literary or hagiographical associations with some of the rulers named earlier would imply a currency of several centuries. We can accept the bare fact of the existence of a line of south-western kings. We can accept the likelihood of the tradition of some of their names, names which look back both to Roman greatness and to Celtic supremacies. This is perhaps the limit of credibility.

Can we refine the locations of these rulers? The father of Cunomorus, Tudwal (or Tutvwlch), presumably in the fifth century, and Constantine in the sixth, bore in medieval literature the subsidiary Welsh title *Corneu.* This, distinct from *Kernyw* ('of Cornwall'; a genitive of place), seems to be an adjective – 'the Cornishman, the man-of-Cornwall' – linking its bearers specifically to the lands west of the Tamar. Cunomorus, who comes between these two, is associated on the one hand with the south coast of Cornwall, on the other with Brittany (Chadwick *1959*). The second Gereint's brothers and nephew spring, in hagiography, from the east of Cornwall, even if dedications in their names are found mostly in the west of the county. At least one legend connects Cato, Gereint's grandson, with mid-Cornwall; another could be used to locate him either in Somerset or, more plausibly, on the north Cornish seaboard. The second Gereint is near enough to history to be real.

The subsequent compression of this king-list into Cornwall – for example, the ninth-century Doniert in the Bodmin Moor area – would be the corollary of the English advance westward, through Devon into the two eastern hundreds of Cornwall, during the later eighth century.

Two points come to mind. Firstly, no one, single, place can be pointed out as a continuous royal seat. Secondly, at a date somewhat earlier than one would have supposed to be dictated by the overall pattern of Britain at this time, the rulers of Dumnonia appear to be connected, not with Exeter, not even with Devon, but with Dumnonia west of the Tamar, the present Cornwall. If these constitute an acceptable hypothesis, rest-ing on what evidence we have and what inferences we can draw from such evidence, does this shed any light at all on the end of the Roman south-west? There would seem to be very little resemblance between the last archaeologically detectable state of the Roman canton, aptly described by a recent chronicler as an area 'backward and resistant to change', and this vague world of the post-Roman Dumnonian princes, ever under pressure from its eastern neighbour.

We might hazard a guess as to how, in the first place, such native rulers emerged. Those figures that I have mentioned are the few that have some claim to be regarded as rulers of the whole province, whatever its actual extent at a given moment. But, just as we glanced at the models of early historic Ireland and Wales to postulate some kind of social stratification in Dumnonia, as one explanation for a diversity of settlement-types, so we can look again in that direction. There would seem to have been other, minor, very local chieftains and *reguli*; they can be spotted in the medieval Lives of saints who are proper to the south-west, and the inscribed memorial stones afford us actual names. One, in the Land's End, commemorates a RIALOBRAN [OS], the first elements being a word meaning 'kingly' or 'royal' (Macalister *1945*, 445). Another, in Devon, labels the dead man as PRINCEPS, which we ought to translate as 'chieftain' here (ibid). There are such Romanised names as IUSTUS, LATINUS, SEVERUS, CIVILIS, and VITALIS, mixed up with (and related to) purely British names. Someone is described as a child of TRIBUNUS, if this is a title and not just a personal name. Here, surely, is a hint of a network of upper-class families, the folk who, elsewhere and in differing circumstances, might have been the grandchildren of late Roman villa-proprietors. Nor is the physical setting lacking. I still feel, as I have argued at length elsewhere (Thomas *1966a* 86), that some distinction within 'Dumnonia', marking off what is now Cornwall by an area-name *Cornouia*, latinised as Cornubia by the early eighth century, goes back to Roman times; and that the traditional further subdivision of Cornwall belongs to the same background. Two of the names of the six ancient 'hundreds' argue for this (Thomas *1964*). Trigg, which was trisected by the Norman Conquest, if not before, appears to have begun as *Tricorios*, '(area of) the three war-bands'; and Pydar, one of four that make up approximate quarters of mid and west Cornwall, has been referred to British *petuariia*, 'a fourth', as elsewhere in Romano-British toponymy.

It is from this specifically, and typically, British background – a province divided and sub-divided, ruled by kings and under-kings – that we can begin to construct a political model; a dominant class, prospering marginally under the *pax Romana*, dwelling in greater or smaller enclosures, and managing a stratified, tenurial, complex social system where wealth resided in cattle and land. From this, we could expect a native line of *tyranni* to emerge in post-Roman times. That such a line should have emerged in the western parts of Dumnonia, those least affected either by Roman *imperium* or by its progressive collapse, strikes me as less improbable than that we should have lost, entirely and without the slightest reflection in tradition and literature, all trace of some continuing rule from Exeter. For a parallel to such a rural, rather than urban, continuance of power, I do not want here to adduce in any detail the contemporary events (as we think we know them) in upland Wales and in southern Scotland; but the outline of post-Roman history seen in those regions is markedly similar.

There are various facets of sub-Roman and post-Roman times so far unmentioned; for example, the Irish settlements (Thomas *1973*), the external contact, shown by trade goods or imports, with the Continent and the Mediterranean (Alcock *1971*), the migrations to Armorica (Jackson *1953*), and the complex history of the early British church with its attendant archaeology (Thomas *1971*). I have omitted full consideration of these because, important though they are, they cannot in this particular context be regarded as absolutely central to my theme – the devolution of supposed political control. But in order to discuss them in an appropriate order, and to summarise the evidence a little more readily, I end by attempting a straight chronological record. Here the model, gratefully borrowed, is that used by Fowler and Rahtz (1972) for Somerset, AD 400–700 – a Somerset that lies mostly beyond Dumnonia, but that exhibits an obviously related sequence. In such a record, centuries are indicated by Roman capitals (V, VI), and half-centuries – though without any commitment to absolute dates – as VIa, VIb, etc.

## SUB-ROMAN: Va

Allowing that, even in late IV, such familiar aspects as money, the market circulation of goods like mass-produced pottery, and any formal maintenance of roads, may have largely lapsed, we picture here a way of life not all that noticeably different from that of IVb. General social unease in southern England may have touched the province, but in Exeter some form of urban life apparently continued, the recent excavations showing structural periods presumably well after 400. In the neighbouring cantons the same may be true of Dorchester and Ilchester. Where there had been vigorous local pottery traditions in IV, they continued (with some devolution) into V as local sub-Roman ceramic styles. Maritime contact with northern or Atlantic France is possible; and small Christian communities, established in IV or even late III, possibly maintained themselves in Exeter and one or two coastal settlements further west.

## A PERIOD OF BREAKDOWN: Vb

This half-century is now commonly seen by students of the period as one of rapid social and political transition. One may prefer the older model of a struggle between adherents to the shades of Roman grandeur, and vigorous neo-Celtic dynasts, or else see such changes as far less formalised. It was, above all, a phase of movement, of settlers into Britain from many quarters. Irish colonists, present in south and west Wales from late IV, and moving eastwards during Va, are (on the evidence of inscribed memorial stones) also present in Devon and Cornwall by the end of Vb. From the south of Britain, perhaps from the centre and south-east as much as from the specific south-west, a migration across the Channel to Armorica (Brittany) began, encouraged by fear of English settlement and social unrest.

In western Dumnonia, an important settlement-shift began in V, one suspects, and may have been spread over VI and even VIIa. This was the progressive abandonment of the enclosed settlements, the 'rounds', in favour of a new pattern that involved considerably greater clearance and intake of lands below the 400ft contour, eventually giving rise to the network of land-holdings indicated (in pre-Norman and medieval times) by the place-name prefix *tre(f)*. This, it can be argued, meant not so much 'farm', in the narrow sense of a farmhouse and curtilage, as something more like 'a share of land, tenement, land-holding'. Local feet were in fact planted on a road that led to Domesday Book. Looking externally, there is now evidence for contact not only with Atlantic France but with the Mediterranean direct, part of a wider nexus involving other regions of Britain and Ireland. This may be shown by metalwork as well as pottery.

## POST-ROMAN TIMES: LATE Vb/EARLY VIa

There is some sort of horizon, loosely centred here, which sees many new features and which takes us into a true post-Roman phase, having increasingly less in common with the end of Roman Britain. We know very little about the fate of Romano-British Christianity in the region, though I have argued that a regional preference for the double-square plan in the oldest chapels may hark back to Roman models (or Gallo-Roman ones?). This hardly affects the advent, towards the end of V, of full monasticism from Mediterranean lands, in part attributable to the spread of ideas along with imported goods, in part to continued contact with western and southern France. Tintagel, possibly Glastonbury, and (added only as a guess) the remarkable site at Oldaport near the south Devon coast, may indeed be the first monasteries in this wave. We can add to this the growth of Christianity generally, the appearance of primary cross-marked stones during VI, and greatly expanded use of inscribed memorial stones (with North African and Gaulish influences). Small enclosed cemeteries, serving specific neighbourhoods, appeared, becoming what I have called 'developed' as this tradition intermingles with that of the isolated rural chapel.

## FULL POST-ROMAN: VIa

In a much wider field, episodes east of Dumnonia, involving Wessex, South Cadbury, Mount Badon, British kingdoms, and whatever one chooses to attach to the name 'Arthur', point to VIa as some period of relative stability. But political stability is not inconsistent with rapid internal change in other directions. During Vb, and especially VI, there was a phase of fairly drastic linguistic evolution, hardly separable from some hypothesis of an imbalance in the social fabric. The general Celtic vernacular inherited from Iron Age times, British, was the descendant of a much older European tongue, and like Latin it possessed inflected terminations, case-structure, final syllables, and so on. This language gave way, apparently with some speed, to what Jackson has described as 'really a medieval one', exhibiting regional dialects that became full divisions (Cumbric in the north-west and southern Scotland; Welsh; Cornish; and by implantation Breton). Final syllables were lost, consonants blurred or softened, vowels shifted; and, again in Jackson's words, 'from the middle of VI we can begin to speak of these [the regional forms of British] as separating languages, and from the end of VI as separate'.

This is important in discussing Brittany, heavily involved with the south-west during VI. Traditionally in 511, certainly in VIa, a

Dumnonian chieftain Riwalus with a large following migrated to Armorica – it is a minor mystery that we still have no archaeological reflection of this episode – and the drain upon the south-western population continued through VI into VII. This movement, doubtless intensified at periods by such events as the British defeat at Dyrham in 577, brought a south-western version of British to Armorica, where it became Breton, developing in a fashion parallel to Cornish.

While VI is the golden period of Christian monastic expansion in the south-west, in Wales, and in Ireland – the 'Age of the Saints' – the large monasteries are not the only major field-monuments involved. Hillforts must be considered. Evidence for re-occupation, refurbishing, and occasionally (as at High Peak, Sidmouth) actual construction, is a feature of VI as well as of V, and preliminary consideration (Fowler *1971a*) makes it clear that much work is needed on this score. Castle Dore, a large round or a small hill-slope fort, exhibits two (successive?) timber palaces during VI, perhaps to be attributed to the Dumnonian king Cunomorus (Radford *1951a*; Rahtz *1972*).

In the extreme west of Cornwall, there is a secondary and limited settlement of Irish, with a totally new domestic pottery style, 'grass-marked' ware (Thomas *1968*). Chun Castle was re-used, perhaps internally rebuilt, by people who left a very Irish-looking grass-marked pot and sherds of Mediterranean (Bi) imported ware. Here, as in south-west Wales, one might adduce onomastic evidence to suggest that Irish immigrants may have introduced their own fashions of stockbreeding and farming (Thomas *1973*); and that the increasing *landnam* postulated in V is maintained in VI, with evidence from as far west as Gwithian for a real plough with fixed mouldboard to break in light soils (Fowler and Thomas *1962*).

## THE BEGINNING OF THE END OF DUMNONIA: VII

The seventh century (not divided) sees the start of a process of retraction, leading inevitably to the extinction of this post-Roman kingdom. By mid-VII or a little later, the English must have reached the Exe: by late VII, the Atlantic coast of north Devon. Exeter re-enters the picture. Whether its British name of Caer Uisc implies continuity of visible structures through V and VI to VII, or continuity of restricted but real urban life, it is perhaps too early to decide. But by the end of VII, Boniface (to give him his Latin name), son of an English settler, was at a monastic school in Exeter. The monastery, if Cyril Fox (*1956*) was right in pinpointing the site, was the predecessor of the cathedral, though one cannot push it back to VI on present evidence.

By VIII, we find the kings of Dumnonia apparently in control of little more than Cornwall and a few sectors of west Devon. By IX one has, at the most, client kings located in the western part of Cornwall. We have moved from the end of the Roman south-west, through a sub-Roman phase, to the close of post-Roman times; the events of VIII and IX are, locally, Anglo-Saxon times, and can be dignified by the label of history.

There are problems throughout, starting with place-names of Devon. The toponymy of Cornwall is primarily Celtic, from Ptolemy to the Tithe Apportionment surveys. Somerset has, in parts, a high proportion of British names – Polden, Chinnock, the Pennards, and Dommett are a few examples. This is also the case in Dorset. Yet in Devon the 1931 volumes of the English Place-Name Society's survey (Gover *et al 1931–2*) could stress that 'the most remarkable fact brought out by the present survey is the prevailingly English character of the local nomenclature of Devon . . . The total number of Celtic names in the county, excluding river-names, is less than one per cent of the whole . . . The whole topographical vocabulary of the region is English'; and the suggestion followed that the Devon encountered by the English in VII was sparsely populated, presumably denuded by huge migrations to Brittany. Today, this smacks of over-simplification. One view is that English settlers took over most of the settlements, by conquest or intermarriage, and re-named them; but why did this not happen elsewhere, as in east Cornwall? Another is that a survey in greater depth – down to field- and rock-names and similar minutiae – might have yielded a higher proportion of surviving British names. This may be doubted. Very complex social and settlement-pattern factors may be involved, and even if we cannot yet solve them, this seems intrinsically more likely than arguments about totally deserted landscapes.

Other mysteries are the fate of the apparently thriving late Roman tin-streaming industry, for which no real evidence is again encountered until the Middle Ages. The over-used story of the sea-captain in the life of St John of Alexandria (written after John's death in 641) should be carefully read by those who cite it; the miraculous overtones apart, it simply fails to specify which part of Britain (or Brittany?) yielded the cargo of tin (Dawes and Baynes *1948* 217–8). Again, there are the challenges of historical demography. One might expect, in view of the increasing evidence for the exploitation of natural resources from V to X, that the most preliminary estimates for the population of Domesday Cornwall should be notably larger than those which increasingly detailed fieldwork permit to be made for the period I to IV. This does not, however, seem to be the case at all. On what scale did the emigration to Brittany really occur? What about the pandemic of plague that began in the eastern Mediterranean in the 540s, and certainly reached Britain a few years later, presumably brought by persons and rats on trading-ships? The refinement of epidemiological studies of medieval and recent occurrences casts doubts on the extent to which this might have affected a predominantly dispersed rural population. Was the very high incidence of infant mortality in the Roman empire, normally linked to insanitary urban life, also a feature of rural areas? We do not know. One can hardly formulate so many of these vital question, let alone begin to answer them. Similarly, the exact course of events in the south-west in late IV and onwards must be beyond all hope of recovery; but we can at least continue our attempts to define the areas of probability, indicated by the (fortunately increasing) evidence available to us.

APPENDIX 1

# A SELECT HANDLIST OF COIN HOARDS
# FROM THE SOUTH-WEST

TERMINUS                              PUBLICATION

*Republican*
Frome (Som)                           *Archaeologia* 54 *1895* 489
Chelvey (Som)                         *VCH Somerset I 1906* 360

*Tiberius*
North Savernake (Wilts)               *VCH Wiltshire I, i 1957*

*Claudius*
Sea Mills (Glos)                      *Trans Bristol Gloucestershire
                                      Archaeol Soc* 68 *1949* 184–7
Chard (Som)                           *VCH Somerset I 1906* 359
Llanelen (Mon)                        *Monmouth Antiq 1961* i, 1
Nunney (Som)                          *Numis Chron 1861* 1–17

*Nero*
Bitterne (Hants)                      *Numis Chron 1908* 'Proceedings', 10

*Vespasian*
Caerleon (Mon)                        *Archaeol Cambrensis* 95 *1940* 123

*Domitian*
Easton Grey (Wilts)                   *Wiltshire Archaeol Natur Hist Mag*
                                      41 *1922* 391
Timsbury (Hants)                      *Numis Chron 1908* 80

*Trajan*
Bath (Som)                            *VCH Somerset I 1906* 287
Caerleon (Mon)                        *Archaeol Cambrensis* 84 *1929* 303

*Hadrian*
Cynwyl Elved (Carm)                   *Archaeol Cambrensis 1875* 407
Y Gaer (Brecon)                       *Y Cymmroddor 1926* 101
'Southants' (Hants)                   *Numis Chron 1911* 42–56

*Antoninus Pius*
Boverton (Glam)                       *Trans Cardiff Natur Soc 1888* 50
Maesbury (Som)                        *Somerset Archaeol Natur Hist* 12
                                      *1865* 60

214

*Marcus Aurelius*
Barton Wood (I o W)      *VCH Hampshire I 1900* 347
Poughill (Devon)      *Numis Chron 1939* 170–5
Ilston (Glam)      *National Museum Wales 27th Report 1934* 28

Mere (Wilts)      *Wiltshire Archaeol Natur Hist Mag 5 1859* 128

*Commodus*
Bream Scowles (Glos)      *Numis Chron 1882* 52–6
Caerleon (Mon)      *Archaeol Cambrensis 87 1932* 101–4

*The Severi*
Denland (Dorset)      A. L–F. Pitt–Rivers, *Excavations in Bokerley Dyke and Wansdyke, III 1892* 279–85

*Severus Alexander*
Warminster (Wilts)      *Wiltshire Archaeol Natur Hist Mag 45 1932* 207

Filwood (Som)      *Proc Soc Antiq ii, 8 1881* 387
Kenfig (Glam)      *Bull Board Celtic Stud 3 1926* 76

*Gordian III*
Y Merydd (Carm)      *Bull Board Celtic Stud 4 1928* 255

*Valerian I*
Baiter, Poole (Dorset)      *Cunobelin 11 1965* 51
Loughour (Glam)      *J Brit Archaeol Ass 12 1857* 158

AD *259–68*
Leigh Down (Som)      *VCH Somerset I 1906* 364
Dorchester (Dorset)      *Numis Chron 1939* 21–61
Ham Hill (Som)      *Somerset Archaeol Natur Hist 86 1940* 25

Kilton (Som)      *VCH Somerset I 1906* 363
Whitchurch (Som)      *Archaeol J 122 1966* 15
Preston (Dorset)      *Gents Magazine 1 1844* 185
Houndsdown Hill (Hants)      *VCH Hampshire I 1900* 345

AD *268–70*
Bridgend (Glam)      *Bull Board Celtic Stud 22 1967* 297–310

Coleford (Glos)      *Trans Bristol Gloucestershire Archaeol Soc 3 1879* 41

Crab Tree Hill (Glos)      *Trans Bristol Gloucestershire Archaeol Soc 6 1882* 108

Romsey (Hants)      *VCH Hampshire I 1900* 346
Pond Head (Hants)      *Numis Chron 1845* 'Proceedings', 5

| | |
|---|---|
| Llanbedr (Mon) | R. Vaughan *The Survey of Monmouth 1667* |
| Marazion (Cornwall) | Gough *Camden I*, 17 |

AD *270–3*

| | |
|---|---|
| Cheddar (Som) | *Proc Univ Bristol Spelaeol Soc 5* 87–9 |
| Clapton-in-Gordano (Som) | *Proc Somerset Archaeol Natur Hist Soc 73 1928* 127 |
| Ham Hill (Som) | *Numis Chron 1936* 30–42 |
| Kingston Seymour (Som) | *Proc Somerset Archaeol Natur Hist Soc 31 1885* 7 |
| Ilchester (Som) | *Archaeol Rev 3 1968* 20 |
| Bridport (Dorset) | *Proc Dorset Natur Hist Archaeol Soc 59 1937* 47–9 |
| Highfield (Wilts) | *Wiltshire Archaeol Natur Hist Mag 48 1939* 292–300 |
| Breague (Cornwall) | *VCH Cornwall V, 1924* 12 |
| Morvah (Cornwall) | *VCH Cornwall V, 1924* 12, 34 |
| Perranworth (Cornwall) | *Numis Chron 1852* 'Proceedings', 12ff |
| Chagford (Devon) | *VCH Cornwall V 1924* 14 |
| Ventnor (I o W) | *VCH Hampshire I 1900* 348 |
| St Donats (Glam) | *Antiq J* 10 *1930* 64 |
| Llandeilo (Carm) | *Bull Board Celtic Stud 22 1967* 297–310 |
| Tintern (Mon) | *Bull Board Celtic Stud 22 1967* 297–310 |
| Fishguard, 1 (Pembroke) | Laws *History of Pembrokeshire* 45 |
| Fishguard, 2 (Pembroke) | Laws *History of Pembrokeshire* 45 |

*Aurelian*

| | |
|---|---|
| Great Chessells (Glos) | *Numis Chron 1960* 275–7 |
| Corton Denham (Som) | *VCH Somerset I 1906* 361 |
| Lydiard St Lawrence (Som) | *Archaeol J 59 1902* 342 |
| Stogumber (Som) | *VCH Somerset I 1906* 364 |
| Netley Over (Hants) | *VCH Hampshire I 1900* 345 |
| Coed y Clorian (Glam) | *Archaeol Cambrensis 47 1892* 247f |
| The Gwindy (Glam) | *Numismatic Journal 1837* 132 |

*Tacitus*

| | |
|---|---|
| Great Cheverell (Wilts) | *VCH Wiltshire, II, i 1957* 74 |

*Probus*

| | |
|---|---|
| Coleford area, 1 (Glos) | *Trans Bristol Gloucestershire Archaeol Soc 6 1882* 109f |
| Coleford area, 2 (Glos) | *Trans Bristol Gloucestershire Archaeol Soc 6 1882* 109f |
| Frocester Court (Glos) | *Trans Bristol Gloucestershire Archaeol Soc 89 1970* 83–6 |

| | |
|---|---|
| Chinnock (Som) | *VCH Somerset I 1906* 360 |
| Carhayes (Cornwall) | *Numis Chron 1900* 209 |
| Ilston (Glam) | *National Museum Wales, 27th Report 1934* 28 |
| Caerleon (Mon) | *Bull Board Celtic Stud* 22 *1967* 297–310 |
| Coygan Camp (Carm) | G. J. Wainwright *Coygan Camp*, 116–26 |

*Numerian*

| | |
|---|---|
| Fishguard (Pembroke) | Laws *History of Pembrokeshire* 45 |

*Carinus*

| | |
|---|---|
| Park End (Glos) | *Trans Bristol Gloucestershire Archaeol Soc* 6 *1882* 110–22 |
| Malpas (Cornwall) | *Antiq J* 3 *1923* 235 |

*Carausius*

| | |
|---|---|
| Cheddar (Som) | *J Brit Archaeol Ass* 2 *1847* 271 |
| Camerton (Som) | *VCH Somerset I 1906* 292 |
| Charterhouse (Som) | *VCH Somerset I 1906* 338 |
| Pucknoll (Dorset) | *Numis Chron 1914* 92 |
| Penard (Glam) | *Bull Board Celtic Stud* 22 *1967* 293 |
| Wentwood Mill (Glam) | *Archaeol Cambrensis* 41 *1886* |
| Coygan Cave (Carm) | *Archaeol Cambrensis* 56 *1901* 21 |

*Allectus*

| | |
|---|---|
| Sapperton (Glos) | *J Brit Archaeol Ass* 2 *1847* 45 |
| Camerton (Som) | *VCH Somerset I 1906* 292 |
| Cocklade (Som) | *J Roman Stud* 17 *1927* 205 |
| Wedmore (Som) | *Antiq J* 8 *1928* 96f |
| Bitterne (Hants) | *VCH Hampshire I 1900* 344 |
| Neath (Glam) | *Numis Chron 1930* 164 |
| Skewen (Glam) | *Numis Chron 1922* 'Proceedings', 9 |
| Caerwent (Mon) | *Archaeologia* 62 *1911* 432 |
| Cynwyl Caio (Carm) | *Archaeologia* 2 *1773* 18 |
| Erw-Hen (Carm) | *Numis Chron 1966* 157–63 |

*Diocletian*

| | |
|---|---|
| Rockbourne, 1 and 2 (Hants) | A. T. Morley Hewitt *Rockbourne Report, 1970* 24 |
| Membury (Devon) | *Trans Devonshire Ass* 23 *1891* 79 |
| Sully (Glam) | *Numis Chron 1900* 27–65 |
| Aberkenfig (Glam) | *Trans Cardiff Natur Soc 1879* 44 |

*Maximian*

| | |
|---|---|
| Maesknoll (Som) | *Proc Somerset Archaeol Natur Hist Soc* 31 *1885* 7 |
| Bisley (Glos) | *Numis Chron 1845* 149 |
| Tickenham (Som) | *VCH Somerset I 1906* 367 |

*The Tetrarchy*

| | |
|---|---|
| Falmouth (Cornwall) | *Numis Chron 1865* 318 |

*Constantine I*

| | |
|---|---|
| Aston Blank, 1 (Glos) | *Archaeol Rev 6 1971* 26 |
| Aston Blank, 2 (Glos) | *Ibid* |
| Easton (Bristol) | *Proc Somerset Archaeol Natur Hist Soc* 31 *1885* 7 |
| Woolaston (Glos) | *Trans Bristol Gloucestershire Archaeol Soc* 19 *1895* 430 |
| Dunster (Som) | J. Ll. W. Page *An exploration of Exmoor 1890* 200f |
| Stoke St Michael (Som) | *Proc Somerset Archaeol Natur Hist Soc* 73 *1917* 119f |
| Wiveliscombe (Som) | L. V. Grinsell *Archaeology of Exmoor 1970* 99 |
| Crewkerne (Som) | *VCH Somerset I 1906* 362 |
| Bath (Som) | *Gents Mag* 96 *1826* 160 |
| Marlborough (Wilts) | *Numis Chron 1890* 282 |
| 'Marlborough Forest' (Wilts) | *Numis Chron 1850* 64–6 |
| East Harnham (Wilts) | *Wiltshire Archaeol Natur Hist Mag* 48 *1939* 48–52 |
| 'Salisbury Plain' (Wilts) | *Numis Chron 1869* 47 |
| Okehampton (Devon) | *VCH Cornwall V 1924* 14 |
| Buddock (Cornwall) | *VCH Cornwall V 1924* 12, 32 |
| Llangarren (Hereford) | *Numis Chron 1929* 334f |
| Caerwent (Mon) | *Archaeologia* 62 *1911* 410 |
| Chepstow (Mon) | *Bull Board Celtic Stud* 14 *1951* 88 |
| Swansea (Glam) | *Bull Board Celtic Stud* 9 *1941* 292 |

*Constantine II*

| | |
|---|---|
| Elm (Som) | *VCH Somerset I 1906* 362 |
| Baynton (Wilts) | *Wiltshire Archaeol Natur Hist Mag* 45 *1932* 185 |
| North Savernake (Wilts) | *Wiltshire Archaeol Natur Hist Mag* 45 *1932* 202 |
| Mawgan (Cornwall) | *VCH Cornwall V 1924* 12 34 |
| Carreg Cennen (Carm) | *Archaeol Cambrensis* 12 *1857* 347 |
| Llangynin (Carm) | *Archaeol Cambrensis Supplement 1911* 59 |

*Constans*

| | |
|---|---|
| Filton (Glos) | *Proc Soc Antiq* 2 *1881* 385 |
| Maiden Castle (Dorset) | R. E. M. Wheeler *Maiden Castle 1943* 334–6 |
| Pembroke (Pembroke) | Laws *History of Pembroke* 46 |

*Magnentius*

| | |
|---|---|
| Easterton (Wilts) | *Wiltshire Archaeol Natur Hist Mag* 45 *1932* 186 |

*Decentius*
Lydney (Glos)                              R. E. M. Wheeler and T. V. Wheeler
                                           *Report on the Excavation of the....*
                                           *Roman.... site in Lydney Park, Glos*
                                           *1932* 112

*Constantius II*
Hanham (Glos)                              *Numis Chron 1954* 213–15
Frome (Som)                                *Numis Chron 1866* 157
Poundbury (Dorset)                         *Numis Chron 1952* 87–95
Tywardreath (Cornwall)                     *VCH Cornwall V 1924* 12, 34
Ross (Hereford)                            *Numis Chron 1896* 209
Llanbethery (Glam)                         *Numis Chron 1960* 253–65
Llwchwr (Glam)                             *J Brit Archaeol Ass 12 1857* 158, 239

*House of Constantine*
Haresfield (Glos)                          *Numis Chron 1896* 237
Nailsworth (Glos)                          *Trans Bristol Gloucestershire*
                                           *Archaeol Soc 35 1912* 109f
Tidenham (Glos)                            *Archaeol Rev 3 1968* 34
Hamble (Hants)                             *Archaeol Rev 3 1968* 18
Chard (Som)                                *VCH Somerset I 1906* 359
Camborne (Cornwall)                        *VCH Cornwall V 1924* 12
Condora (Cornwall)                         *VCH Cornwall V 1924* 12, 34
Chepstow (Mon)                             *Numis Chron 1862* 230

*Julian II*
Willersley (Glos)                          *Numis Chron 1971* 203–6

*Valentinian I*
Rodmarton (Glos)                           *Archaeologia 18 1817* 115
Kelston (Som)                              *VCH Somerset I 1906* 363

*Valens*
Yatesbury (Wilts)                          *Wiltshire Archaeol Natur Hist Mag*
                                           18 *1879* 331
Constantine (Cornwall)                     *VCH Cornwall V 1924* 12, 34

*Gratian*
East Harptree (Som)                        *Somerset Archaeol Natur Hist 34*
                                           *1878* 21–8

*Valentinian II*
Cheddar (Som)                              *Numis Chron 1957* 231–7

*House of Valentinian*
Bath area (Som)                            *VCH Somerset I 1906* 355
Cheddar (Som)                              *Numis Chron 1957* 231–7
Polden (Som)                               *VCH Somerset I 1906* 354
Uphill (Som)                               *Gents Mag 1846* 633

| | |
|---|---|
| Wookey Hole (Som) | *VCH Somerset I 1906* 356 |
| Kenchester (Hereford) | *Trans Woolhope Natur Fld Club 1912–13* 210 |

*Theodosius I*

| | |
|---|---|
| Charlton Mackrell (Som) | *VCH Somerset I 1906* 356 |
| Shapwick (Som) | *Numis Chron 1938* 53–8 |

*Magnus Maximus*

| | |
|---|---|
| Shapwick (Som) | *Numis Chron 1939* 128–42 |
| Bristol area (Som) | *Numis Chron 1840* 144 |

*Arcadius*

| | |
|---|---|
| Sea Mills (Glos) | *Trans Bristol Gloucestershire Archaeol Soc 66 1945* 285–7 |
| Milverton (Som) | *Archaeol J 90 1933* 300f |
| Wiveliscombe (Som) | *Numis Chron 1946* 163–5 |
| Amberwood (Hants) | *Numis Chron 1845* 'Proceedings', 5 |

*Honorius*

| | |
|---|---|
| Cirencester (Glos) | *Archaeol J 40 1933* 298f |
| Camerton (Som) | *Archaeol J 40 1933* 300f |
| Holway, 1 (Som) | *VCH Somerset I 1906* 363 |
| Holway, 2 (Som) | *Ibid* |
| North Curry (Som) | *VCH Somerset I 1906* 356 |
| North Mendips (Som) | *Numis Chron 1915* 433–519 |
| Shapwick (Som) | *Numis Chron 1936* 245–50 |
| Worle Camp (Som) | *Ibid* |
| Marlborough (Wilts) | *Numis Chron 1884* 348 |
| Grovely Wood (Wilts) | *Numis Chron 1906* 329 |
| Dorchester (Dorset) | *Numis Chron 1922* 134–9 |
| Weymouth Bay (Dorset) | *Proc Dorset Natur Hist Archaeol Soc 51 1929* 158–82 |
| Cliff (I o W) | *Numis Chron 1845* 'Proceedings', 18 |
| Zennor (Cornwall) | *VCH Cornwall V 1924* 42 |
| Caerwent, 1 (Mon) | *Archaeol J 40 1933* 300f |
| Caerwent, 2 (Mon) | *Ibid* |
| Caerwent, 3 (Mon) | *Ibid* |

*House of Theodosius*

| | |
|---|---|
| Cirencester (Glos) | *Numis Chron 1952* 128f |
| Colerne (Wilts) | *Wiltshire Archaeol Natur Hist Mag 45 1932* 172 |
| Haven Street (I o W) | *VCH Hampshire I 1900* 348 |

# APPENDIX 2

# A HANDLIST OF VILLA SITES
# IN THE WEST COUNTRY

In the following list, which includes those sites considered in the writing of chapter 7, it has been impossible to give more than one published reference to each site. In most cases the reference chosen is the most recent, which will carry reference to earlier papers, but in some cases where the most recent references are brief and of little consequence, earlier, major descriptions or discussions are cited. The sites are listed in alphabetical order; where a site is known by two different names the second is given in brackets before the county.

Abbey Mead (Witchampton, Dorset) ST 9906 *J Roman Stud* 15 (1925), 238
Allington (Wilts) SU 206383 *Archaeol Rev* 5 (1970), 28
Alton (Wilts) SU 138618 *Wiltshire Archaeol Natur Hist Mag* 65 (1970), 207
Ampney St Peter (Glos) SP 0801 OS Map
Askerswell (Dorset) SY 529936 *Proc Dorset Natur Hist Archaeol Soc* 78 (1956), 9
Atworth (Wilts) ST 856665 *Wiltshire Archaeol Natur Hist Mag* 49 (1942), 46–95
Aylburton (Glos) SO 6201 *J Roman Stud* 46 (1956), 141
Badbury (Chiseldon, Wilts) SU 195810 *Archaeol Rev* 6 (1971), 34
Badminton Park (Glos) ST 8083 *J Brit Archaeol Ass* 2 (1846–7), 90
Banwell (Winthill, Som) ST 397584 *Archaeol Rev* 2 (1967), 16
Barnsley Park (Glos) SP 083067 *Trans Bristol Gloucestershire Archaeol Soc* 86 (1967), 74–87
Barrington Park (Glos) SP 204138 OS Map
Barton Farm (Glos) SP 017022 *Trans Bristol Gloucestershire Archaeol Soc* 70 (1952), 51–3
Bathampton (Som) ST 7766 BM MSS Skinner 1830
Bathford I (Som) ST 787666 *VCH Somerset I,* 300–1
Bathford II (Som) ST 784657 *VCH Somerset I,* 301
Bayford Lodge (Som) SU 7229 *VCH Somerset I,* 320
Bedminster (Bristol) ST 5769 *Proc Univ Bristol Spelaeol Soc* 2 (1926), 298
Bedwyn Brail (Wilts) SU 283629 *Wiltshire Archaeol Natur Hist Mag* 48 (1938), 318–20
Bibury (Glos) SP 1206 R. Gough, *Camden's 'Britannia'* 1 (1789), 282
Birdlip (Glos) SO 9214 *Trans Bristol Gloucestershire Archaeol Soc* 45 (1923), 294–5

Bishopstone (Wilts) SU 260815 *Britannia* 4 (1973) 317

Bisley (Glos) SO 913043 *J Brit Archaeol Ass* 2 (1847), 324–7

Bowood House (Wilts) ST 976699 *Wiltshire Archaeol Natur Hist Mag* 45 (1943), 181

Box (Wilts) ST 824685 *Wiltshire Archaeol Natur Hist Mag* 43 (1927), 335

Bradford Abbas I (Dorset) ST 593152 *RCHM Dorset I*, 30

Bradford Abbas II (Dorset) ST 577153 *Proc Dorset Natur Hist Archaeol Soc* 80 (1958), 98

Bratton Seymour (Som) ST 668295 *Archaeol Rev* 6 (1971), 32

Brenscombe (Dorset) SY 979827 *RCHM Dorset III*, 598

Brislington (Bristol) ST 6170 *Somerset Archaeol Natur Hist* 116 (1972), 78–85

Bristol (Greyfriars) ST 5873 *Bull Bristol Archaeol Res Grp* 4, 8 (1973), 219

Brockham End (Hanging Hill, Glos) ST 716698 OS Map

Bromham (Mother Anthonys Well, Wilts) ST 998642 *VCH Wilts I, i*, 51

Brookthorpe with Waddon (Glos) SO 833124 *Trans Bristol Gloucestershire Archaeol Soc* 90 (1971), 50–3

Brownshill (Glos) SO 8507 *Trans Bristol Gloucestershire Archaeol Soc* 77 (1958), 155–6

Burnett (Som) ST 6664 *VCH Somerset I*, 303

Calne (Studley, Wilts) ST 984709 *Wiltshire Archaeol Natur Hist Mag* 45 (1932), 180

Cambridge Batch (Som) ST 522699 *Trans Bristol Gloucestershire Archaeol Soc* 86 (1967), 102–6

Carrow Hill (Monmouth) ST 446910 OS Map

Castleton (Sherborne Park, Dorset) ST 652170 *RCHM Dorset I*, 63

Castle Tump (Caerwent, Monmouth) ST 480911 *Archaeologia* 62 (1911), 406

Catsgore (Som) ST 500260 *Archaeol Rev* 6 (1971), 33

Chard (Som) ST 3408 *VCH Somerset I*, 333

Charlton Marshall (Dorset) ST 904033 *RCHM Dorset III, i*, 59

Charminster (Dorset) SY 668949 *RCHM Dorset III, i*, 72

Chedworth (Glos) SP 054135 R. Goodburn, *Chedworth* (1972)

Cherhill (Wilts) SU 038705 *Wiltshire Archaeol Natur Hist Mag* 48 (1939), 390

Cherington (Glos) ST 9096 *Archaeologia* 18 (1817), 117

Chesterblade (Som) ST 6641 *VCH Somerset I*, 319

Chew Park (Som) ST 568515 *J Roman Stud* 45 (1955), 139; P. Rahtz, *Excavations at Chew Valley Lake* (1976)

Church Knowle (Creech, Dorset) SY 935827 *RCHM Dorset III, iii*, 595

Clear Cupboard (Farmington, Glos) SP 134158 *Trans Bristol Gloucestershire Archaeol Soc* 90 (1971), 224

Cold Knap (Glamorgan) ST 099664 *J Roman Stud* 51 (1961), 138

Colerne (Wilts) ST 811718 *Wiltshire Archaeol Natur Hist Mag* 45 (1932), 184

Coln St Aldwyns (Glos) SP 151053 R. Goodburn, *Chedworth* (1972), 12

Combe Down (Som) ST 7662 *VCH Somerset I*, 309–10

Combe Hay (Som) ST 729612 *Archaeol Rev* 7 (1972), 36

Combend (Stockwood, Glos) SO 984111 *Archaeologia* 18 (1817), 112–13

Compton Grove (Glos) SP 048163 *J Roman Stud* 22 (1932), 214–15

Cromhall (Glos) ST 685896 *Proc Soc Antiq* 23 (1910), 20–3

Daglingworth (Glos) SO 998045 O Griffiths and J Toynbee, *Daglingworth* (1959) 3–7

Dewlish (Dorset) SY 768973 *RCHM Dorset III, i,* 88

Didbrook (Glos) SP 046310 *Archaeol Rev* 4 (1969), 39

Discove (Bruton, Som) ST 6933 *VCH Somerset I,* 320 (possibly a temple site)

Ditcheat (Som) ST 634341 *VCH Somerset I,* 320

Ditteridge (Wilts) ST 812697 *Wiltshire Archaeol Natur Hist Mag* 45 (1932), 186

Donnington (Broadwell, Glos) SP 199279 *J. Roman Stud* 12 (1922), 262

Downton (Wilts) SP 182213 *Wiltshire Archaeol Natur Hist Mag* 58 (1963), 303–41

Drayton (Som) ST 400247 *VCH Somerset I,* 329

Dryhill (Glos) SO 932169 *Archaeol Rev* 5 (1970), 20

Duntisbourne Abbots (Glos) SO 974086 *Trans Bristol Gloucestershire Archaeol Soc* 45 (1923), 295

Dyrham (Glos) ST 730752 *J Roman Stud* 17 (1927), 205

East Aberthaw (Glamorgan) ST 034666 *J Roman Stud* 51 (1961), 158–9

East Brent (Som) ST 357506 *Archaeol Rev* 5 (1970), 9

East Coker (Som) ST 546138 *VCH Somerset I,* 329

East Grimstead (Wilts) SU 233274 *VCH Wilts I, i,* 75

Eastington (Whitminster, Glos) SO 779066 *Trans Bristol Gloucestershire Archaeol Soc* 90 (1971), 57–60

Ebrington (Glos) SP 1840 *Proc Cotteswold Natur Fld Club* 36 (1971–2), 87–93

Ely (Glamorgan) ST 147762 *Trans Cardiff Natur Soc* 55 (1925), 19–45

Enford (Wilts) SU 136519 *Wiltshire Archaeol Natur Hist Mag* 62 (1967), 126

Farleigh Hungerford (Som) ST 797583 *VCH Somerset I,* 301

Farley (Wilts) SU 2330 *Wiltshire Archaeol Natur Hist Mag* 45 (1932), 188

Fifehead Neville (Dorset) ST 773112 *Proc Dorset Natur Hist Archaeol Fld Club* 50 (1928), 92–5

Forest Hill (Wilts) SU 2068 *VCH Wilts I, i,* 88

Frampton (Dorset) SY 616954 *RCHM Dorset I,* 150

Frampton Mansell (Glos) SO 9302 *RCHM* (forthcoming)

Frocester Court (Glos) SO 785029 *Trans Bristol Gloucestershire Archaeol Soc* 89 (1970), 15–86

Frocester St Peter (Glos) SO 784033 *Trans Bristol Gloucestershire Archaeol Soc* 82 (1963), 149

Froxfield (Rudge Farm, Wilts) SU 275689 *VCH Wilts I, i,* 71–2

Fyfield (Wilts) SU 1468 *Wiltshire Archaeol Natur Hist Mag* 45 (1932), 189

Goathill (Dorset) ST 670178 *Proc Dorset Natur Hist Archaeol Soc* 80 (1958), 97

Great Barrington (Glos) SP 217132 OS Map

Grittleton (Wilts) ST 8479 J. E. Jackson, *Grittleton* (1843)

Halstock (Dorset) ST 533076 *Proc Dorset Natur Hist Archaeol Soc* 88 (1967), 125–6

Ham Hill (Som) ST 489165 *J Roman Stud* 3 (1913), 127–33

Hannington Wick (Wilts) SU 181958 *Wiltshire Archaeol Natur Hist Mag* 45

(1932), 190

Havyatt (Som) ST 480614 *Proc Univ Bristol Spelaeol Soc* 12, ii (1970), 195–202

Hazelbury (Wilts) ST 8368 *Wiltshire Archaeol Natur Hist Mag* 45 (1932), 177

Hemsworth (Dorset) ST 9605 *Proc Dorset Natur Hist Archaeol Soc Fld Club* 30 (1909), 1–12

High Bridge (Cricklade, Wilts) SU 102941 *VCH Wilts I, i,* 61

High Ham (Som) ST 422295 *VCH Somerset I,* 328

Hinton St Mary (Dorset) ST 7816 *Proc Dorset Natur Hist Archaeol Soc* 87 (1966), 102–3

Holcombe (Uplyme, Devon) SY 315928 *Proc Devon Archaeol Soc* 32 (1974), 59–161

Holcombe (Som) ST 6750 *VCH Somerset I,* 301

Hucclecote I (Glos) SO 877175 *Trans Bristol Gloucestershire Archaeol Soc* 80 (1961) 42–9

Hucclecote II (Glos) SO 869168 *Trans Bristol Gloucestershire Archaeol Soc* 79 (1960) 159–63

Huish (Draycot Farm, Wilts) SU 146632 *Wiltshire Archaeol Natur Hist Mag* 65 (1970), 206–7

Huish Episcopi (Brooklands, Som) ST 429277 *J Roman Stud* 37 (1947), 173

Hurcot (Pitney Pavement 5, Som) ST 511298 *Proc Somerset Archaeol Natur Hist Soc* 96 (1951), 47

Ilchester Mead (Som) ST 512222 *Somerset Dorset Notes Queries* 29 (1970), 121–3

Keynsham (Som) ST 645693 *Archaeologia* 75 (1926), 109–38

Kingsdon I (Som) ST 525274 *VCH Somerset I,* 325 (number 2)

Kingsdon II (Som) ST 528275 *VCH Somerset I,* 325 (number 1)

Kingshill (Cricklade, Wilts) SU 118926 *VCH Wilts I, i,* 61

Kings Weston (Bristol) ST 532775 *Trans Bristol Gloucestershire Archaeol Soc* 69 (1950), 5–58

Lacock (Wilts) ST 9369 *Wiltshire Archaeol Natur Hist Mag* 45 (1932), 194

Langridge (Som) ST 725703 *Proc (Bath Br) Somerset Archaeol Natur Hist Soc* 2 (1909–13), 246–7

Lansdown (Upper Langridge Farm, Som) ST 7368 *Proc Soc Antiq* 22 (1909), 34–5

Laverton (Som) ST 770534 *Bristol City Museum* card index

Lechlade (Glos) SP 216006 *J Roman Stud* 52 (1962), 179–80

Lenthay Green (Dorset) ST 625153 *RCHM Dorset I,* 63

Limpley Stoke (Som) ST 7761 *Proc (Bath Br) Somerset Archaeol Natur Hist Soc* 4 (1921), 167, 215

Listercombe Bottom (Glos) SP 070118 *J Roman Stud* 21 (1931), 240

Littlecote (Wilts) SU 2970 *VCH Wilts I, i,* 98

Littleton I (Som) ST 490304 *VCH Somerset I,* 323–4

Littleton II (Som) ST 492311 *Proc Somerset Archaeol Natur Hist Soc* 96 (1951), 44

Llantwit Major (Glamorgan) SS 958699 *Archaeol Cambrensis* 102 (1953), 89–163

Locking (Som) ST 3660 *Locking Review* (1967)

Long Newnton (Glos) ST 917916 *Archaeol Rev* 1 (1966), 20

Lower Langford (Som) ST 458608 *Proc Univ Bristol Spelaeol Soc* 12, ii (1970), 195–202

Lower Swell (Glos) SP 185262 *Trans Bristol Gloucestershire Archaeol Soc* 4 (1888), 209

Low Ham (Som) ST 436288 *J Roman Stud* 44 (1954), 99–100

Lufton (Som) ST 515178 *Somerset Archaeol Natur Hist* 116 (1972), 59–77

Lye Hole (Som) ST 502622 *Proc Univ Bristol Spelaeol Soc* 12, ii (1970), 177

Magor (Cornwall) SW 6342 *J Brit Archaeol Ass* 39 (1933), 117–75

Melbury (Som) ST 479275 *Proc Somerset Archaeol Natur Hist Soc* 96 (1951), 47

Minchington (Handley, Dorset) ST 9614 (information from Miss M. Willoughby)

Moulton (Glamorgan) ST 0770 *J Roman Stud* 49 (1959), 102

Netheravon House (Wilts) SU 148482 *Wiltshire Archaeol Natur Hist Mag* 45 (1932), 490

Newberry Terrace (Weymouth, Dorset) SY 679783 *RCHM Dorset III, iii,* 615

Newton Nottage (Glamorgan) SS 8077 *Archaeol Cambrensis* 4 (1853), 90–8

Newton St Loe (Som) ST 713655 *Somerset Archaeol Natur Hist* 112 (1968), 104–5

North Stoke (Som) ST 703692 *VCH Somerset I,* 302

North Wraxall (Wilts) ST 8376 *Wiltshire Archaeol Natur Hist Mag* 7 (1862), 59–74

Norwood Farm (Dorset) ST 532059 *Proc Dorset Natur Hist Archaeol Soc* 77 (1955), 136

Nuthills (Wilts) ST 968683 *Wiltshire Archaeol Natur Hist Mag* 45 (1932), 181

Olga Road (Dorchester, Dorset) SY 687901 *RCHM Dorset III, iii,* 570

Painswick (Ifold, Glos) SO 858102 *Trans Bristol Gloucestershire Archaeol Soc* 27 (1904), 156

Pamphill (Dorset) ST 978043 *Britannia* 4 (1973) 315

Piddletrenthide (Dorset) SY 706999 *RCHM Dorset III, ii,* 219

Pit Meads (Warminster, Wilts) ST 9043 *VCH Wilts I, i,* 110

Pitney I (Som) ST 451301 *VCH Somerset I,* 326–8

Pitney II (Som) ST 448293 *VCH Somerset I,* 328

Portskewett (Monmouth) ST 498888 OS Map

Preshute (Wilts) SU 170704 *VCH Wilts I, i,* 97

Preston (Weymouth, Dorset) SY 703827 *RCHM Dorset III, iii,* 618

Priddy, North Hill (Som) ST 541508 *Archaeol Rev* 3 (1968), 20

Purton (Wilts) SU 0887 *Wiltshire Archaeol Natur Hist Mag* 45 (1932), 201

Rampisham (Dorset) ST 557037 *RCHM Dorset I, i,* 191

Rodmarton (Glos) ST 946987 *Archaeologia* 18 (1817), 113–16

Seaton (Devon) SY 237909 *Britannia* 1 (1970), 297

Seavington (Som) ST 407138 *VCH Somerset I,* 332

Shepherds Mead (Hinton Charterhouse, Som) ST 7658 OS Map

Shipton Gorge (Dorset) SY 484919 *Proc Dorset Natur Hist Archaeol Soc*

79 (1957), 114

Sock Dennis (Som) ST 516213 *Somerset Dorset Notes Queries* 25 (1948), 109

Somerdale (Som) ST 658695 *Archaeologia* 75 (1925), 136

Somerton (Som) ST 497291 *VCH Somerset I,* 324

South Petherton (Som) ST 449180 *VCH Somerset I,* 332

South Stoke (Som) ST 750614 *Bristol City Museum* File 5496M

Spaxton (Som) ST 2436 A. Rainey, *Mosaics in Roman Britain,* 144

Spoonley Wood (Glos) SP 0425 *Archaeologia* 52 (1891), 651–68

Springhill (Glos) SO 159223 *Archaeol Rev* 6 (1971), 28

Stanbridge (Dorset) SO 0004 *Proc Dorset Archaeol Natur Hist Soc* 71 (1949), 66

Stanchester (Curry Rivel, Som) ST 398256 *VCH Somerset I,* 329

Stancomb Park (Glos) ST 742971 *Trans Bristol Gloucestershire Archaeol Soc* 4 (1880), 208

Stanton Fitzwarren (Wilts) SU 173900 *Archaeol Rev* 5 (1970), 29

Stanton Park Wood (Wilts) ST 897797 *Wiltshire Archaeol Natur Hist Mag* 45 (1932) 203

Star (Shipham, Som) ST 435587 *Proc Somerset Archaeol Natur Hist Soc* 108 (1964), 52

Stockend (Glos) SO 8409 *Trans Bristol Gloucestershire Archaeol Soc* 83 (1964), 147

Stowford (Wingfield, Wilts) ST 8157 *VCH Somerset I,* 301

Street (Som) ST 488346 *Proc Somerset Archaeol Natur Hist Soc* 96 (1951), 43

Swindon (Victoria Rd, Wilts) SU 156847 *VCH Wilts I, i,* 112

Swindon (Westlecott, Wilts) SU 146831 *Wiltshire Archaeol Natur Hist Mag* 45 (1932), 204

Tarlton (Glos) SO 964004 *J Roman Stud* 59 (1969), 128

Tarrant Hinton (Dorset) ST 927118 *Proc Dorset Natur Hist Archael Soc* 93 (1971), 161–3

Tatworth (Som) ST 327053 *Somerset Dorset Notes Queries* 28 (1966), 279–82

Thornford (Dorset) ST 594136 *Proc Dorset Natur Hist Archaeol Soc* 87 (1965), 104

Tockington Park (Glos) ST 627856 *Trans Bristol Gloucestershire Archaeol Soc* 13 (1889), 196–204

Tottenham House (Gt Bedwyn, Wilts) SU 2463 *Wiltshire Archaeol Natur Hist Mag* 45 (1932), 174

Truslowe Manor (Wilts) SU 083700 *Wiltshire Archaeol Natur Hist Mag* 45 (1932), 173

Upham (Albourne, Wilts) SU 215782 OS Map

Upton Grove (Tetbury Upton, Glos) ST 8794 *Archaeol Rev* 6 (1971), 28

Upton St Leonards (Glos) SO 866159 *Trans Bristol Gloucestershire Archaeol Soc* 90 (1971), 44–9

Wadeford (Som) ST 309105 *VCH Somerset I,* 333–4

Wadfield (Glos) SP 023261 *Trans Bristol Gloucestershire Archaeol Soc* 90 (1971), 124

Wanshouse (Wilts) ST 968675 *VCH Wilts I, i,* 51

Wellow I (Som) ST 728580 *VCH Somerset I, 312–14*
Wellow II (Som) ST 7258 *VCH Somerset I, 315*
Wells Bridge (Glos) SO 865190 *Archaeol Rev 6 (1971), 26*
Westbury (Heywood, Wilts) ST 863523 *Wiltshire Archaeol Natur Hist Mag* 36, 465
West Coker (Som) ST 5213 *J Roman Stud 49 (1959), 130*
West Cranmore (Som) ST 6643 *VCH Somerset I, 319*
Westland (Yeovil, Som) ST 5415 *Proc Somerset Archaeol Natur Hist Soc* 74 (1928), 122–43
West Park Field (nr Bromham, Wilts) ST 973658 *VCH Wilts I, i, 51*
Westwood (Wilts) ST 802593 *VCH Wilts I, i, 121*
West Woodlands (Som) ST 789419 *Archaeol Rev 6 (1971), 34*
Whatley (Nunney, Som) ST 744470 *Somerset Archaeol Natur Hist* 114 (1970), 37
Whitestaunton (Som) ST 2810 *VCH Somerset I, 334*
Whittington Court (Glos) SP 016206 *Trans Bristol Gloucestershire Archaeol Soc* 71 (1952), 13–87
Whitton (Glamorgan) ST 081713 *J Roman Stud 59 (1969), 200*
Wick (Glos) ST 706719 *Proc Bath Natur Hist Antiq Fld Club 1 (1868), 1–22*
Willington Court (Glos) SO 837241 *Archaeol Rev 3 (1968), 17*
Wimborne Minster (Dorset) SZ 014998 *Proc Dorset Natur Hist Arch Soc* 84 (1962)
Wincanton (Som) ST 6927 *Proc Somerset Archaeol Natur Hist Soc* 16 (1871), 14–16
Winscombe (Som) ST 402579 *Archaeol Rev 4 (1969), 47*
Winterslow (Wilts) SU 228326 OS Map
Witcombe (Glos) SO 8914 *Trans Bristol Gloucestershire Archaeol Soc* 73 (1954) 5–69
Withington (Glos) SP 031148 *Archaeologia 18 (1817), 118–21*
Woodchester (Glos) SO 839031 D. J. Smith, *The Great Pavement and Roman Villa at Woodchester, Glos* (1973)
Woodlands (Som) ST 4464 *VCH Somerset I, 307*
Woolaston (Glos) ST 596986 *Archaeol Cambrensis 93 (1938), 93–125*
Woolverton (Som) ST 783549 BM MSS Skinner 32681
Wraxall (Som) ST 479716 *Proc Somerset Archaeol Natur Hist Soc* 105 (1961), 37–51
Wynford Eagle (Dorset) SY 575953 *RCHM Dorset I, 269*
Yanworth (Glos) SP 059138 *Trans Bristol Gloucestershire Archaeol Soc* 47 (1925) 77
Yatton (Wemberham, Som) ST 405653 *VCH Somerset I, 306*

# APPENDIX 3

# A SELECT HANDLIST
# OF LARGER AGRICULTURAL SETTLEMENTS

## GLOUCESTERSHIRE

Barrington (SP 217132) RCHM *Gloucestershire* forthcoming
Bourton-on-the-Water (SP 157206) ibid
Coln St Aldwyns (SP 140055) ibid
Duntisbourne Rouse (SO 997074) ibid
Elkstone (SO 984127) ibid
Elmstone Hardwicke (SO 902259) *Trans Bristol Gloucestershire Archaeol Soc* 90 (1971) 42–3 (site 5)
Farmington (SP 129166) RCHM *Gloucestershire* forthcoming
Kingscote (ST 808953–807963–810961) ibid
Long Newton (ST 91639156) ibid
North Cerney (SO 996093) ibid
Northleach (SP 129156) ibid
Poulton (SP 097006) ibid
Quenington (SP 135054) ibid
Sherborne (SP 18821456) ibid
Siddington (SU 028988 and SU 047997) ibid
Temple Guiting (SP 13252830) ibid
Tredington Rise (SO 913289) *Trans Bristol Gloucestershire Archaeol Soc* 90 (1971) 26–34 (site 2)
Uley (ST 790996) RCHM *Gloucestershire* forthcoming
Whitminster (Eastington) (SO 777068) *Trans Bristol Gloucestershire Archaeol Soc* 90 (1971) 57–60 (site 18)
Winson (SP 076069) RCHM *Gloucestershire* forthcoming
Yanworth (SP 06051390–06151395) ibid

## SOMERSET

Bancombe Hill (ST 473297) *Notes Queries Somerset Dorset* 29 (1969)
Bush Marsh (ST 326404) *Archaeol Rev* 6 (1971) 9
Catsgore (ST 506264) *Somerset Archaeol Natur Hist* 114 (1970) 104; 115 (1971) 57–8; 116 (1972) 111
Charlton Mackrell (ST 532294) *Notes Queries Somerset Dorset* 27 (1957) 206–7
Chew Park (ST 568594) P. Rahtz, *Excavations at Chew Valley Lake, Somerset* (1976)
Clapton in Gordano (ST 472737) *Archaeol Rev* 4 (1969) 17

East Brent (ST 362532) *Archaeol Rev* 5 (1970) 9
Golds Cross (ST 595610) P. Rahtz, *Excavations at Chew Valley Lake, Somerset* (1976)
Herriot's Bridge (ST 571582) ibid
Holway (ST 246231) *Archaeol Rev* 6 (1971) 10
Littleton (ST 49053045) R. Colt Hoare, *The Pitney Pavement* (1832)
Monk Moor (ST 454498) *Archaeol Rev* 4 (1969) 45
Montacute (Ham Hill) (ST 487164) *Personal observation*
Podimore (ST 545247) *Proc Somerset Archaeol Natur Hist Soc* 97 (1952) 189
Puriton (ST 314417) *Archaeol Rev* 4 (1969) 18
St Algars (ST 789491) *Archaeol Rev* 6 (1971) 34
Stoodham (ST 434177) *Archaeol Rev* 3 (1968) 21
Sutton (ST 618333) *Personal observation*
Upton (ST 454268) *Ordnance Survey cards*
Wearne (ST 428278) *Ordnance Survey cards*

## WEST DORSET

Bradford Abbas I (ST 593152) *Proc Dorset Natur Hist Archaeol Soc* 80 (1958) 98
Bradford Abbas II (ST 577153) ibid 98
Chorlock Hill (ST 614184) ibid 98
Goathill (ST 670178) ibid 97
Pinford Lane (ST 652170) ibid 95

# APPENDIX 4

# A LIST OF THE ROMANO-BRITISH
# PIGS OF LEAD FROM THE MENDIPS

All measurements are in centimetres. The following abbreviations are used:

*Gowland:* M. Gowland, 'The Early Metallurgy of Silver and Lead', *Archaeologia* 57 (1901) 11

*Skinner:* J. Skinner, BM MSS Add 33673, 33717

*Webster:* G. Webster, 'The Lead Mining Industry in North Wales in Roman Times', *Flintshire Hist Soc Publ* 13 (1952–3)

1  Found in 1544 at Wookey Hole, near Wells, Som, but now lost. Weight and measurements unknown.
*CIL* VII.1201; *VCH Som I* 340; *Gowland* no 17; *Webster* no 27
Face (moulded):   Ti(beri) Claud(i) Caesar(is) Aug(usti) P(ontificis) M(aximi) trib(unicia) p(otestate) VIIII Imp(eratoris) XVI de Britan(nicis argentariis).
'(product) of Tiberius Claudius Caesar Augustus, Pontifex Maximus, in the ninth year of his tribunician power, and sixteen times acclaimed Imperator, from the British lead-silver works'
*Date:* AD 49

2–4  Three pigs of lead found in 1822 by Farmer Stephens when ploughing in Raynes Batch, Charterhouse. They were melted down almost immediately. Measurements unrecorded. Weight: 'one weighed over 200 lb, one less, and one half as much'.
*Skinner* 33673, f 103, 105, 117; 33717, f 166; *Webster* nos 40, 41, 42
Face (moulded) *said to be*:   DB *or* OB (not interpreted)

5  Found in 1853 near Blagdon, on the Mendips, and now in the British Museum.
Weight: 161 lb; height: 9.2; base: 60 × 14.6; face: 51.2 × 7
*VCH Som I* 341; *Gowland* no 14; *Webster* no 28
Face (moulded):   Britannic[i] Aug(usti) fi(li)
Front (incuse):   V(eranio) et P(ompeio) c(onsulibus)
'(product) of Britannicus, true son of Augustus'
'in the consulship of Veranius and Pompeius'
*Date:* AD 49

6  Found in 1783, at Bossington, Stockbridge, Hants, and now in the British Museum.
Weight: 166 lb; height: 12.1; base: 57.5 × 14.6; face: 53.4 × 8.2; silver content: 0 oz 12.6 dwt
*VCH Hants I* 323; *Gowland* no 27; *Webster* no 29

Face (moulded): Neronis Aug(usti) ex k(alendis) ian(uariis) quartum
co(n)s(ulis) (plumbum) Brit(annicum)

Front (moulded): Ex k(alendis) Iul(iis) P(ontificis) M(aximi)
co(n)s(ulis)

Back (incuse): Ex argent(ariis) G(ai) N[i]pi Asca(ni) XXX

'(product) of Nero Augustus from the first of January in his fourth
consulship, British (lead)'

'From the first of July, Pontifex Maximus, Consul'

'From the lead-silver works of Gaius Nipius Ascanius' '30'

*Date:* AD 60

7   Found in 1883, at St-Valéry-sur-Somme, Boulogne, France, and now in
the museum at St-Germaine-en-Laye.

Weight: 165.3 lb; height: 10.2; base: 60 × 17.2

*Révue Archaeol* 12 *1920* no 45

Face (moulded): Neronis Aug(usti plumbum) Britan(nicum) L(egio)
II

'(product) of Nero Augustus, British lead. The Second Legion (produced
it)'

*Date:* AD 54–68

8.  Found in 1952 at Syde, Glos, and now in the Corinium Museum,
Cirencester.

Weight: 174 lb; height: 10.2; base: 57.5 × 16.9; face: 52.2 × 7.6

*J Roman Stud* 53 *1963* 162

Face (moulded): Imp(eratore) Vesp(asiano) Aug(usto) VIIII
(plumbum) Brit(annicum) ex ar(gentariis)

Left end (impressed): G(aius) P(ublius) C(——) *(five times)*

Front (incuse): Soc(ietatis) Nov(a) ec

'(Cast) while the Emperor Vespasian Augustus was consul for the ninth
time; British lead from the lead-silver works'

'Gaius Publius C(——) (produced this)'

'(product of) the Novaec Company'

*Date:* AD 79

9   Found in 1918 with no 10 at *Clausentum*, Bitterne, Southampton, and
now in a private museum there.

Weight: 174 lb; height: 10.2; base: 58.8 × 14.7; face: 49.8 × 8; silver
content: 0 oz 3 dwt

*Proc Soc Antiq* 31 *1918* 37; *Webster* no 55

Face (moulded): Imp(eratoris) Vespasian(i) Aug(usti)

Front (moulded): (plumbum) Brit(annicum) ex arg(entariis) Veb.

(incuse): Nov(a)ec Soc(ietatis) No(vaec) IIVI

'(product of) the Emperor Vespasian Augustus'

'British (lead) from the Veb. lead-silver works'

'(product of) the Novaec Company 8'

*Date:* AD 69–79

10  Found in 1918 with no 9, but now lost.

Height: 10.5; base: 57.5 × 14; face: 49.8 × 8

Weight said to be 166 lb, but inaccurate scales may have been used, and

162 lb is probably a more accurate figure (information from R. P. Wright).
*Proc Soc Antiq* 31 *1918* 37; *Webster* no 56
Face (moulded):    as for no 9
Front (moulded):    as for no 9
            (incuse):    Soc(ietatis) No(vaec) *(twice)*
Back (incuse):        VIII
Translations as for no 9
*Date:* AD 69–79

11  Found in 1876, at Charterhouse, and now in the City Museum, Bristol (pl 32).
Weight: 182 lb; height: 12.8; base: 60 × 15.4; face: 51 × 8.3; silver content: 0 oz 13.2 dwt
*VCH Som I* 341; *Webster* no 31
Face (moulded):    Imp(eratoris) Vespasiani Aug(usti)
'(product) of the Emperor Vespasian Augustus'
*Date:* AD 69–79

12  Found in 1874 at Charterhouse, and now lost.
Weight: not recorded. Measurements: 'approximately 38.3 long, 9 wide, and 5 thick'
*VCH Som I* 341
Face (moulded):    Imp(eratoris) Vespasia[ni Aug(usti)]
'(product) of the Emperor Vespasian Augustus'
*Date:* AD 69–79

13  Found in 1875 at Charterhouse, and now in the Priory, Roehampton.
Weight: 171 lb; height: 11.5; base: 59.4 × 16; face: 51 × 8.2; silver content: 0 oz 0.3 dwt
*VCH Som I* 341; *Gowland* no 18; *Webster* no 30
Face (moulded):    Imp(eratoris) Vespasian(i) Aug(usti)
Front (moulded):    (plumbum) Brit(annicum) ex arg(entariis) Veb
Translations and date as for no 9

14–17  Four pigs of lead were discovered together in 1956 at Vespasian Farm, Green Ore. They are now in the Wells Museum (pl 30).
*Proc Somerset Archaeol Natur Hist Soc* 102 *1957* 52–88; *J Roman Stud* 47 *1957* 230

14  Weight: 187 lb; height: 12.8; base: 58.8 × 15.4; face: 52.2 × 9; silver content: nil
Face (moulded):    Imp(eratoris) Vespasian(i) Aug(usti)
Front (moulded):    (plumbum) Brit(annicum) ex arg(entariis) Veb
Right end (incuse):    LXV (incuse and inverted) Ti(berius) Cl(audius) Trif(erna)
Back:                (Applied strip)
Front and face moulded translations as for no 9; final figure '65'

15  Weight: 197½ lb; height: 12.8; base: 60 × 14.7; face: 51.5 ×9; silver content: a trace
Front and face moulded as no 14
Right end (incuse):    LXXIIX (incuse and inverted) LRΛD

Front and face moulded translations as for no 9; final figure '78'

16   Weight: 189½ lb; height: 12.8; base: 60 × 15.3; face: 51.5 × 9; silver content: a trace

Face and back moulded as were the face and front of no 14

Back (incuse transversely):   Ti(berius) Cl(audius) Trif(erna)

(Applied strip):          V (overlaying the *A* of *ARG*)

Right end (incuse):   Ti(berius) C(laudius) Trifer(na)

Left end (incuse):   LXIIX

Face and back moulded translations as for no 9 (face and front).

'Tiberius Claudius Triferna (produced this)'

'Tiberius Claudius Triferna (produced this)'

'68'

17   Weight: 187 lb; height: 12.8; base: 60 × 15.3; face: 51 × 9; silver content: 18 oz 12 dwt

Face and front moulded as no 14

Front (incuse and inverted): IMP

Back (incuse):   Ti(berius) Cl(audius) Trif(erna) *(twice)*

Left end (incuse and inverted):   Ti(berius) C(laudius) Trifer(na) *(twice)*

Face and front moulded translations as for no 14

incuse translations as for no 16

*Dates:* AD 69–79

18   Found in 1819 at Claverton Down, Bath, but since melted down.

Weight: 'about 150 lb'; measurements unknown.

*Skinner* 33673, f 105

Face (moulded):   Imp(erator) Hadrianus Aug(ustus)

'The Emperor Hadrian Augustus (produced this)'

*Date:* AD 117–38

19   Found in 1822 at Sidney Place, Bath, and now in the Roman Baths Museum, Bath.

Weight: 195 lb; height: 11.5; base: 58.8 × 15.3; face: 51.5 × 8.3; silver content: 0 oz 13 dwt

*VCH Som I* 342; *Gowland* no 21; *Webster* no 52

Face (moulded):   Imp(eratoris) Hadriani August(i)

'(product of) the Emperor Hadrian Augustus'

*Date:* AD 117–38

20   Found in 1873 at Charterhouse, and now at the Priory, Roehampton.

Weight: 223 lb; height: 12.5; base: 58.8 × 17.2; face: 49.8 ×7; silver content: 0 oz 18 dwt

*VCH Som I* 342; *Gowland* no 19; *Webster* no 33

Face (moulded):     Imp(eratoris) Caes(aris) Antonini Aug(usti) P [ii]

                         p(atris) p(atriae)

Right end (moulded):   a circle   a hammer mark

Left end (moulded):   a palm branch

'(product) of the Emperor Caesar Antoninus Augustus Pius, *pater patrae*'

Official marks not interpreted

*Date*: AD 139–61

21　Found in 1865 in the river Frome, at Bristol, and now in the City Museum, Bristol (pl 31)
　　Weight: 89 lb; height: 7.6 tapering to 6.4; base: 54.8 × 14; face: 48 × 7; silver content: 0 oz 15.8 dwt
　　*VCH Som I* 342; *Gowland* no 16; *Webster* no 35
　　Face (moulded):　Imp(eratoris) Caes(aris) A[nto]nini Aug(usti) Pii
　　　　　　　　　　p(atris) p(atriae)
　　Translation as for no 20
　　*Date:* AD 139–61

22　Found in 1865 with no 21, and now in the British Museum.
　　Weight: 76 lb; height: 6.3; base: 53 × 12.8; face: 49.8 × 7; silver content: 1 oz 2 dwt
　　*VCH Some I* 342; *Gowland* no 15; *Webster* no 34
　　Inscription, translation and date as for no 21

23　A fragment of lead found in the eighteenth century at Bruton, but since lost.
　　Weight: about 50 lb; about ¾″ thick, 20″ long, and 3¼″ wide.
　　*VCH Som I* 342; *Gowland* no 15; *Webster* no 34
　　Face (moulded):　Imp(eratorum) duor(um) Aug(ustorum) Antonini et
　　　　　　　　　　Veri Armeniacorum
　　'(product) of the two Emperors Augustus Armeniacus, Antoninus and Verus'
　　*Date:* AD 164–9

24　Found in about 1530, at Wells, but since lost.
　　Weight and measurements: unknown
　　Leland *BM MSS Cotton Julius* C VI f 37. *Webster* no 37
　　Inscription and translation and date as for no 23 (by analogy)

25–6　Two fragments of lead found in 1874 at Charterhouse, and now at the Castle Museum, Taunton:

25　Measurements: 20.4 long; 9.6 wide, and 1.9 thick
　　*VCH Som I* 342–3; *Webster* no 38–9
　　Face (moulded):　[Imp(eratorum) duor(um) Aug(ustorum) A]ntonini
　　　　　　　　　　| [et Veri Armenia]corum
　　Translation and date as for no 23

26　Measurements: 14 long; 6.3 wide; almost 0.6 thick
　　Face (moulded):　[Imp(eratorum) duor(um) Au] g[(ustorum)
　　　　　　　　　　Antonini] | [et Veri Ar] menia[corum]
　　Translation and date as for no 23

27　Half a lead pig found in 1840 in the south-west corner outside the Roman theatre at Lillebonne, Normandy, and now in the museum at Rouen.
　　Weight: 31 lb 6 oz; height: 13.4; base: 28.5 long; face: 24.8 long
　　*Révue Arch* 13 *1921* 68, no 46
　　Back (moulded and inverted):　I[mp(eratoris) Caes(aris)] L[uci
　　　　　　Septimi Severi | Perti]nacis Aug(usti) Pa[(rthici Adiabenici
　　'(product) of the Emperor Caesar Lucius Septimius Severus Pertinax Augustus Parthicus Adiabenicus'
　　*Date:* AD 195–211

234

# BIBLIOGRAPHY

Alcock, L. *1971 Arthur's Britain*
——. *1972 'By South Cadbury Is That Camelot . . .': The Excavation of Cadbury Castle 1966–70*
Allen, D. *1944* 'The Belgic Dynasties of Britain and Their Coins', *Archaeologia* 90, 1–46
——. *1958* 'The Origins of Coinage in Britain: A Reappraisal' in S. S. Frere (ed), *Problems of the Iron Age in Southern Britain*, 97–308
——. *1961* 'A Study of the Dobunnic Coinage' in Clifford *1961*, 75–147
——. *1967* 'Celtic Coins', Ordnance Survey *Map of Southern Britain in the Iron Age*, 19–32
Annable, F. *1966* 'A Late First Century Well at Cunetio', *Wiltshire Archaeol Natur Hist Mag* 61, 9–24
Applebaum, S. *1966* 'Peasant Economy and Types of Agriculture' in Thomas *1966*, 99–107
Ashbee, P. *1970* 'Excavations on Halangy Down, St Mary's, Isles of Scilly, 1969–70', *Cornish Archaeol* 9, 69–76
Ashworth, H. *1970 Report on Romano-British Settlement and Metallurgical Site, Vespasian Farm, Green Ore*
Baker, A. *1966* 'Aerial Reconnaissance over the Romano-British Town of Magna (Kenchester)', *Trans Woolhope Natur Fld Club* 38, 192
Barker, P. *1969* 'The Origins of Worcester', *Trans Worcester Archaeol Soc* 2, 7–116
Bean, C. E. *1958* 'Some Roman Sites and Miscellaneous Finds from the Sherborne District', *Proc Dorset Natur Hist Archaeol Soc* 80, 96–98
Beecham, K. *1886 History of Cirencester and the Roman City of Corinium*
Birley, A. R. *1967* 'The Roman Governors of Britain', *Epigraphische Studien* 4, 65–6
Birley, E. R. *1952* 'Roman Garrisons in Wales,' *Archaeol Cambrensis* 102, 9–19
——. *1953 Roman Britain and the Roman Army*
Bonney, D. *1968* 'Iron Age and Romano-British Settlement Sites in Wiltshire. Some Geographical Considerations', *Wiltshire Archaeol Natur Hist Mag* 63, 27–38
Boon, G. C. *1945* 'The Roman Site at Sea Mills 1945–6', *Trans Bristol Gloucestershire Archaeol Soc* 66, 258–95
——. *1949* 'A Claudian Origin for Sea Mills', *Trans Bristol Gloucestershire Archaeol Soc* 68, 184–88

———. *1967* 'The Coins' in G. Wainwright, *Coygan Camp*, 110–26

———. *1969* 'Belgic and Roman Silchester: the Excavations of 1954–8 with an Excursus on the Early History of Calleva', *Archaeologia* 102, 1–82

———. *1971* 'Aperçu sur la Production des Metaux non Ferreux dans la Bretagne Romaine', *Apulum* 9, 453–503

Boon, G. C., and Rahtz, P. *1966* 'Third Century Counterfeiting in Somerset', *Archaeol J* 122, 13–51

Bowen, H. C. *1961* *Ancient Fields*

———. 'The Celtic Background' in Rivet *1969*, 1–48

Bowen, H. C., and Fowler, P. J. *1966* 'Romano-British Settlements in Dorset and Wiltshire', in Thomas *1966*, 43–67

Branigan, K. *1968* 'The North-East Defences of Roman Gatcombe', *Proc Somerset Archaeol Natur Hist Soc* 112, 40–53

———. *1971* 'Gatcombe', *Current Archaeol* 25, 41–4

———. *1972* *Latimer. Belgic, Roman, Dark Age and Early Modern Farm*

———. *1972a* 'The Romano-British Villa at Brislington', *Somerset Archaeol Natur Hist* 116, 78–85

———. *1973* *Town and Country (Verulamium and the Roman Chilterns)*

———. *1974* 'Vespasian and the South-West', *Proc Dorset Natur Hist Archaeol Soc* 95, 50–7

———. *1974a* 'Gauls in Gloucestershire', *Trans Bristol Gloucestershire Archaeol Soc* 92, 82–95

Brill, R., and Wampler, J. *1967* 'The Isotope Studies of Ancient Lead', *American J Archaeol* 71, 63–77

Brown, P. D. *1970* 'A Roman Pewter Mould from St Just, Penwith, Cornwall', *Cornish Archaeol* 9, 107–10

Brown, P. D., and McWhirr, A. D. *1966* 'Cirencester 1965', *Antiq J* 46, 240–54

———. *1967* 'Cirencester 1966', *Antiq J* 47, 185–97

———. *1969* 'Cirencester 1967–8', *Antiq J* 49, 222–43

Brunt, P., and Moore, J. *1967* *Res Gestae Divi Augusti*

Buckman and Newmarch *1850* *Illustrations of the Remains of Roman Art, Cirencester*

Calkin, B. *1935* 'An Early Romano-British Kiln at Corfe Mullen, Dorset', *Antiq J* 15, 42–55

Chadwick, N. K. *1969* *Early Brittany*

Christie, P. *1970* 'Carn Euny: Sixth Interim Report', *Cornish Archaeol* 9, 63–7

Clarke, D. L. *1973* 'A Provisional Model of an Iron Age Society and Its Settlement System' in Clarke, D. L. (ed), *Models in Archaeology,* 801–69

Clifford, E. *1938* 'Roman Altars in Gloucestershire', *Trans Bristol Gloucestershire Archaeol Soc* 60, 297–307

———. *1955* 'Stamped Tiles Found in Gloucestershire', *J Roman Stud* 45, 68

———. *1961* *Bagendon: A Belgic Oppidum*

Collingwood, R. and Myres, J. N. L. *1937* *Roman Britain and the English Settlements*

Collingwood, R. and Richmond, I. *1969 The Archaeology of Roman Britain*

Collis, J. *1972 Exeter Excavations: The Guildhall Site*

Cullen, P. *1970* 'Cirencester: The Restoration of the Roman Town Wall', *Britannia* 1, 227–39

Cunliffe, B. *1966* 'The Somerset Levels in the Roman Period' in Thomas *1966*, 68–73

——. *1967* 'Excavations at Gatcombe, Somerset, in 1965 and 1966', *Proc Univ Bristol Spelaeo Soc* 11, 126–60

——. *1969 Roman Bath*

——. *1971 Excavations at Fishbourne*

Dawes, E., and Haynes, H. *1948 Three Byzantine Saints*

Dewar, H. S. *1955* 'Note on a New Range of Buildings and a Roman Well at Low Ham', *Somerset Dorset Notes Queries* 27, 58–60

Donovan, H. *1933* 'Excavations at Bourton-on-the-Water', *Trans Bristol Gloucestershire Archaeol Soc* 55, 377

——. *1934* 'Excavations at Bourton-on-the-Water', *Trans Bristol Gloucestershire Archaeol Soc* 56, 99, 133

——. *1935* 'Excavations at Bourton-on-the-Water', *Trans Bristol Gloucestershire Archaeol Soc* 57, 234 260

Douch, H., and Beard, S. 'Excavations at Carvossa, Probus, 1968–70', *Cornish Archaeol* 9, 93–8

Dudley, D. *1954* 'Sub-rectangular Earthworks with Rounded Corners', *Proc West Cornwall Fld Club* 1, 2, 54–8

Dudley, D., and Webster, G. *1965 The Roman Conquest of Britain* AD *43–57*

Dyggve, E., and Vetters, H. *1966 Mogorjelo. Ein spätantiker Herrensitz im römischen Dalmatien*

Eagles, B., and Swann, V. *1973* 'The Chessalls, a Romano-British Settlement at Kingscote', *Trans Bristol Gloucestershire Archaeol Soc* 91, 60–91

Eichholz, D. *1972* 'How Long did Vespasian Serve in Britain?', *Britannia* 3, 149–63

Evison, V. *1965 The Fifth Century Invasions South of the Thames*

Finberg, H. P. *1957 Gloucestershire Studies*

Fowler, P. J. *1962* 'A Native Homestead of the Roman Period at Porth Godrevy, Gwithian', *Cornish Archaeol* 1, 17–60

——. *1968* 'Excavation of a Romano-British Settlement at Row of Ashes Farm, Butcombe, N Somerset', *Proc Univ Bristol Spelaeo Soc* 11, 209–36

——. *1969* (Ed) *Archaeol Rev* 3

——. *1970* 'Fieldwork and Excavation in the Butcombe Area, N Somerset', *Proc Univ Bristol Spelaeo Soc* 12, 169–94

——. *1970a* (Ed) *Archaeol Rev* 4

——. *1970b* 'Grass-tempered Pottery', *Trans Bristol Gloucestershire Archaeol Soc* 89, 50–2

——. *1971* (Ed) *Archaeol Rev* 5

——. *1971a* 'Hill-forts, AD 400–700' in D. Hill and M. Jesson (eds), *The Iron Age and its Hill-Forts*, 203–13

——. *1972* (Ed) *Archaeol Rev 6*

——. *1972a* (Ed) *Archaeology and the Landscape*

——. *1975* 'Continuity in the Landscape?' in P. J. Fowler (ed), *Recent Work in Rural Archaeology,* 121–36

——. *forthcoming* 'Agriculture and Rural Settlement' in D. M. Wilson (ed), *Anglo-Saxon Archaeology*

Fowler, P. J., and Bennett, J. M.  *1973* 'Archaeology and the M5 Motorway: 2nd Report', *Trans Bristol Gloucestershire Archaeol Soc 92*, 21–81

Fowler, P. J., and Thomas, C.  *1962* 'Arable Fields of the pre-Norman Period at Gwithian, Cornwall', *Cornish Archaeol 1*, 61–84

Fowler, P. J., and Walthew, C.  *1970* 'M5, M4 and Archaeology', *Archaeol Rev 5*, 5–10

——. *1971* (Eds) 'Archaeology and the M5 Motorway', *Trans Bristol Gloucestershire Archaeol Soc 90*, 22–63

Fox, A.  *1955* 'A Dark Age Trading Site at Bantham, South Devon', *Antiq J 35*, 55–68

——. *1968* 'Excavations at the South Gate, Exeter, 1964–5', *Proc Devon Archaeol Soc 26*, 1–20

——. *1969* 'Prehistoric and Roman Settlement' in *Exeter and Its Region* (Exeter), 137–49

——. *1971* *Exeter in Roman Times*

——. *1973* *South-West England, 3500* BC–AD *600*

Fox, A., and Pollard, S.  *1973* 'A Decorated Bronze Mirror from an Iron Age Settlement at Holcombe, Devon', *Antiq J 53*, 16–41

Fox, A., and Ravenhill, W.  *1959* 'The Stoke Hill Signal Station', *Trans Devonshire Ass 91*, 71–82

——. *1966* 'Early Roman Outposts on the North Devon Coast, Old Burrow and Martinhoe', *Proc Devon Archaeol Expl Soc 24*, 3–39

——. *1968* 'Trevinnick, St Kew', *Cornish Archaeol 8*, 89–97

——. *1972* 'The Roman Fort at Nanstallon, Cornwall', *Britannia 3*, 56–111

Fox, C.  *1956* 'The Siting of the Monastery of St Mary and St Peter in Exeter' in D. Harden (ed), *Dark Age Britain,* 202–17

Frere, S. S.  *1967* *Britannia: A History of Roman Britain*

Fulbrook-Leggatt, L. E.  *1968* *Roman Gloucester*

Gingell, G.  *1971* *A Penny for Your Past*

Glos Roman Res Comm  *1934* 'Report on Excavations during 1934 in the Barbican and Bon Marché Sites, Gloucester', *Trans Bristol Gloucestershire Archaeol Soc 56*, 65–81

Goodall, I.  *1972* 'Industrial Evidence from the Villa at Langton', *Yorks Archaeol J 44*, 32–7

Goodburn, R.  *1972* *The Roman Villa at Chedworth*

Gordon, A. E.  *1953* '938. Q. Veranius', *Pauly-Wissowa,* VIIIA, 398

Gowland, W.  *1901* 'The Early Metallurgy of Silver and Lead', *Archaeologia 57*, 359–422

Gover, J. E., Mawer, A., and Stenton, F. M.  *1931–2* *The Place-Names of Devon*

# Bibliography

Gracie, H. S. *1970* 'Frocester Court Roman Villa, Gloucestershire', *Trans Bristol Gloucestershire Archaeol Soc* 89, 15–86

Green, C. *1942* 'Glevum and the Second Legion', *J Roman Stud* 32, 39–52

Greene, J., and Greene, K. *1971* 'A Trial Excavation on a Romano-British Site at Clanacombe, Thurlestone', *Proc Devon Archaeol Soc* 28, 130–6

Griffiths, M. *1972* *The Cathedral Close*

Grimes, W. *1951* *The Prehistory of Wales* (2nd ed)

——. *1960* *Excavations on Defence Sites, 1939–1945*

Guthrie, A. *1969* Excavation of a Settlement at Goldherring, Sancreed, 1958–61', *Cornish Archaeol* 8, 5–39

Hannan, A. *1973* *Tewkesbury District. A Preliminary Archaeological Survey*

Haverfield, F. *1906* 'Romano-British Somerset' in *VCH Somerset I,* 207–371

——. *1906a* *Ancient Town Planning*

——. *1920* 'Roman Cirencester', *Archaeologia* 69, 161

Haverfield, F., and MacDonald, G. *1924* *The Roman Occupation of Britain*

Hawkes, C. F. *1961* 'The Western Third C Culture and the Belgic Dobunni' in Clifford *1961*, 43–74

Hawkins, A. B. *1973* 'Sea Level Changes in South West England' in D. J. Blackman (ed), *Marine Archaeology* (Colston Papers 23)

Heys, F., and Thomas, M. *1959* 'Excavations on the Defences of the Romano-British Town at Kenchester, 1956–8', *Trans Woolhope Natur Fld Club* 36, 100, 116

——. *1963* 'Excavations on the Defences of the Romano-British Town at Kenchester. Final Report', *Trans Woolhope Natur Fld Club* 37, 149

Hirst, F. C. *1936* 'Stone Mortaria in West Cornwall', *Proc West Cornwall Fld Club* I, i, 12–16

Hoare, R. C. *1821* *Ancient Wiltescire. Roman Aera*

Hodder, I. *1972* 'Locational Models and the Study of Romano-British Settlements' in D. L. Clarke (ed) *Models in Archaeology*, 887–909

Hunter, A. *1968* 'The Westminster Bank, Westgate Street, Gloucester, 1959', *Trans Bristol Gloucestershire Archaeol Soc* 87, 56–64

Hurst, H. R. *1972* 'Excavations in Gloucester 1968–71', *Antiq J* 52, 24–69

Jack, G. H. *1916* *The Romano-British Town of Magna (Kenchester) Herefords*

——. *1923* 'Excavations on the Site of Ariconium', *Trans Woolhope Natur Fld Club* 1

Jack, G. H., and Hayter, A. G. *1926* *The Romano-British Town of Magna (Kenchester), Herefords*

Jackson, K. H. *1953* *Language and History in Early Britain*

——. *1970* 'Appendix on the Place Names' in A. L. Rivet, 'The British Section of the Antonine Itinerary', *Britannia* 1, 68–82

Jarrett, M. *1964* 'Early Roman Campaigns in Wales', *Archaeol J* 120, 23

# Bibliography

Jones, G. D. *1973* 'Civil War and Society in Southern Etruria' in M. R. D. Foot (ed), *History, War and Society*, 277–88

Kutzbach, F. *1935* 'Das ältere Hochschloss in Pfalzel bei Trier', *Germania* 19, 40

Laing, L. *1969* *Coins and Archaeology*

Laur-Belart, R. *1966* *Fuhrer durch Augusta Raurica*

Lawrence, W. C. *1863* 'Wycomb', *Proc Soc Antiq* 2, ii, 302–7

——. *1864* 'Wycomb', *Proc Soc Antiq* 2, ii, 422–6

Leech, R. H. *1970* 'Excavations at Catsgore, 1970', *Somerset Archaeol Natur Hist* 114, 104

——. *1971* 'Excavation at Catsgore, Somerton, Somerset, 1971', *Somerset Archaeol Natur Hist* 115, 57–8

——. *1972* 'Excavation at Catsgore, Somerton, Somerset, 1972', *Somerset Archaeol Natur Hist* 116, 111

——. *1972a* 'Excavations on Bradley Hill, 1972', *Somerset Archaeol Natur Hist* 116, 110

Lilley, D., and Usher, G. *1972* 'Romano-British Sites on the North Somerset Moors', *Proc Univ Bristol Spelaeo Soc* 13, 37–40

Lysons, S. *1817* *Reliquiae Britannico Romanae III*

Macalister, R. A. *1945* *Corpus Inscriptionum Insularum Celticarum I*

McWhirr, A. D. *1973* 'Cirencester 1969–72. Ninth Interim Report', *Antiq J* 53, 191–218

Manning, W. H. *1972* 'Ironwork Hoards in Iron Age and Roman Britain', *Britannia* 3, 224–50

Masson-Phillips, E. *1965* 'Excavations at Lower Well Farm, Stoke Gabriel', *Proc Devon Archaeol Soc* 23, 3

Medland, M. H. *1895* 'An Account of Roman and Medieval Remains Found on the Site of the Tolsey at Gloucester in 1893–4', *Trans Bristol Gloucestershire Archaeol Soc* 19, 142

Miles, D., and Fowler, P. J. *1973* *Tewkesbury: the Archaeological Implications of Development* (2nd ed)

Miles, H., and Miles, T. *1969* 'Settlement Sites of the Late pre-Roman Iron Age in the Somerset Levels', *Somerset Archaeol Natur Hist* 113, 17–55

——. *1973* 'Trethurgy', *Current Archaeol* 40, 142–7

Morley-Hewitt, A. T. *1971* *Roman Villa, Rockbourne, Hants. 1971 Report*

Morris, J. *1973* *The Age of Arthur*

Nash-Williams, V. E. *1969* *The Roman Frontier in Wales* (2nd ed, ed M. G. Jarrett)

Ogilvie, R., and Richmond, I. *1967* (eds) Cornelii Taciti *De Vita Agricolae*

O'Neil, H. E. *1952* 'Whittington Court Roman Villa, Gloucestershire', *Trans Bristol Gloucestershire Archaeol Soc* 71, 13–87

——. *1962* 'Friar's Orchard, Technical College, Gloucester, 1961', *Trans Bristol Gloucestershire Archaeol Soc* 81, 11–40

——. *1965* 'Excavations in the King's School Gardens, Gloucester, 1964',

# Bibliography

*Trans Bristol Gloucestershire Archaeol Soc* 84, 15–27

——. *1966* 'Archaeological Observations on the Jurassic Way in North Oxfordshire and the Cotswolds', *Proc Cotteswold Natur Fld Club* 35, 42–9

——. *1968* 'The Roman Settlement on the Fosse Way at Bourton-on-the-Water, Glos', *Trans Bristol Gloucestershire Archaeol Soc* 87, 29–55

O'Neil, H. E. and B. H. *1952* 'The Roman Conquest of the Cotswolds', *Archaeol J* 109, 23–38

O'Neil, H. E., and Saunders, A. D. *1959* 'Wycombe Roman Site, Andoversford', *Trans Bristol Gloucestershire Archaeol Soc* 88, 161–2

O'Neil, H. E., and Toynbee, J. M. *1958* 'Sculptures from a Romano-British Well in Gloucestershire', *J Roman Stud* 48, 49

Palmer, L., and Ashworth, H. *1957* 'Four Pigs of Lead from Green Ore', *Proc Somerset Archaeol Natur Hist* 102, 52–88

Parlasca, K. *1959* *Die romischen Mosaiken in Deutschland*

Peacock, D. P. *1969* 'A Romano-British Salt-working Site at Trebarveth, St Keverne', *Cornish Archaeol* 8, 47–65

Pearce, S. M. *1971* 'The Traditions of the Royal King-List of Dumnonia', *Trans Hon Soc Cymmrodorion,* 1971, 128–39

Pollard, S. *1974* 'A Late Iron Age Site and a Romano-British Villa at Holcombe, near Uplyme, Devon', *Proc Devon Archaeol Soc* 32, 59–161

Probert, L. *1969* 'Excavations at Abergavenny, 1962–69', *Monmouthshire Antiq* 2, iv, 163–98

Radford, C. A. R. *1951* 'The Roman Site at Catsgore, Somerton', *Proc Somerset Archaeol Natur Hist Soc* 96, 41–79

——. *1951a* 'Report on the Excavations at Castle Dore', *J Roy Inst Cornwall* ns 1, appendix 1

——. *1955* 'The Tribes of Southern Britain', *Proc Prehist Soc* 20, 1–26

Rahtz, P. A. *1963* 'A Roman Villa at Downton, Wilts', *Wiltshire Archaeol Natur Hist Mag* 58, 303–41

——. *1972* 'Castle Dore – a Re-appraisal of the Post-Roman Structures', *Cornish Archaeol* 10, 49–54

——. *1976* *Excavations at Chew Valley Lake, Somerset*

Rahtz, P. A., and Fowler, P. J. *1972* 'Somerset AD 400–700' in Fowler *1972a,* 187–221

Reece, R. *1971* 'Cirencester Grammar School', *Trans Bristol Gloucestershire Archaeol Soc* 89, 11–14

——. *1971a* 'Two Lost Mosaics at Cirencester', *Trans Bristol Gloucestershire Archaeol Soc* 89, 175–76

Rennie, D. *1972* 'Excavations in Parsonage Field, Watermoor Road, Cirencester', *Trans Bristol Gloucestershire Archaeol Soc* 90, 64–94

Rhodes, J. *forthcoming* Excavation report in preparation

Richardson, K. M. *1962* 'Excavations in Parsonage Field, Watermoor Road, Cirencester, 1959', *Antiq J* 42, 160

Richmond, I. A. *1946* 'The Four Coloniae of Roman Britain', *Archaeol J* 103, 57–84

——. *1950* 'Excavations at the Roman Fort of Newstead, 1947', *Proc Soc Antiq Scot* 84, 1–38

——. *1955 Roman Britain*

——. *1957* 'Roman Britain in 1957', *J Roman Stud* 48, 130–50

——. *1968 Hod Hill II. Excavations carried out between 1951–1958*

Richmond, I. A., and Crawford, O. G. S. *1949* 'The British Sections of the Ravenna Cosmography', *Archaeologia* 93, 1–50

Rivet, A. L. F. *1966 Town and Country in Roman Britain* (3rd impression)

——. *1969 The Roman Villa in Britain*

——. *1969a* 'Social and Economic Aspects' in Rivet *1969*, 173–216

Royal Commission on Historical Monuments, England (RCHM) *1952 An Inventory of the Historical Monuments in Dorset, I. West*

——. *1970 An Inventory of the Historical Monuments in Dorset III*

——. *forthcoming An Inventory of the Historical Monuments in Gloucestershire I*

Rudder, *1800 The History of Cirencester* (2nd ed)

Saunders, C. *1972* 'The Excavations at Grambla, Wendron, 1972: interim report', *Cornish Archaeol* 11, 50–3

Sherwin White, A. N. *1959* 'Review of Syme *Tacitus*', *J Roman Stud* 49, 140–6

Smith, D. J. *1965* 'Three Fourth Century Schools of Mosaics in Roman Britain in *Mosaique Greco-Romaine* (Centre National de la Recherche Scientifique)

——. *1969* 'The Mosaic Pavements' in Rivet *1969*, 71–125

——. *1974* 'Roman Mosaics in Britain Before the Fourth Century' in *Actes du IIeme Colloque la Mosaique Antique, Vienne (Isere), 1971*

Smith, I. *1972* 'Ring-Ditches in Eastern and Central Gloucestershire' in Fowler *1972a*, 157–67

Smythe, J. *1940* 'Roman Pigs of Lead from Brough', *Trans Newcomen Soc* 20, 139–45

Stevens, C. E. *1951* 'The will of Q. Veranius', *Class Rev* 1, 4–7

——. *1952* 'The Roman Name of Ilchester (Lindiniae)', *Proc Somerset Archaeol Natur Hist Soc* 96, 188–92

——. *1966* 'The Social and Economic Aspects of Rural Settlement' in Thomas *1966*, 108–28

Stanford, S. C. *1970* 'Credenhill, Herefordshire: An Iron Age Hill-Fort Capital', *Archaeol J* 127, 82

——. *1974 Croft Ambrey*

St Joseph, J. K. S. *1973* 'Air Reconnaissance in Roman Britain, 1969–72', *J Rom Stud* 63, 214–46

Sutherland, C. H. V. *1937 Coinage and Currency in Roman Britain*

——. *1963* 'A Late Julio-Claudian *Aes* Hoard from Worcester', *Numis Chron* 7, iii, 57–9

Syme, R. *1958 Tacitus*

Taylor, M. *1961* 'Roman Britain in 1960', *J Rom Stud* 51, 132

Thomas, C. *1958 Gwithian: Ten Years' Work, 1949–58*

——. *1964* 'Settlement-History in Early Cornwall, 1: The Antiquity of the Hundreds', *Cornish Archaeol* 3, 70–6

# Bibliography

——. *1966* (Ed) *Rural Settlement in Roman Britain*
——. *1966a* 'The Character and Origins of Roman Dumnonia' in Thomas *1966*, 74–98
——. *1968* 'Grass-marked Pottery in Cornwall' in J. M. Coles and D. D. Simpson (eds), *Studies in Ancient Europe*, 311–13
——. *1971* *The Early Christian Archaeology of North Britain*
——. *1972* 'The Present Significance of Fieldwork in the Light of the Cornish Parochial Check-List Survey' in Fowler *1972a*, 75–94
——. *1973* 'Irish Colonists in South-West Britain', *World Archaeol* 5, 5–12
Thomas, N. *1974* *A Guide to Roman Sites in the Bristol Region*
Todd, M. *1970* 'The Small Towns of Roman Britain', *Britannia* 1, 114
Townend, G. *1959* 'The Date of the Composition of Suetonius' Caesares', *Class Quart* 53, 285
Toynbee, J. M. *1964* *Art in Britain under the Romans*
Tratman, E. K. *1970* 'The Glastonbury Lake Village: a reconsideration', *Proc Univ Spelaeol Soc* 12, 146–67
Wacher, J. *1962* 'Cirencester, 1961, Second Interim Report', *Antiq J* 42, 1–14
——. *1963* 'Cirencester, 1962, Third Interim Report', *Antiq J* 43, 15–26
——. *1964* 'Cirencester, 1963, Fourth Interim Report', *Antiq J* 44, 9–18
——. *1965* 'Cirencester, 1964, Fifth Interim Report', *Antiq J* 45, 97–110
——. *1971* *Corinium*
Wainwright, G. *1968* 'The Excavation of a Durotrigian Farmstead near Tollard Royal in Cranbourne Chase, Southern England', *Proc Prehist Soc* 34, 102–47
Walters, H. B. *1908* 'Roman Herefordshire' in *VCH Herefordshire I*, 167–98
Warmington, B. H. *1969* *Nero, Reality and Legend*
Waterman, D. *1952* 'A Group of Claudian Pottery from Clausentum', *Proc Hampshire Fld Club Archaeol Soc* 17, 253
Webster, G. *1957* 'Excavations on the Defences of the Romano-British Town at Kenchester, 1956', *Trans Woolhope Natur Fld Club* 35, 138
——. *1959* 'Cirencester, Dyer Court Excavation, 1957', *Trans Bristol Gloucestershire Archaeol Soc* 78, 44–85
——. *1959a* 'An Excavation at Nunnington Park, Wiveliscombe', *Proc Somerset Archaeol Natur Hist Soc* 103, 81–91
——. *1960* 'The Roman Military Advance under Ostorius Scapula', *Archaeol J* 115, 49–98
——. *1967* 'Excavations at the Romano-British Villa in Barnsley Park, Cirencester, 1961–66', *Trans Bristol Gloucestershire Archaeol Soc* 86, 74–87
——. *1969* 'The Future of Villa Studies' in Rivet *1969*, 217–49
——. *1970* 'The Military Situation in Britain between AD 43 and 71', *Britannia* 1, 179–97
Wedlake, W. J. *1958* *Excavations at Camerton, Somerset*
——. *forthcoming* *Excavations at Nettleton Shrub, Wilts*, Soc Antiqs Res Rpt forthcoming

243

## Bibliography

Wells, C. M. *1972 The German Policy of Augustus*
Wheeler, R. E. M. *1943 Maiden Castle, Dorset*
Whittick, G. C. *1931* 'Notes on some Romano-British Pigs of Lead', *J Roman Stud* 21, 264
——. *1961* 'The Casting Techniques of Romano-British Lead Ingots', *J Roman Stud* 51, 105
Wightman, E. *1970 Roman Trier and the Treveri*
Wilson, D. R. *1970* 'Roman Britain in 1969', *Britannia* 1, 269–305
——. *1971* 'Roman Britain in 1970', *Britannia* 2, 243–88
——. *1972* 'Roman Britain in 1971', *Britannia* 3, 299–351

# ACKNOWLEDGEMENTS

*Chapter 1 The Conquest of the West Country*
The preparation of this chapter would not have been possible without information and advice from many people, to all of whom I am most grateful. They include Professor L. Alcock, P. J. Ashmore, P. J. Casey, Dr J. Collis, Professor B. W. Cunliffe, Dr J. Diggle, P. J. Fowler, Lady Aileen Fox, M. Griffiths, H. Hurst, Dr M. G. Jarrett, Professor G. D. B. Jones, A. D. McWhirr, Mrs H. Miles, W. G. Putnam, R. Reece, Professor J. K. St Joseph, Mrs V. Swann and Dr G. Webster. I am particularly indebted to Professor F. R. D. Goodyear for his advice on certain passages in classical writers, and to Professor S. S. Frere who read the draft text, to its great benefit. For provision of photographs I am grateful to M. Griffiths and P. J. Fowler.

W. H. M.

*Chapter 4 Gloucester (Glevum) : A Colonia in the West Country*
At the time of writing, much of the information mentioned in this chapter was used before publication. I am much indebted to M. W. Hassall and J. F. Rhodes for allowing use of their then unpublished paper on work at the New Market Hall Site, and for much helpful discussion. Later publications of my own excavations are in *Antiq J* 1974, 1975. I am grateful also for information and helpful comment to K. Greene, A. G. Hunter, D. C. Mynard, B. G. Rawes, Miss J. Reynolds, and J. S. Wacher.

H. H.

*Chapter 6 The Vici of Western England*
I am indebted to J. Bennett and K. Branigan for information about Sea Mills and Gatcombe respectively. In each case, however, the interpretation offered is my own. For the provision of photographs I am grateful to K. Branigan and J. Hancock.

M. T.

*Chapter 7 Villa Settlement in the West Country*
I am grateful to Dr D. J. Smith for supplying copies of plates 19–20 and to the British Museum for plates 21–2. I am pleased to acknowledge helpful information and comment from Mr and Mrs B. Rawes, R. H. Leech, and Miss M. Willoughby.

K. B.

# Acknowledgements

*Chapter 8   Larger Agricultural Settlements in the West Country*
I am much indebted to the Royal Commission on Historical Monuments, England, for the use of unpublished material collected during its recent Cotswold survey (RCHM forthcoming), and to the M5 Research Committee for the use of both published and unpublished material.

R. H. L.


*Chapter 9   Farms and Fields in the Roman West Country*
My general debt to colleagues, amateur and professional, working on the Roman West Country is all too clear and is as clearly acknowledged. I would thank for specific help here the M5 Research Committee, the Department of Extra-Mural Studies, University of Bristol, H. and T. Miles, R. H. Leech, the Royal Commission on Historical Monuments, England, and my aerial partners J. E. Hancock, J. White and S. Sharpe.

P. J. F.


*Chapter 10   The Mendip Lead Industry*
My acknowledgements are gratefully given in particular to Mr R. P. Wright, Reader in Epigraphy at Durham University, for his guidance and generous advice when I undertook this study. Any mistakes that may have crept in are my own. I also record my gratitude to the curators of the many museums that house Romano-British lead and pewter objects for allowing me to study and photograph these objects. I am particularly grateful to the Director and staff of Bristol Museum for giving permission and providing facilities to take the photographs that comprise plates 30–33. My thanks are also due to my wife for so carefully preparing the difficult typescript.

H. D. H. E.

# INDEX

247